HIMALAYA ALPINE-STYLE

The most challenging routes on the highest peaks

Andy Fanshawe & Stephen Venables

THE
MOUNTAINEERS

Published in the United States in 1996 by The Mountaineers
1001 SW Klickitat Way, Suite 201, Seattle WA 98134

Published simultaneously in Canada by Douglas & McIntyre Ltd.
1615 Venables St., Vancouver BC V5L 2H1

ISBN 0-89886-456-9 (North America)

Book interior designed by Design/Section
Printed and bound in Italy by LEGO

Picture Credits
Front endpapers: A climber on the lower section of Ama Dablam's South-West
Ridge, with the unclimbed Mingbo peaks in the background. (*Alex McNab*)
Back endpapers: The Trango group photographed from high on Biale. (*Mike Searle*)
Previous page: A lone figure negotiates the wild knife-edge of Gaurishankar's
South-West Ridge during the first ascent of the South Summit in 1979 (*Peter
Boardman/Chris Bonington Library*)
This page: The Chinese side of Broad Peak photographed during a bold alpine-
style attempt on the West Face of Skyang Ka___ in 1990 (*Michael Kennedy*)

CONTENTS

INTRODUCTION Grand Alpinism

Lightweight climbing in the Greater Himalaya

In April 1982, Alex MacIntyre, Roger Baxter-Jones and Doug Scott travelled through Tibet to the foot of the huge unclimbed South-West Face of Shishapangma, 8046m, the thirteenth highest peak in the world. On 25 May, without having ever before set foot on the mountain, they started to climb the steep snow and icefields at the bottom of the 2500m high face. On their backs were heavy rucksacks with food for four days, a sleeping bag each and a stove and tent between them. They also carried ropes and a small rack of essential climbing gear. On the 28th, after three bivouacs on the face, they reached the summit and by the 29th were safety back at base camp.

This, in its purest form, had been an alpine-style ascent. The climbers had treated their Himalayan wall like a traditional climb in the European Alps, leaving base and moving up the mountain continuously, eschewing any further contact with the ground. There was no support from back-up teams, pre-placed camps, fixed ropes or supplementary oxygen; self-sufficiency was paramount.

Mountaineering historians tend glibly to describe 'alpine-style' as a uniquely modern phenomen, oust-ing the 'traditional' Himalayan tactics of massive, quasi-military expeditions sieging mountains into submission by sheer force of logistics. This simplistic view ignores two important points. First, those huge 'sieges' were the obvious reaction to the sheer colossal scale of the Himalaya and its unique problems of altitude – not to mention isolation – which put the range in a completely different league from the Alps. Just because people operated (and often still do operate) in large, highly organised teams, it does

▲

'The face was the ambition;
the style became the obsession'

Alex MacIntyre, 1982

not mean their exploits lacked adventure. Second, the alpine-style approach is not as radical chic as many suppose. It has been with us from the start, ever since Alfred Mummery made his futuristic attempt on the Diamir Face of Nanga Parbat a hundred years ago.

Mummery and Raghobir Thapa reached nearly 7000m on that gigantic ice wall in 1895, before retreating from their brave, naive step into the unknown. A few years later, Dr Alexander Kellas made

several first ascents in Sikkim, including 7065m Pauhunri, in similar lightweight style, with a small band of Sherpa servants. It was he, in preparation for the Everest Reconnaissance of 1921, who insisted that the world's highest mountain could be climbed without supplementary oxygen. On the basis of laboratory calculations he estimated a possible ascent rate above 8000m of about 100m per hour, exactly what Peter Habeler and Reinhold Messner were to achieve when they made their historic ascent of Everest without supplementary oxygen in 1978.

The desire to do more with less, to keep things simple, to travel light and fast, to give the mountain a sporting chance, is not new. Colin Kirkus and Charles Warren climbed Bhagirathi III alpine-style in 1933; they just didn't have a label for it. Fine notions of ethical purity came later, in the mid-seventies. The great walls like Nanga Parbat's Rupal Face and Makalu's West Pillar had succumbed to heavyweight campaigns; now people began to think light, even on the much prized eight-thousanders, starting in 1975 with Peter Habeler's and Reinhold Messner's swash-buckling three-day dash up and down the North-West Face of Hidden Peak. Hot on their heels came the charismatic Pole, Wojciech Kurtyka, known to all as 'Voytek', and his various European associates, including the ambitious young Englishman, Alex

(Left) One of the most single-minded proponents of alpine-style at extreme altitude, Pierre Béghin, took this photo of Christophe Profit during a two-man attempt on the gigantic South Face of Lhotse in October 1990. *(Pierre Béghin/Foc Photo)*

MacIntyre. They were committed, almost dogmatic, about alpine-style, yet MacIntyre, writing in *Mountain* magazine about their audacious 1980 ascent of the North-East Face of Dhauligiri, was able to look wryly at the accompanying contortions and manoeuvres:

'Our plan, in the best of tradition, was simple. We would place the two natty pieces of nylon acquired for the purpose in downtown Kathmandu up on the North-East Col and designate the spot Advance Base. Always a good move this. The presence of a Camp 1 on an alpine-style ascent can be embarrassing. However, by dint of an imaginative use of nomenclature quite a bit of ground can be gained: Rest & Recreation Camp, Operations Logistical HQ, Glacier Camp, Advanced Mountain Base etc. … From our Advance Base we would make forays up the ridge above until such a time as we had had sufficient rare air to be declared fit, whereupon we could belt up the face and go home.'

Which is exactly what they did, with brilliant success. MacIntyre died two years later on Annapurna. Kurtyka went on to achieve even harder ascents with fellow Pole Jerzy Kukuczka, Austrian Robert Schauer and the formidable Swiss duo, Jean Troillet and Erhard Loretan. Other names that stand out are the Catalans Nil Bohigas and Enric Lucas, who completed MacIntyre's presumptuous line up the South Face of Annapurna, and the Slovenians, Marko Prezelj and Andrej Stremfelj, whose string of climbs includes an on-sight ascent of Kangchenjunga's stupendous South Ridge.

Some of these routes are included in this book, as examples of alpine-style taken to the extreme. To climb unsupported on one of the very highest peaks, treading close to the edge of what is physiologically possible, will always be exciting, but not necessarily

enjoyable. For many people the real interest lies on smaller peaks, in the shadow of the giants, or in regions like Kishtwar or Kulu, where the highest peaks do not even reach 7000m. Some of the most attractive climbs in the book are around 6000m, where a well-acclimatised party can move continuously for several days on end, up steep technical

Pragmatism on Everest – Stephen Venables in 1988 using fixed ropes to climb a new route on the immense, complex Kangshung Face. (*Ed Webster*)

ground, without suffering the stultifying effects of more extreme altitudes.

A glance through the action shots in the book will show several instances of climbers on fixed ropes. The plain truth is that some of the most compelling routes in the Himalaya are, like it or not, draped with ropes, making a genuine alpine-style ascent virtually impossible. The tremendous West Pillar of Makalu is a good example. However, even if all the ropes were stripped, it would need a very strong party, blessed with long

spells of fine weather, to achieve the climb in a single push. The present reality is that people either make sparing use of existing old ropes (extremely dangerous with deterioration from ultra-violet) or they add their own new ones, creating more mess.

It is fashionable to dismiss fixed ropes but, in 1988, both authors of this book found them useful. On Menlungtse, Andy Fanshawe's ascent of the West Summit was aided by short sections of rope, fixed previously over awkward sections. On a more lavish scale, I fixed 1500m of rope with my American/ Canadian companions on a new route on the Kangshung Face of Everest. We felt that it was the only way to tackle the complexities of an, initially, very steep climb. It was also the most *enjoyable* way, for we could relish the most spectacular situations during the day and return to the comparative comfort of advance base during the night. Even with the benefit of that initial fixing, the four of us were stretched to the very limit on our final push to the summit and back; grand intentions of removing the ropes were abandoned in our desperate, headlong flight back to safety.

If there had been six, not four, of us we might have managed to remove the ropes and with them, any unease about the style of our ascent, leaving the route unsullied for future parties. Instead we left a mess. I would never denounce fixed ropes *per se*, just avoid them whenever possible and plead with people to build into their calculations the time, manpower and energy to remove ropes at the end of a climb.

Andy Fanshawe started work on this book during the winter of 1991/2 shortly before his death on Lochnagar in the Scottish Highlands. During that hectic winter, discussing the project with Voytek, Jean Troillet and Pierre Béghin, another of the great Himalayan adventurers of recent years, he became inspired by

Changabang, with the awesome West Wall on the left, the South-West Ridge facing the camera and the South Pillar profiled on the right. Kalanka is behind on the right. (*Doug Scott*)

their commitment to extreme adventure. However, he recognised that a book like this should also reflect the gentler side of Himalayan mountaineering, with a sprinkling of more moderate routes. When I took over the project, I bore that aim in mind, but decided not to include very straightforward climbs like, for instance, the normal route on Nepal's popular Mera Peak. The criteria were that the mountain should be an inspiring summit and that the route up it should be

either an irresistibly compelling line or redolent with historical association; it should also be a sporting route where success will never be a foregone conclusion.

'Alpine-style' covers a multitude of sins and is rarely adhered to in its purest form. On very long, complex, technical climbs with few reasonable bivouac sites the single continuous push can be very impractical. Often the better tactic is what Peter Boardman termed 'capsule-style', moving up the route in a series of mini-sieges, lifting the fixed ropes from one section when complete, then using them to work on the next stage. This was the tactic he used to brilliant effect on

his ascent of Changabang's West Wall with Joe Tasker in 1976, and three years later on his tight-rope walk along along the gravity-defying knife-edge of Gaurishankar's South-West Ridge. What counted far more than semantic dogma was the fact that in each case a small, self-contained team was stretched to the limit in a great adventure, which had minimal impact on the mountain and surrounding area.

So 'alpine-style' is here more an ideal than a set of rules. It is the basic principle of trying to do more with less. To start a great Himalayan climb and continue in one single, committed push to the summit is proba-

▲

bly the most satisfying – and often the most effective – tactic, but there are cases where the risk seems unjustified and some compromise may well be desirable. This book is intended to celebrate the joy of Himalayan climbing, not promulgate dogma.

Readers will notice the inclusion of more than one climb in which the authors were closely involved. We tried of course to be objective, but a little personal bias was bound to creep in. I make no

Andy Fanshawe greets a new day in the mountains during his 1989 expedition to the Makalu region. The photo was taken at a bivouac on Peak 4, with Tutse in the background. (*Ulric Jessop*)

apologies for sharing our enthusiasm for particularly memorable adventures. At one stage Andy hoped to include outlying areas of Central Asia, like the Pamirs and Yunnan. I decided to limit the scope to the main Karakoram/ Himalaya chain, moving west to east from Rakaposhi in northern Pakistan to Kangchenjunga on the Nepal/Sikkim border. There are obvious omissions, such as the Hindu Kush in the west and the beautiful peaks of Sikkim and Bhutan in the east, but with just forty routes to play with, limits had to be drawn. Many of the climbs are concentrated deliberately in fairly tight areas. The reasons for this are first, to give scope for cross-referencing between chapters and, second, to concentrate mainly on areas of proven popularity. Throughout the massive ranges of Central Asia there are still immense tracts of land hardly known by mountaineers, whole glacier systems awaiting exploration, countless summits untouched. It would be a shame to detract from their mystery with premature popularisation, so I have stuck deliberately to well-known regions. Even within these regions, though, many summits remain unclimbed and the scope for new routes is almost limitless.

This is a climber's book. It concentrates inevitably on the bald geology of the mountains and on the lines which we weave up those mountains. I hope though that it also hints at the huge varied wealth of experience that makes the Himalaya so much more than a mere climbing ground. On a purely egotistical level a great Himalayan route enriches the climber with lasting satisfaction but, long before an expedition sets foot on the route, there are all the dramas, frustrations, pleasures and excitements of travelling through magnificent country, experiencing whole new cultures.

It is now three years since I was asked to complete this book. I would like to thank Caroline Fanshawe for her patience and support during all the tantalising delays. I would also like to thank my editor Maggie Body for keeping track of a thousand erudite details and enlivening the proceedings with her customary wit. The designers, Graham Webb, Pippa Martin, and Caroline Wilson, learned very quickly to understand the esoteric complexies of Himalayan mountaineering and it has been a real pleasure to work with such consummate professionals. Ken Wilson, who first suggested the book, has been an invaluable fund of advice, as have the many climbers, historians and photographers acknowledged opposite. Without their advice, debate, enthusiasm, generosity – and of course their photographs – the project would never have been completed. I have no doubt that their support has been inspired more than anything by the boundless enthusiasm of Andy Fanshawe, to whom this book is dedicated.

Stephen Venables, Bath, March, 1995

ANDY FANSHAWE MEMORIAL FUND

Some of the profits from this book will be given to the Andy Fanshawe Memorial Fund. Set up in 1992, the fund enables young people, who would not otherwise have the means, to visit the mountains. Each year a group of youngsters is given qualified assistance and instruction in mountaineering-based activities. They are helped to develop competence in climbing and hill craft, and encouraged to foster a love of the mountains in the same spirit which inspired Andy.

Enquiries and donations should be sent c/o British Mountaineering Council, 177-9 Burton Road, Manchester M20 2BB

ACKNOWLEDGEMENTS

Caroline Fanshawe and Stephen Venables acknowledge gratefully the help received from so many people, who gave generously of their time, enthusiasm, expertise and advice, and who loaned their precious, unique photographs. We apologise to any people who may inadvertently have been omitted from the list.

Kurt Albert, Jan Babicz, Manu Badiola, Mike Banks, Kobus Barnard, Bob Barton, Pierre Béghin, Annie Béghin, Steve Bell, Steven Berry, Robin Beadle, David Breashears, Barry Bishop, Ernest Bladé, Barry Blanchard, Nil Bohigas, Chris Bonington, Tony Brindle, Joe Brown, Carlos Buhler, Kitty Calhoun-Grisson, Adams Carter, Giovanni Casiaghi, Greg Child, John Cleare, Ingeborga Cochlin, Rob Collister, Noel Craine, Giorgio Daidalo, Frances Daltrey, Madelaine David, Henry Day, Victor Dedi, Monesh Devjani, Kurt Diemberger, Mal Duff, Glenn Dunmire, Bill Durtler, Margaret Ecclestone, Xavier Eguskitza, Roger Everett, Michel Fauquet, Foc Photo, Mick Fowler, Jeanne Franco, Peter Ganner, Michael Germann-Bauer, René Ghilini, Maurizio Giordano, Dennis Gray, Colin Grisson, Nick Groves, Mark Gunlogson, Peter Habeler, Christoph Hainz, Brian Hall, Rob Hall, David Hamilton, Elizabeth Hawley, Stuart Hepburn, Tilmann Hepp, Alan Heppenstall, Alan Hinkes, Christian Hocke, David Hopkins, Philip Horniblow, Andy Hughes, Tsunemicki Ikeda, Ulric Jessop, Hans Kammerlander, Harish Kapadia, Nick Kekus, Michael Kennedy, Dag Kolsrud, Wojciech Kurtyka, Stephen Jones, Ferran Latorre, Michael Lendtrodt, Dorjee Lhatoo, Jeff Lowe, Mark Lowe, Enric Lucas, Randy Leavitt, Natalie Lecable, Erhard Loretan, Tim Macartney-Snape, Alex McNab, Claire Marvin, Roger Mear, Mark Miller, Terris Moore, Hideki Nagata, Jill Neate, Bill O'Connor, Sally O'Connor, Oshio Ogata, Attila Ozváth, Roger Payne, Iain Peter, Bob Pettigrew, Bernard Pierre, Sieghard Pircher, John Porter, Marko Prezelj, Paul Pritchard, Gillian Quinn, Steve Razzetti, Al Read, Simon Richardson, Ann Roberts, André Roch, Dario Rodriguez, Malte Roeper, John Roskelley, Enrico Rosso, Maria Rosso, Galen Rowell, Glenn Rowley, Balwant Sandhu, Victor Saunders, Franci Savenc, Robert Schauer, Mike Searle, Andy Selters, Sean Smith, Rosie Sanchez, Charlie Sassara, Doug Scott, Donna DeShazo, Hukam Singh, Alex Straber, Dhiren Toolsidas, Fiona Treble, Jean Troillet, Maggie Urmston, Carles Valles, Rosie Venables, Charles Warren, Ed Webster, Mike Westmacott, Jim Wickwire, Simon Yates.

GRADES: This book uses the UIAA grading system, except for some mixed climbs where Scottish winter grading seems more appropriate.

Balti porters near the confluence of the Dumordo and Biaho rivers, with the Masherbrum peaks in the background.
(*John Cleare/Mountain Camera*)

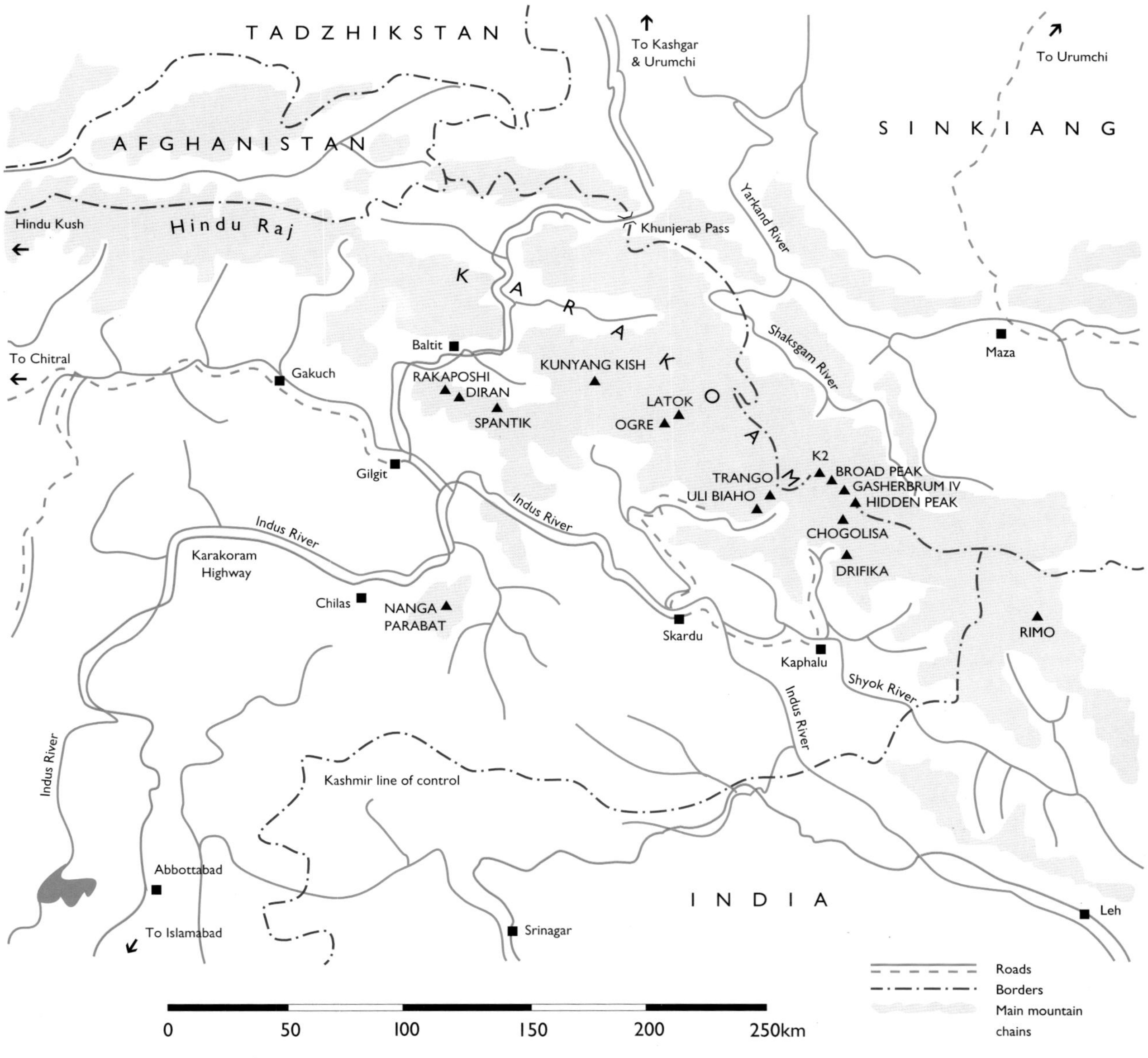

T A D Z H I K S T A N

↑ To Kashgar & Urumchi

↗ To Urumchi

A F G H A N I S T A N

S I N K I A N G

Hindu Kush

Hindu Raj

← To Chitral
←

Hindu Kush

↑ Khunjerab Pass

Yarkand River

K A R A

Baltit ■

Shaksgam River

Maza ■

KUNYANG KISH ▲

RAKAPOSHI ▲
▲ DIRAN
SPANTIK ▲

LATOK ○
OGRE ▲ ▲

K

Gakuch ■

← To Chitral

Gilgit ■

Indus River

Indus River

K2 ▲

TRANGO ▲ ▲ BROAD PEAK
ULI BIAHO ▲ ▲ GASHERBRUM IV
▲ HIDDEN PEAK

Karakoram Highway

Chilas ■ NANGA ▲
PARABAT

CHOGOLISA ▲

DRIFIKA ▲

Skardu ■

Kaphalu ■

Shyok River

RIMO ▲

Indus River

Kashmir line of control

Indus River

Abbottabad ■

I N D I A

Leh ■

To Islamabad
↙

Srinagar ■

Roads
Borders
Main mountain chains

| 0 | 50 | 100 | 150 | 200 | 250km |

▲

PAKISTAN

RAKAPOSHI 7788m

North Spur

Rakaposhi is the western bastion of the Karakoram Range, a massive pyramid whose shimmering ice walls seem to hang in the sky above the legendary orchard terraces of the Hunza valley. This North Face is immense, stretching 20km across and at its highest point rising in a single sweep of nearly 6000m from the Hunza river. Looking at the wall from Karimabad, the capital of Hunza, the mountaineer's eye is drawn to one single compelling feature, the razor-sharp spur which cuts clean through a mass of dangerous séracs, leading with direct and irresistible logic to the summit. This route, the North Spur of Rakaposhi, first climbed in 1979, is one of the most challenging mountain lines in the world.

Before discussing the North Spur, let us look briefly at Rakaposhi's early climbing history. Martin Conway, on the first real mountaineering expedition to the Karakoram, in 1892, explored Rakaposhi's southern approaches but found no practical way to the summit. Forty-six years passed before Campbell Secord attempted the immense North-West Ridge in 1938, reaching about 5800m. He returned in 1947 with that tireless explorer, Bill Tilman, to make a further reconnaissance of the narrow valley on Rakaposhi's west flank, the Jaglot nullah. Their work was consolidated in 1954 when a Cambridge University expedition, led by the Swiss Alfred Tissières, identified the best route from this side up the Gunti Glacier, on to the long South-West Spur and over the dark tower of the Monk's Head. This was the

route finally completed to the summit in 1958, when Tom Patey and the leader of the British/ Pakistani expedition, Mike Banks, reached Rakaposhi's prestigious summit.

The original route up Rakaposhi, although not particularly difficult by modern standards, is long and convoluted. Equally long and rather harder is the route of the second ascent, the North-West Ridge, which was climbed from the Biro Glacier in 1979 by a Polish/Pakistani expedition. Meanwhile, in the early 'seventies, as mountaineers began to look at the great unclimbed walls on the world's highest peaks, the controversial German expedition organiser, Karl Herrligkoffer, was drawn to the obvious challenge of the North Spur. He organised attempts in 1971 and 1973, but both were defeated by the logistical problems of sieging what proved to be a long and difficult route. Success came finally to a Japanese team from Waseda University in 1979.

The Japanese expedition of seven climbers was led by Eiho Ohtani. Their base camp was just one day's walk above the Karakoram Highway, on a grassy meadow at 3700m, east of the Ghulmet Glacier. It was from this glacier, from the west, that the spur was

(Left) The immense North Face of Rakaposhi catches the day's first light, while the Hunza valley still sleeps in darkness. The North Spur slants from right to left, reaching the skyline just left of the summit block. The more rounded spur on the left, rising to the snowy East Summit was first climbed by Edi Koblmüller's Austrian team in 1985, after they had first acclimatised on Diran. (Stephen Venables)

(Below) The North Spur from the west, showing the camps of the Canadian 1984 ascent.

7788m
Top bivouac ▲
7300m C6 ▲
C5 ▲
Rockband
6400m C4 ▲
C3 ▲
4800m
C1 ▲
Dangerous direct start
Ghulmet Glacier
— — Original start

(Left) The Canadian Camp 2 in 1984. This convoluted section of the lower ridge was bypassed by a more direct and dangerous line on the final summit push. Behind the camp, on the north side of the Hunza valley, is the Ultar Massif. The prominent summit at centre with the cloud plume is Ultar I, still unclimbed, after numerous attempts, in 1994. Behind, at the far left, is the summit of Shispare (7611m), first climbed in 1974 by Janusz Kurczab's Polish expedition. (Barry Blanchard)

gained. Over a period of six weeks the climbers laid siege to the spur, safeguarding its spectacular crest with 5000m of fixed rope and placing six camps. In the final push, Ohtani and Matsushi Yamashita had to make a further bivouac at 7600m before continuing up the final rocks of the East Ridge to the summit.

That first ascent in 1979 received virtually no publicity in the west and it was only after 1984, when a team from Canada repeated the North Spur, that mountaineers in Europe and North America began

to realise that this was one of the great modern Himalayan climbs. The eight* who arrived in Hunza that summer were young, fit and ambitious. They planned to push a new route up the face to the right of the spur, hoping for fast, alpine-style face climbing, but soon realised that the knife-crest of the North Spur was the only safe line amidst a battlefield of open slopes raked by sérac avalanches. So they opted to repeat the Japanese route.

It soon became obvious what a challenge they had

*Steve Langely & Chris Dale (British/Canadian), Dave Cheesmond (South African/Canadian), Gregg Cronn (American), Barry Blanchard, Kevin Doyle, Tim Friesen & Dr Vern Sawatsky (Canadian)

the Canadians found frequent patches of rotten snow overlaying ice. Faced with a long exposed traverse, they decided to secure this section with their minimal supply of 600m of fixing rope.

Later, they lifted the ropes and took them up to an awkward rockband which starts at about 6700m.

(*Right*) A foreshortened view up the long ice ridge, the rockband, the upper slopes and, on the right, the summit block. (*Barry Blanchard*)
(*Below*) The sting in the tail! Barry Blanchard leading hard, delicate mixed terrain on the summit rock tower at 7650m. (*Dave Cheesmond*)

taken on. From the Japanese Camp 1, at 4800m on the spur, they faced a vertical interval of 3000m to the summit. The initial towers and crests leading to Camp 3 at 5500m were long and difficult, with pitches of grade V. Then they faced the long central ice arête. This arête is the dominant feature in the classic view of Rakaposhi. From a safe distance the aesthete can admire the elegant snow flutings which drape its eastern flank; for the committed climber, close up, the reality is very different and the best route lies up the smoother slopes on the west flank. Even here, though,

Above the rockband the terrain changed to more open hanging glacier slopes. Up here, in their top camp at 7400m, running out of energy and supplies, threatened by bad weather without the reassurance of a safety line of fixed ropes stretching down to the valley, the Canadians decided to retreat. They painstakingly reversed the long spur, downclimbing and abseiling, returned to base camp and packed up to leave. Then a week later, on their last day in the Hunza valley before leaving for Canada, the weather suddenly improved. In a sudden, wonderful, mad fit of opti-

mism, Dave Cheesmond said, 'Why don't we give it one more try?' And they did.

This time just three climbers, Dave Cheesmond, Barry Blanchard and Kevin Doyle, climbed all the way back up the spur. To save time they took a dangerous short-cut, climbing further up the Ghulmet Glacier, close under the immense séracs of the North Face, then cutting left up a couloir, to reach the spur at the site of their old Camp 3. Blanchard advises any future climber taking this short-cut to 'run like a starving jackal'!

From base camp they took four days to reach their previous top camp at 7400m. On the fifth day they bivouacked, like the Japanese, at 7600m on the East Ridge. On the final day, 17 July, they discovered the sting-in-the-tail of this epic route – three pitches of very hard rock and mixed climbing. The middle pitch involved climbing at grade VI and A2, including a pendulum to reach a vital corner, extremely strenuous work at 7700m. Above the rocks an easier snow arête led to the summit. They returned to the bivouac that night and took another two days of intense concentration to descend to base.

Himalayan climbing has advanced since 1984 and today's top mountaineers might consider a pure, two-man, alpine-style ascent of Rakaposhi's North Spur. However, it is worth remembering that the Canadians, despite their experience, fitness and motivation, felt compelled to work slowly on the route, adopting a capsule-style, moving up the mountain with a limited amount of fixed rope to safeguard each section. Given the huge length, height and complexity of this route, with long sections of traversing, it is always going to be a time-consuming proposition; faced with the reality of the terrain, even the boldest climbers may abandon the alpine-style dream in favour of pragmatism. On their final impromptu push, the Canadians reached the summit in just seven days from the Karakoram Highway, but that was with the benefit of several weeks' prior work on the route; seven days on sight would be a very different proposition.

A detailed description of the route is not relevant here and each party will make its own minor variations, but the broad outline is as follows. From the Ghulmet Glacier the North Spur is gained at 4700m just south of some prominent rock pinnacles. The climb from the glacier is safe provided there is good snow cover; in lean conditions rockfall can be a problem. Once on the spur, two snow plateaus and narrow snow ridges lead to the site of the Japanese Camp 2. Then the Step Ridge – four big rock steps – leads to a col at the start of the main snow arête. (This point was reached direct by the Canadians' dangerous short-

cut in 1984). The crest of the arête is festooned with spectacular cornices, and it is usually best to traverse on the West Flank. At about 6700m the arête runs into a 150m high rockband clearly visible from the valley. Mixed climbing up this band leads to a broadening of the spur, where convex slopes may present windslab danger and there are also crevasses. The route here will vary from year to year, but the general trend is rightward, across steep snow slopes, to reach the crest of the East Ridge just beneath the final summit rock tower. This final rockband is climbed by its skyline crest in three hard pitches (one of grade VI and A2), then an easier snow arête leads to the summit. Barry Blanchard summed up the North Spur's universal appeal when he called it 'the Cassin Ridge of the Himalaya'.

SUMMARY STATISTICS AND INFORMATION

Mountain	Rakaposhi
Height	7788m
Location	Rakaposhi Range, Western Karakoram, Pakistan.
Route	North Spur.
First ascent of mountain	Mike Banks & Tom Patey (UK) reached summit on 25 June 1958.
First ascent of route	Summit reached 2 August 1979, by Eiho Ohtani & Matsushi Yamashita. A semi-alpine-style ascent was made by Barry Blanchard (Can), David Cheesmond (RSA/Can) & Kevin Doyle (Can), 12-17 July 1984.
Height of b/c	At 3800m, beside the Ghulmet Glacier.
Roadhead	The hamlet of Ghulmet on the Karakoram Highway.
Length of walk-in	Approx 5km and one day from Ghulmet.
Season	The two successful ascents were made during June and July. Later in the summer, bare ice and rockfall could make the route harder and more dangerous.
Permission	Ministry of Tourism, Islamabad.
Success rate	Up to 1994 there had been five attempts on the route of which two, in 1979 and 1984 were successful. Herrligkoffer's 1971 and 1973 attempts failed and a Slovenian team failed in 1987.
Bibliography	The first ascent of the route is described in *Iwa To Yuki* 72. The *AAJ* vol. 27 (1985) pp 52-60 carries an illustrated article by David Cheesmond, describing the 1984 repeat. For background information on the western approaches to Rakaposhi, see Tilman's *Two Mountains and a River* (included in Tilman, *The Seven Mountain-Travel Books*, Diadem/Mountaineers, 1983) and Mike Banks' *Rakaposhi*, Secker & Warburg, 1959.

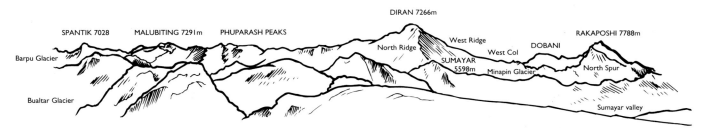

Rising due south from the Hunza, the Sumayar valley leads by a pleasant walk, then steep scrambling, to the Silkiang Glacier, which is enclosed by a fine cirque of alpine scale peaks. This panorama, taken from an easy snow summit in that cirque, Peak Dawson (c.5200m), shows some of the giants aligned along the main southern axis of the Karakoram, sometimes referred to as the Lesser Karakoram. (*Stephen Venables*)

DIRAN 7266m

North Face / West Ridge

For centuries travellers have been intoxicated by the miracle of Hunza's gold and green terraces, carved out of arid desert rubble. With only 14cm of rainfall a year in the valley, the fields and orchards depend entirely on the irrigation channels which siphon off meltwater from thundering glacial torrents. These rivers are in turn fed by the snows of the high peaks which enclose the valley so dramatically. Immediately behind the village of Karimabad, grossly foreshortened, towers the oppressive cirque of Hunza Peak, Bojohaghur Duanasir and Ultar. Further west, the wall continues unbroken to the equally daunting Batura peaks. Looking across to the south side of the valley, the eye is drawn inevitably to Rakaposhi's sharp profile, but a little to the left, rising beyond the Sumayar valley is an altogether gentler white dome, the summit of Diran Peak.

Diran is the perfect foil to Rakaposhi, lower and easier, but still a serious mountain on which success will never be assured. In 1954 Matthias Rebitsch's wide-ranging Hunza expedition explored the southern approaches, concluding that it would be possible to gain the West Ridge from the Bagrot Glacier. In fact, subsequent parties decided on the more obvious approach from the north, up the Minapin valley. In 1958 the British climbers Chris Hoyte and Ted Warr found a way up the glacier slopes of the North Face and continued up the West Ridge. They were last seen only about 100m from the summit. The following year a German attempt was defeated low down on the mountain. In 1964 an Austrian expedition only reached 5500m before succumbing to deep snow and avalanche danger. A year later the Japanese reached Hoyte's and Warr's highpoint, but they were defeated by strong winds. Finally, in 1968, Austrians Rainer Goschl, Hans Schell, and Rudoph Pischinger succeeded in completing the route to the summit of Diran.

Since the opening of the Karakoram Highway in 1978 the mountain has become increasingly popular. Several teams attempted the harder North Ridge, also from the Minapin Glacier, and it was actually descended in 1985, before it was finally climbed by Ken Takahashi's six-man Japanese team in 1989. Other teams opted to repeat the original route up the North Face and West Ridge and it has now had several ascents. With a base camp just two days from the main road and a comparatively straightforward snow and ice route to a 7000m summit, set amongst some of the world's most dramatic mountain scenery, it should remain popular.

The mountain lies on the south side of the Hunza river, in the Shia district of Nagar, traditional rival of the Ishmaeli district of Hunza. The men of Nagar have long held a reputation for obduracy, but recent reports suggest an improved working relationship between Nagar porters and foreign expeditions, so it should be possible to enjoy a harmonious approach from the village of Minapin. It is a delightful walk through fields and forests of juniper, willow and rose bushes, up the west bank of the Minapin Glacier. The journey to Tagafari camping ground can be done in a day, but counts as two porter stages. A third stage takes you across the glacier to Kacheli, a more convenient base camp site at 3750m, closer to the mountain, on the north bank of the glacier. The scramble up Kacheli Peak makes for perfect acclimatisation and an even better view of the route up Diran. Another, more serious, peak for acclimatising is Sumayar Peak (5598m). Trevor Braham and Dennis Kemp, who made the first ascent in 1958, called it Snow Dome, and climbed the snowy south face, initially 45°, then steepening to the

North Ridge

West Col

North Col

Minapin Glacier

(Opposite page) Diran at sunset, rising above the Minapin Glacier. *(Doug Scott)*

West Ridge, which they followed to the summit.

Diran itself is a classic exercise in glacier travel. From base camp the route crosses the glacier, usually dry, then heads up the right-hand side of the north slope of the mountain towards the broad saddle of the West Col. The route will vary from year to year, zigzagging its way through a maze of crevasses. It is not particularly steep or difficult and with good snow conditions it should be little more than a glacier walk. But a few days' snowfall can make progress almost impossible and very dangerous. As Barry Blanchard commented in 1994, 'It's just steep enough to avalanche.' There are also one or two dangerous séracs to pass. Add to that the problems of route-finding in a whiteout, and you have a potential death-trap in a big storm. Blanchard, guiding clients on a traditional ascent with three camps on the mountain, marked the route with 150 wands and recommended 200-300 to be on the safe side. Others, without the responsibility of clients and blessed with crisp snow, will prefer to travel light, using speed to minimise the risk of entrapment. Doug Scott's very strong party, making the fourth ascent in 1985, reached the summit in just two days from the glacier, with a further day for the descent.

Whatever tactics you choose, it is worth remembering that this is a long route. The glacier is at 4000m and the West Col at about 6350m, exposed to ferocious winds in bad weather. From the col there is still another 900m to climb up the West Ridge to the summit. The first ascent party placed a Camp 3 at the col and a final camp further up the ridge at about 6350m where there is a comparatively sheltered balcony on the east side of the ridge.

On a fine day the final ridge, steepening to about 45° in the last 400m, is a magical place, with magnificent views back along the immense connecting ridge to Rakaposhi, north over the Hunza valley to Batura,

(*Top*) Mark Miller, Alastair Reid and Mike Scott above the West Col on a perfect morning in 1985. Behind them the Bagrot Glacier sweeps down left of the 10km ridge linking Diran to Rakaposhi. Profiled on the right is the North Spur of Rakaposhi East, which was climbed by Edi Koblmüller's team a few days after this picture was taken. (*Doug Scott*) (*Below*) A Canadian team weaves its way up the lower crevassed slopes of the North Face. (*Barry Blanchard*)

SUMMARY STATISTICS AND INFORMATION

Mountain	Diran (also known as Minapin)
Height	7266m
Location	Rakaposhi Range, Western Karakoram, Pakistan.
Route	North Face and West Ridge. 3250m of ascent from the Minapin Glacier, entirely on snow, first up the glaciated slopes of the North Face, then on the broad, exposed West Ridge.
First ascent of mountain	Austrians Rainer Goschl, Hans Schell & Rudolph Pischinger reached summit via North Face and West Ridge, 17 August 1968.
First ascent of route	As above.
First alpine-style ascent of route	Mark Miller, Alastair Reid, Doug Scott & Mike Scott (UK), over three days in 1985.
Height of b/c	3750m at Kacheli, in the ablation valley on the north bank of the Minapin Glacier.
Roadhead	Minapin village, a short jeep-ride from the Karakoram Highway.
Length of walk-in	2 days and 3 porter-stages.
Season	June to August.
Permission	Ministry of Tourism, Islamabad.
Success Rate	By 1993 the route had had at least seven ascents, with as many unsuccessful attempts. Given a fit party, success seems to depend largely on the weather.
Bibliography	Trevor Braham's *Himalayan Odyssey* (George Allen & Unwin, 1974) is an inspiring reference work for many areas of the Himalaya. Chapter VI describes in some detail the 1958 expedition which reconnoitred and climbed virtually the entire route on Diran. The actual first ascent is recorded in the 1968 *AAJ* and *HJ*. Subsequent attempts on this route and the North Ridge are written up in later journals.

Shispare and Ultar, and east up the great gash of the Hispar to Kunyang Kish, Kanjut Sar and the distant turrets of the Ogre. They are not as famous as the 8000m giants of the Baltoro, but they are all majestic summits. Ultar remained unclimbed in 1994; most of the others had still had just one ascent; all are difficult mountains with a wealth of possibilities for future pioneers.

SPANTIK 7028m

The North-West (Golden) Pillar

A typical Karakoram pastoral scene at Nagar, with crops ripening amongst apricot, walnut and poplar trees. Thirty kilometres to the south-east the upper section of the Golden Pillar of Spantik is clearly visible. (*Steve Razzetti*)

So called because its orange-pink marble catches perfectly the evening alpenglow, the Golden Pillar of Spantik is a massive sweep of rock and ice. You wonder whether, in fact, it shouldn't belong to a bigger peak; the mountain does look rather shocked by its own immense northern precipice.

Spantik is barely 30km from the Karakoram Highway at Karimabad. Yet you have to drive a few kilometres up the jeep track to Nagar, en route to the Hispar Glacier, to catch a view of the mountain and its pillar. This was the approach of the first ascencionists, Britons Mick Fowler and Victor Saunders in 1987, but all previous activity on the mountain had taken place on the other side.

In 1906, the irrepressible American Fanny Bullock Workman and her husband William, made an attempt on the extremely long South-East Ridge, from near the head of the Chogo Lungma Glacier. She estimated that they reached 6700m, with a good distance still to go to reach the top. In July 1955, German climbers led by Karl Kramer reached the summit by the same route, placing four camps. Subsequently there have been three more ascents from the Chogo Lungma, all using this ridge for all or some of its length: two in 1978 and another in 1984. These climbs were remote adventures at the head of a little visited glacier system. However, our concern here is not really with the summit, but with one of the most striking features in the Karakoram.

There is a tendency to compare the Golden Pillar of Spantik to the great lines of the European Alps such as the Walker Spur or the North-East Pillar of the Droites, but there is an important difference: the Walker starts at 3000m and finishes at 4000m; this line starts at 5000m and finishes at 7000m.

In the classic view from Nagar, only the upper 1100m is visible which, conveniently enough is the extent of the very hard climbing. From base camp, however, at a place beneath the pillar known by locals as Suja Bassa, one sees that the route is split into four

A heart-stopping view down the pillar on the third day of the climb, as Mick Fowler traverses across into the base of the Shale Chimney. Two-day-old tracks are clearly visible on the snow arête far below. (*Victor Saunders*)

barely comprehensible sections: a 400m high tower; a 900m high ridge, less steep but well defined, with an elegant snow arête running its full length; a hanging glacier and snow apron cut by a bergschrund; and,

finally, as Saunders put it 'the point of the exercise: 1100m of wall, like a great spear thrust into the sky'.

The rock on this upper pillar is marble, a crystalline metamorphosed limestone, which also crops up further east in the Karakoram on Gasherbrum IV, Skyang Kangri and, right over in Ladakh, on the Saser Kangri massif. From a distance its orange-pink glow is alluring; close up it is a different story. Although often sound, the marble can be disturbingly compact, with few reassuring cracks. In the case of Spantik, the marble layer is one of many bedding planes tipped vertically and interlayered with dark shale. For Mick Fowler, a devotee of the crumbling sea cliffs of Britain's south-west coastline, there was a perverse pleasure in finding a shale chimney sandwiched high on the Spantik climb.

Before starting the pillar in 1987, Fowler and Saunders wisely investigated a separate descent on this side of the mountain — a prominent parallel spur of snow and ice falling from the South-West Ridge of the mountain about 1500m to the west of the pillar. They then turned their attention to the pillar itself. A gully with pitches of Scottish II/III mixed climbing led up the initial tower to the long serpentine snow arête. At the top of this an awkward mixed step led out on to the hanging glacier. On the first

recce Fowler and Saunders continued up the snow apron and fixed the first two pitches of the upper pillar before caching most of their gear and descending to rest at base camp. The next attempt was stopped by bad weather and they retreated again to base camp. Finally, on 5 August they returned to advance base beneath the pillar. On the 7th they started work on the pillar. Four days later, after forty pitches of intricate, sustained and totally committing climbing, they emerged at the top of the pillar. On 11 August they reached the summit.

In detail, their route climbed directly from the top of the snow apron aiming for the Amphitheatre (a hanging icefield hemmed in by vertical walls rather like the Spider on the North Face of the Eiger). The climbing to here, essentially on the very front face of the pillar, comprised around ten pitches on delicate, poorly protected slabs. In August 1987 they were covered in powder snow and were very difficult (around Scottish IV/V) but, with more ice in the cracks or forming streaks on the slabs, the difficulties would be fewer. The Amphitheatre is an obvious place to bivouac. Saunders and Fowler sat (allegedly comfortably) on a flake that they excavated to form a small ledge.

From the Amphitheatre an obvious chimney line led rightwards to the right-hand edge of the pillar. First there was a long pitch (Scottish VI) with thin smears of ice on compact marble. Then came the Shale Chimney, a shallow 75° gully line cutting steeply in 90m (V) to the right edge of front face and a small bivouac ledge.

The route now followed the right edge of the pillar. Sixty degree slabs, smothered in 20cm of powder snow, led to an obvious vertical corner which gave access to the top of the Giant Jammed Block, where they found the only comfortable ledge on the

entire upper pillar. Above, aid climbing up the shortest of a series of overhanging grooves led to a series of snowy ramp lines slanting rightwards. The ramps were extremely awkward – smooth 55° rock covered in 20cm of powder – and led to a feature called the Shield where the snowy diagonals ran out and began again higher up. Luckily a steep chimney, invisible from below, made the link. This pitch (Scottish V) was again extremely poorly protected and, to make matters worse, Saunders couldn't find a single useful belay point at its top. Instead, he wedged himself across the

Evening light on the North-West Face of Spantik highlights the Golden Pillar, one of the most compelling lines in the whole Karakoram. Seen from a distance, the pinkish glow of the rock suggests granite and it was only discovered in 1987, when Mick Fowler and Victor Saunders climbed the route, that the upper pillar is composed of disconcertingly compact marble. In this photo it is liberally dusted with powder snow which rarely, if ever, disappears. The summit of Spantik itself is just visible, set back, in the cloud. (*Victor Saunders*)

chimney and instructed Fowler not to fall off!

After a fairly stressful day the pair then had to endure a hanging bivouac on an ice ramp not far above, supported by a solitary nut in a crack. On the fourth and final day on the upper pillar, the snow-covered ramps continued, with more difficult, poorly protected pitches to reach the foot of the Open Book Corner. This pitch (Scottish VI) was a dramatic climax, leading directly beneath a huge overhanging and precariously supported sérac, called the Ice Ear, to an exit left. A final 30m wallow through deep snow took the pair back right to the top of the Ice Ear and well deserved level ground.

The summit of Spantik lies 200m above the top of the pillar. In 1987, after long periods of heavy snowfall, this final section consisted of thigh-deep snow. It took Fowler and Saunders a whole day to reach the summit and regain their bivouac at the top of the pillar. They then descended the South-West Ridge for about 1500m to the point (c.6500m) where a well defined snowy spur descends rightward to the glacier. Cornices guarding the top of the spur and windslab conditions further down made for a nerve-racking descent.

Few would argue that the original ascent of the Golden Pillar of Spantik ranks as one of the hardest

achievements ever accomplished in the Karakoram. Although neither as big nor as high as some of the Karakoram giants, this route is distinguished by its sustained, technical nature, at least twenty pitches of mixed climbing at Scottish grade V and above. One feature of the climb was its paucity of protection. Saunders comments in his own route description that at one place (above the unprotected chimney through the Shield), 'this was an irreversible section. No safe pegs equals no safe abseils.' Given that in bad weather downclimbing the chimney would be impossible, and given also that there are at least two pitches of Scottish grade V+ above, you could say that this

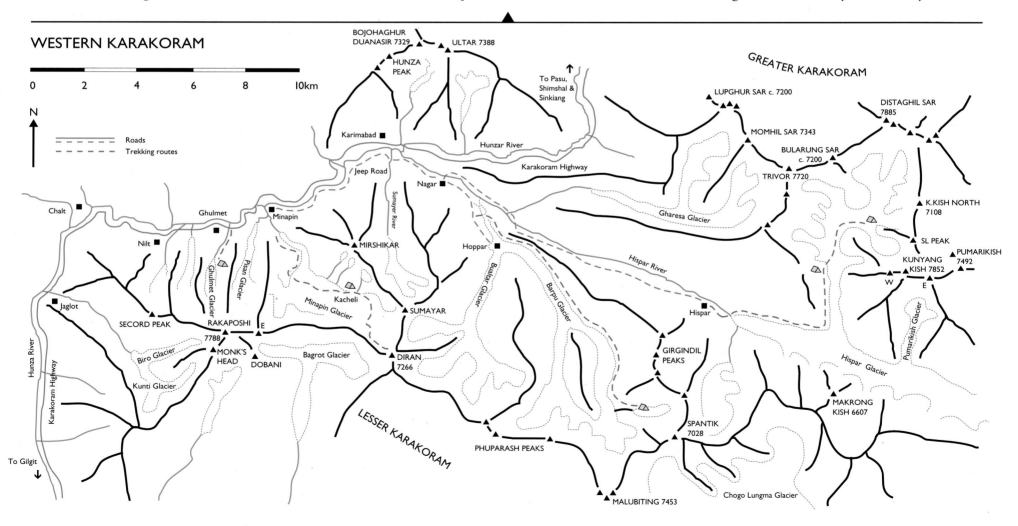

WESTERN KARAKORAM

route is kind of committing.

Conditions in August 1987 were particularly hard, after long spells of heavy snowfall, but it may be that, given the north-west aspect of the pillar, there will never be sufficient sun to consolidate or remove the powder snow. It is likely that the upper pillar will always be characterised by precarious moves on snow-covered rock, demanding considerable skill and nerve. In 1991 another team attempted to repeat the Golden Pillar by taming it with bolts, but they did not get very far. Let us hope that future parties will respect the clean, bold style in which the pillar was first climbed and leave their bolt kits at home.

▲

SUMMARY STATISTICS AND INFORMATION

Mountain	Spantik
Height	7028m
Location	Rakaposhi Range, Western Karakoram, Pakistan.
Route	North-West Pillar. 2100m of ascent, the upper 1100m on steep and very difficult rock and mixed climbing, typically Scottish grade V/VI.
First ascent of mountain	Summit reached 5 July 1955, by K. Kramer and party (Ger) via the South-East Ridge.
First ascent of route	5-11 August 1987, by Mick Fowler & Victor Saunders (UK).
Height of b/c	4000m, at Suja Bassa near the head of the true right branch (Sumayar Bar Glacier) of the Barpu Glacier.
Roadhead	Hoppar, on the edge of the confluence of the Barpu and Bualtar Glaciers, half an hour's drive above Nagar.
Length of walk-in	Approx 35km and 5 stages from Hoppar - traditional porter-stages in this region are very short, and the walk could easily be done in 3 days.
Season	July to September.
Permission	Ministry of Tourism, Islamabad.
Bibliography	Victor Saunders' book *Elusive Summits*, (Hodder & Stoughton, 1990) and the 1987 *AJ* contain humorous, if modest accounts of their ascent. Mick Fowler's article in *Mountain* 118 does likewise. The climb was also recorded in the *AAJ* and *HJ*.

(*Above*) On the fifth and final day on the pillar, Mick Fowler follows a pitch up the snow ramps. The smooth, compact marble, with only the sparsest protection, makes this route a very serious undertaking. (*Victor Saunders*)

(*Left*) Fowler continues up the final pitch on the pillar, right up under the menacing Ice Ear of the summit séracs. Describing Fowler on this section, Victor Saunders said that it was like watching a vacuum cleaner at work, hoovering its way up the powder-choked cracks. (*Victor Saunders*)

▲

KUNYANG KISH 7852m

North-West Spur / North Ridge

Kunyang Kish stands guard like a colossus over the Hispar Glacier. An immense peak, it rises nearly 4000m from base camp and covers an area three or four times that of K2. With Trivor (7720m) and Distaghil Sar (7885m) it forms a mighty triptych, enclosing one of the Hispar's major tributaries, the Kunyang Glacier.

The first climbing team to enter the Kunyang cirque was led by Alfred Gregory, who took our lead photo from the slopes of Distaghil Sar in 1957 (his expedition failed and Distaghil Sar was climbed three years later by Wolfgang Stefan's Austrian expedition). The picture captures perfectly the heroic architecture of Kunyang Kish's northern flank, with the North-West Spur rising in one single sweep to the North Ridge on the left skyline. It is the obvious compelling line up the mountain, yet it was strangely ignored during early attempts on the summit.

The British expedition of 1962 chose the distressingly long 8km South Ridge from the Hispar Glacier. The attempt was abandoned low down after two climbers were killed by a windslab avalanche. Disaster also struck a Japanese attempt in 1965 when another climber died. Then in 1971 a Polish team led by Andrzej Zawada chose a more direct line on to the South Ridge, starting from the Pumarikish Glacier, but even this improved version was very extended. The

route was sieged as far as Camp 4, from where the four summit climbers set off on a bold rising traverse of over 2 kilometres, bivouacking just below the summit, which they reached the following day at sunrise.

That first ascent of Kunyang Kish, by a long highly complex route, was a landmark in Polish Himalayan climbing, but early in the expedition the mountain had once again fulfilled its killer reputation when Jan Franczuk died in a crevasse accident.

Nine years later a British team arrived to try a new route up the mountain. It was Dave Wilkinson who had spotted the classic line on Gregory's photo and who invited Phil Bartlett and Stephen Venables to join him in the first attempt from the north. That 1980 attempt was unsuccessful, but succeeded in pushing a route right up the spur to the start of the North Ridge at 7000m. Influenced by the bold alpine-style successes of the late 'seventies, the British climbers travelled light, eschewing fixed ropes and sheltering in snowholes instead of tents. With greater speed, better timing and kinder weather they would probably have completed the route up the North Ridge; instead they were repulsed twice by massive snowfalls.

A second British attempt failed in 1981, as did a French effort in 1982. In 1987, in a retrograde step, Japanese climbers fixed ropes on the spur, but they too were defeated and a climber was killed, the fifth

person to die on Kunyang Kish. Then finally, in 1988, the route was completed to the summit.

There were five climbers in the successful 1988 British team but bad health stopped all except two, Mark Lowe and Keith Milne, making the final push to the summit. After thorough reconnaissance of the lower spur, they set off on 9 July from Camp 4, a snowcave at about 6900m, emerged on to the North Ridge and continued to make Camp 5 at 7150m. The following evening they made the sixth camp at 7530m and on 11 July, climbing light without rucksacks, reached the summit.

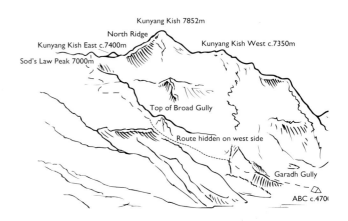

Kunyang Kish, a majestic peak to rival any of the eight-thousanders, with a height gain from base camp to summit of nearly 4000m. Alfred Gregory's picture was taken from the flanks of Distaghil Sar in 1957. Twenty-three years later it inspired Dave Wilkinson to organise an attempt on the classic line of the North-West Spur and North Ridge. The East Summit of Kunyang Kish, appearing behind the North Ridge, and the West Summit both remain unclimbed. (*Alfred Gregory*)

Seventeen years after Zawada's success, the mountain had finally been climbed again, this time by a more logical, direct and perhaps easier line. That is the appeal of this route: it is aesthetically pleasing and it is the line of least resistance, but on this giant of a peak even the easiest line is a serious undertaking with over 3000m of height rise from the glacier.

Advance base lies at about 4700m on the Upper Kunyang Glacier, at the foot of the North-West Spur.

The route reaches the spur from the huge basin on its right, beneath the North-West Face. Huge avalanches crash down regularly from this massive wall, but our route is cunningly protected. First it climbs a narrow gully through rock cliffs on the left side of the icefall. From the top of the gully it traverses right, along the edge of the basin, until another broader snow gully leads up left, to reach the North-West Spur at a little col (c.5700m). There

are good camp sites just above this col.

From here the route follows the left flank of the spur. It is hanging glacier terrain, varying from year to year, but rarely difficult. However, crevasses need care and after heavy snowfalls the entire slope can form lethal windslab. Most parties will need at least one bivouac on this section. The slope eventually steepens to 50° ice, leading directly to the summit of Sod's Law Peak. The 1980 expedition had hoped to find a way

round the back of this 7000m mini-summit, but was forced to climb over the top of it, confirming that 'Sod's Law' always rules. It was tiresome but the reward was an immediate dramatic opening up of new vistas to the north and east, and the first clear view of the North Ridge – a beautiful white ribbon, leading inexorably, like a vast Himalayan version of the famous alpine Biancograt, to the summit.

In reality it is no Biancograt, but an altogether more complex creation. From the top of Sod's Law Peak the dangerously corniced ridge descends slightly to a broader, level section, often laden with deep snow. The first ascent team camped at the end of this level section. The ridge then rises in one 800m sweep to the summit. The precise climbing line will depend on snow conditions and cornices. The angle rarely exceeds 45° but in 1988 Lowe and Milne found an awkward rock step (grade III) at c.7600m and a difficult bergschrund at c.7750m.

The climbing is not particularly technical, but the situation on this final snow ribbon in the sky is stunning. The tiny green oasis of base camp is just visible, nearly 4000m below; beyond it lie all the great peaks of Hunza and Nagar. Far away to the north Kongur and Muztagh Ata rise from the desert of Sinkiang and, as you approach Kunyang Kish's summit, a whole new vista opens to the south-east, towards Snow Lake and the very heart of the Karakoram.

(*Above*) Carlos Buhler enjoying a perfect morning at the start of the North-West Spur, just above the top of Broad Gully. All the lower section of the spur is avoided on the left. The traversing slope between Garadh Gully and Broad Gully can be seen at the bottom left. The skyline is dominated by the huge unclimbed South Face of Trivor (7720m) on the right. The distant white pyramid of Rakaposhi is just visible between the two double-summited peaks on the left, both around 6500m and both unclimbed. (*Stephen Venables*)

Figures in a landscape. Phil Bartlett and Dave Wilkinson on the 1980 attempt, descending from Sod's Law Peak to the start of the North Ridge, where a snowcave (Camp 3) was dug. That night the clouds developed into a storm which kept the climbers pinned down in the snowcave for six days. (*Stephen Venables*)

▲

28

SUMMARY STATISTICS AND INFORMATION

Mountain	Kunyang Kish
Height	7852m
Location	Hispar Muztagh, West Karakoram, Pakistan.
Route	North-West Spur & North Ridge. 3150m of ascent almost entirely on snow and ice. Seriously affected by heavy snowfalls, with some avalanche danger.
First ascent of mountain	Zygmunt Heinrich, Jan Stryczynski, Ryszard Szafirski & Andrzej Zawada (Pol) reached summit 26 August 1971.
First ascent of route	Summit reached 11 July 1988, by Mark Lowe & Keith Milne (UK).
Height of b/c	4000m at Bularung, a camping ground on the west bank of the Kunyang Glacier. Higher, closer sites available beneath Bularung Sar, but porters reluctant to carry that far.
Roadhead	Somewhere between Nagar and Hispar, depending on state of jeep track.
Length of walk-in	Only 20km, but 3 official porter-stages from Hispar, 6 from Nagar.
Season	Fine weather is possible in late autumn, but for vital good snow conditions July & August are probably the best months.
Permission	Ministry of Tourism, Islamabad.
Success rate	By 1994 the route had only been climbed once, despite five attempts. The key to success will usually be speed. A very fit team could climb the route up and down in four days, maximising on a typical short Karakoram weather window.
Bibliography	*Gipfelsturm im Karakoram* by Andrzej Zawada (VEB F.A.Verlag Leipzig, 1977) describes the first ascent, lavishly illustrated. See also *Mountain* 22 & 44. For articles and reports on the North Ridge see *AJ* vol.88 ('West of Baltoro' by S. Venables) & vol. 94, *Mountain* 77 & 126, *HJ* 46.

Calm after the storm. Sunrise gilds the unclimbed East Ridge on the left, while the North Ridge rises directly to the summit, photographed on the return over Sod's Law Peak. In the bottom left corner is the faint impression of the snowcave at 7000m and a powdery trench stopping just above it, representing half an hour's futile attempt to continue up the ridge. The route was completed eventually in 1988 by Mark Lowe and Keith Milne. (*Stephen Venables*)

The massive ramparts of the Ogre's South Face towering over the Uzun Brakk Glacier, photographed from near the campsite at Baintha. On the left, obscuring part of the Ogre, is Lukpilla Brakk (5380m), or Ogre's Thumb, one of the myriad smaller granite towers in the area. It was first climbed in 1984 by Rob Milne, Galen Rowell, Jack Tackle and Gray Thompson. (*Steve Razzetti*)

THE OGRE 7285m

The South Pillar

Baintha Brakk, a magnificent three-summited peak towering above the immense snowfields at the heart of the Central Karakoram, has been climbed only once. Given the tempting challenge of technical rock climbing at 7200m, it is puzzling that such a wonderful and relatively accessible mountain has seen so few visitors. It is known to most as the Ogre – the site of the famous epic in which Doug Scott broke both his legs on the first abseil from the summit (with Chris Bonington later on the descent breaking two ribs and contracting pneumonia). Scott's strength of character, crawling for seven days in a dreadful storm back to a deserted base camp, and the dedication of his companions through the ordeal, make this story one of the most gripping in recent Himalayan exploration.

With its three summits and its battery of granite pillars and hanging icefields, the Ogre is a complex mountain. Early attempts concentrated on the south-western aspect above the Uzun Brakk Glacier, and it was from this side that Scott's party, the fourth to attempt the mountain, made the first ascent in 1977. The six-man team had multiple objectives and Scott himself hoped to climb the impressive prow of rock on the left of the South Face, the South Pillar. However, he had to abandon this route when his companion, Tut Braithwaite, was injured by a falling stone, and join the rest of the team on their easier line up the South-West

Face. The South Pillar, our selected route, was eventually climbed by a French team in 1983 though the climbers who completed the pillar, Michel Fauquet and Vincent Fine, did not actually reach the summit. Before describing the pillar, we will look at the less direct route of the first ascent.

In 1977 Mo Anthoine, Clive Rowland, Chris Bonington and Nick Estcourt chose the route attempted the previous year by a Japanese team, the 1200m high mixed spur which leads to the broad glacier terrace supporting the rock tower of the West Summit. This spur alone is equivalent to a major alpine mixed climb, but it is probably the easiest breach in the Ogre's defences and it stands clear of sérac avalanches. From the glacier terrace above, two options were tried. First Bonington and Estcourt traversed round to the right, on to the upper slopes of the South Face. Over-extended and short of supplies, they ignored the Main Summit on this foray, settling for the first ascent of the lower West Summit.

A week later Bonington returned with Anthoine, Rowland and Scott. This time, instead of the insecure traverse round on to the South Face, they climbed up to the West Ridge, overlooking the Sim Gang Glacier. The ridge, rising in two huge granite steps, gave excellent climbing with pitches of grade V, and provided a safer route to the West Summit. However, this time,

the real goal was the monolithic turret of the Main Summit itself and the four climbers now descended the far side of the West Summit to dig a cave in the hanging icefield at the top of the South Face.

The final day to the Main Summit proved unexpectedly long and difficult. Bonington and Scott went ahead, traversing across the top of the snowed-up icefield, then on to the crest of the ridge above before tackling the final turret. Scott's lead up five pitches of hard free and aid climbing – some of the hardest technical climbing ever attempted at that altitude – was a tour de force of bold commitment on a truly inaccessible summit. He and Bonington finally reached the top at sunset and it was nearly dark by the time Scott set off down on the first abseil. It was whilst reversing a difficult pendulum that he skidded on newly frozen verglas, swung across the face and broke both his ankles. On any summit it would have been alarming; at 7200m on the Ogre it was a nightmare, compounded the following day by the arrival of a major storm. Luckily Scott had enormous mental and physical reserves and, although his ankles were broken, he was still able to use his knees. He also had three highly competent partners with him. And he had the benefit of occasional fixed ropes and camps to aim for on the gruelling traverse back over the West Summit. If this had been a pure alpine-style ascent the outcome might perhaps have been less happy. As it was, the whole team was stretched to the limit to escape alive from the Ogre and return to tell the tale of one of the most remarkable first ascents of all time. Bonington summed it up nicely when he wrote, 'I felt that the Ogre had allowed us to climb it and then, like a great cat, had played with us all the way down, finally

is essentially a rock climb, with 1000m of beautiful, rough, red granite providing a direct approach to the upper icefields of the South Face. Looking up from the Uzun Brakk Glacier, one sees a prominent rocky ridge, or rognon, descending from the pillar, dividing the upper glacier. The dangerous right-hand glacier branch leads to the col between Baintha Brakk I and Baintha

obvious. The first section is almost horizontal, with easy ground, then three aid pitches, followed by an airy traverse left into a gap. Then the main pillar begins to rear up, with easy pitches at first, then several excellent pitches of grade V as the rock steepens. An awkward offwidth (V+) leads to a very exposed ledge. To the left of the ledge easier pitches (IV) with

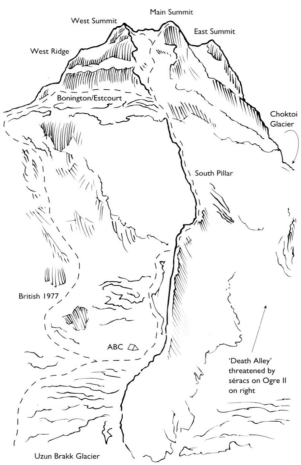

The entire South Face with the South Pillar highlighted by early morning sunshine. (*Chris Bonington*)

allowing us to escape, mauled but in one piece to play more games with other mountains in the future.'

The original route over the West Summit is probably the easiest way of getting to the Ogre's Main Summit tower. However it is a long and circuitous approach. More elegant perhaps is the line of the South Pillar, first climbed in 1983 by Fauquet and Vine. This

Brakk II (itself an inspiring peak, but festooned with lethal séracs on this side). Our route takes the left-hand branch, passing under the 1977 original route and reaching the South Pillar by a gully. There is some stonefall danger here, but the terrain is easy, allowing fast movement to the safer crest of the pillar.

Once the pillar is reached the line becomes quite

some snow and a tension traverse lead to a much bigger ledge and snowpatch – the best bivouac site so far.

Above the big ledge, several pitches of IV and V and more easy ground lead to another obvious ledge above a prominent chandelle. Above this ledge comes the hardest climbing (VI+) up compact slabs, avoiding an obvious roof on the left. Further pitches of grade V lead to the top of the pillar where there is a comfortable bivouac ledge. From the start of the pillar

▲

(*Below*) One of those pictures that answers the question 'Why do we do it?' From a high camp on the West Ridge in 1977, Clive Rowland looks out across the Uzun Brakk Glacier. The peak on the right with the prominent streak of sunlit snow, is Uzun Brakk or Conway's Ogre (6422m). In 1980 Victor Saunders and Will Tapsfield climbed the wall facing the camera, taking the narrow slanting gully. Further back on the right, the jagged summit of Sosbun Brakk (6413m) rises above the Biafo Glacier. The two rounded summits on the horizon left of centre are Ganchen (left) and Hikmul. (*Doug Scott*)

(*Above*) Nick Estcourt finding a way on to the upper slopes of the South Face in 1977. On this occasion he and Bonington had traversed in from left, but teams climbing the South Pillar also reach the same point, from where there is still 350m to climb to the main summit on the right. (*Chris Bonington*)

to here is about twenty-four rope-lengths.

The top of the pillar is at about 6500m. Despite at least three ascents of the pillar itself, no party on this route has yet succeeded in reaching the summit of Baintha Brakk. Fauquet and Vine made a brave try, sitting out a day of poor weather, then wading through metre-deep snow to reach the base of the final tower. The route slants rightward across 40-50° ice or snow-fields, crossing a small rockband at about 7000m.

(*Left*) Malte Roeper leading one of the aid pitches at the start of the South Pillar. (*Hans-Christian Hocke*)

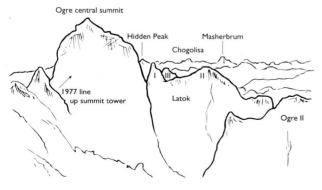

Although never desperate, the terrain up here, first explored by Bonington and Estcourt in 1977, is delicate and a lot of care is needed to secure good belays. And of course it leads to a remarkable sting-in-the-tail — the final vertical granite tower of the Main Summit.

The summit tower has not yet been climbed direct by its South Face and the best option may be to follow the Bonington/Scott route. From the top icefield (usually snow-covered) they climbed an obvious gully and rocks (IV) on to the ridge between the West and Main Summits. They then followed the ridge crest over the pinnacle just west of the summit tower and abseiled down its east side to reach the little col immediately left of the tower. From here the real fun started.

There are five pitches. The first is a long groove (V) leaning slightly rightwards to reach (in 1977) a patch

(*Far left*) Evening light on the Main Summit tower, photographed from the West Summit. (*Chris Bonington*)

(*Left*) Chris Bonington following the aid crack on the summit tower on the first ascent in 1977. It is already late and the huge sweep of the South Face below is in shadow, except for a streak of light at the foot of the South Pillar. By the time Bonington and Scott reached the top it was dusk. Shortly after that Scott broke both his legs on the first abseil from the summit. (*Doug Scott*)

(*Below*) Three days later Scott, helped by Anthoine, Bonington and Rowland, crawls painfully through the storm, back over the West Summit, with 2000m of descent still to go. (*Chris Bonington*)

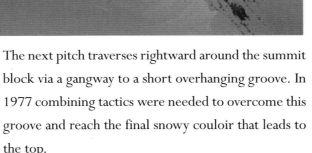

(*Above left*) Unfinished business. A distant view of the Ogre/Latok group from the Khurdopin Pass after heavy snowfall. On the left is the much-tried North Face of Latok I. Right of that is the broader summit of Latok II and in the centre is the top of the untouched North Face of the Ogre. (*Stephen Venables*)

of snow. The wall above provides the next. Split by a single crack, this is climbed (good nut and Friend placements) for about 25m to where it peters out. A pendulum swing right for 5-10m reaches a continuation crack, followed for the rest of the rope-length to the small snowy shoulder (V/A1). (It may be possible to avoid this pitch by abseiling diagonally rightward from the snow patch into an adjacent chimney system.)

The next pitch traverses rightward around the summit block via a gangway to a short overhanging groove. In 1977 combining tactics were needed to overcome this groove and reach the final snowy couloir that leads to the top.

Few summits are as commanding. The panorama from this, the highest peak for scores of kilometres in all directions, extends from K2 to Nanga Parbat. Nor

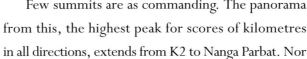

are many as remote, with a great deal of difficult down-climbing and abseiling still required to regain terra firma. The epic descent in 1977 demonstrated just how vulnerable a small party is on this complex mountain. For that reason, most teams on the South Pillar, will think very carefully about their tactics.

In 1990 a German team used big-wall techniques, complete with haul sacks and portaledges, on the South

An aerial view of the Ogre/Latok group, looking across the great highway of the Biafo Glacier which, together with the connecting Hispar, is over 70km long. In this shot the glacier is still snow-covered, but by July it is usually bare gritty ice, blessedly free of moraine debris. (*Galen Rowell*)

Pillar. In their own estimation, this was a mistake. Too many of the pitches are easy-angled to allow for efficient sack-hauling and the four climbers spent far too long on the route, leaving no time or energy for the upper face. So it is actually more efficient to move in a more alpine-style, as did Fauquet and Vine on their 1983 ascent. After initial preparation of the lower pitches, they set off in a single push, taking five days on the pillar, waiting a day at the top, then taking another day to reach the foot of the summit tower. The descent, including twenty-four abseils down the pillar, took another three days. Although they did not reach the summit, they showed that a ten-day round trip is feasible; with a little more

speed on the rock pillar (now that many of the abseil anchors are in position, rock climbing racks could be kept quite light), ten days could include the summit tower. Alternatively, it might be best to spend time fixing the pillar and caching supplies near the top, before jumaring back up at high speed to give oneself a better chance on the summit slopes. Provided the ropes were removed on the descent, it would harm nobody.

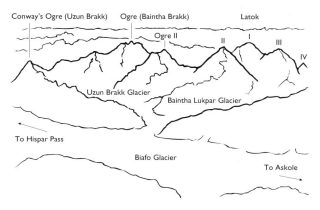

On Baintha Brakk no system will ever be perfect. The variety of steep technical problems on this huge complex mountain is always going to present the Himalayan dilemma of speed versus weight. But that is what makes this kind of mountain so stimulating. By any route it is always going to demand skill, determination and luck. There are still many other possibilities for exploration, particularly the daunting North Face, brooding over the quasi-arctic Sim Gang Glacier and the sunnier South-East Face, rising from the Choktoi Glacier to the still untouched East Summit. However, with at least five attempts since 1983, the South Pillar seems to be the most popular objective. It has the advantage of a comparatively short approach from Askole and delightful base camp, surrounded by a myriad rock towers and spires, ideal for acclimatisation before setting foot on the Ogre itself, a true mountaineer's mountain.

Mountain	The Ogre (Baintha Brakk)
Height	7285m
Location	Panmah Muztagh, Central Karakoram, Pakistan.
Route	South Pillar. Glacier approach to 5500m and start of 1000m pillar. Technical granite climbing to grade VI and A2, followed by 600m snow, ice and mixed slopes and finally 5 pitches technical rock and mixed climbing (V & A2) on the summit tower.
First ascent of mountain	West Summit reached by Chris Bonington & Nick Estcourt (UK) 1 July 1977. Main Summit reached by Bonington & Doug Scott (UK) 13 July via South-West Spur and West Ridge of West Summit.
First ascent of route	Michel Fauquet & Vincent Fine reached top of South Pillar at c.6500m on 15 June 1983, but failed to reach summit.
Height of b/c	At c.4500m, on the true left bank of the Uzun Brakk Glacier below the south-western slopes of Ogre's Thumb and Lukpilla Brakk. The 1990 Dutch attempt on the pillar was thwarted by bears stealing all the expedition food from base camp; bear-proof storage barrels are strongly recommended in this area!
Roadhead	Askole, a day's jeep drive from Skardu.
Length of walk-in	Approx 45 kilometres and four days, via Namla, Mango and Baintha, camping sites on the Biafo Glacier
Season	Conditions are best in July/August.
Permission	Ministry of Tourism, Islamabad.
Success rate	Of five attempts between 1977-1993, two reached the top of the pillar, but none reached the summit. Despite its obvious dangers, the Ogre had only claimed one victim by 1993, when a German climber was killed on the South Pillar after becoming unclipped from his ropes.
Bibliography	Bonington wrote a concise account of the first ascent of Baintha Brakk in the *AAJ* vol. 21 (1978). Bonington's book *Mountaineer* and Scott's *Himalayan Climber*, both published by Diadem, contain picture essays of this expedition. The *AAJ* vol. 26 (1984) details the French ascent of the South Pillar in 1983.

LATOK III 6949m

South-West Ridge

Trekking up the Biafo Glacier, one's eye is drawn unavoidably to the side valley of the Uzun Brakk Glacier and the imposing Ogre peaks. However, if you look back as you pass the valley entrance, you see another glacier, the Baintha Lukpar; clustered around the head of this glacier are yet more gloriously gothic towers – the Latoks – and from this viewpoint the most impressive is Latok III, bounded on the right by the soaring buttress of its South-West Ridge.

Like the Ogre, the Latoks are difficult, complex mountains, composed of granite, with large ice cliffs often threatening potential climbing routes. Latok II (7108m) was climbed in 1977 by an eighteen-person Italian expedition led by Prof. Arturo Bergameschi, following a series of buttresses and ice slopes from the south-east, with prolific rope-fixing along the way. The expedition also had a field day on smaller peaks, climbing most of the five-thousanders on the true left bank of the Baintha Lukpar Glacier.

Latok I (7145m) was climbed in 1979 by Naoki Takada's Japanese expedition, also from the Baintha Lukpar side, ascending the buttress left of the danger-

Latok III from the Baintha Lukpar Glacier. The West Face on the left is unclimbed and the only route to date, the South-West Ridge, is the line between light and shade. The route mainly follows the right-hand side of the ridge. (*Victor Saunders*)

ous couloir between Latoks I and III, and then up the East Ridge. Meanwhile on the other side of the mountain, operating from a base camp on the Choktoi Glacier in 1978, a strong team of young American alpinists had made the first of many attempts, by many different nationalities, on the tremendous 2500m high North Ridge. 'Ridge' is perhaps a misleading term for this very steep spur, bristling with difficulties on rock, snow and ice. In 1978, Jim Donini and Michael Kennedy, with George and Jeff Lowe, very nearly completed the route, claiming to be within 100m of the summit ridge when they eventually turned back. The decision to retreat was prompted by one member's illness, but the whole team was near breaking point after sitting out a five-day storm at the highpoint. By the time they regained the Choktoi Glacier the four climbers had been on the spur for twenty-six continuous days, almost four weeks!

The American effort of 1978 has not been equalled since and, with depressing inevitability, some teams have now draped fixed ropes where the Americans managed without. Despite those ropes, the route remains one of the most sought-after uncompleted lines in the Himalaya.

Returning to the Baintha Lukpar side of the group, Latok IV (6456m) was climbed by a Japanese expedition in 1980. The South-West Face was climbed alpine-style and on the final push Motomo Ohmiya and Koji Okano reached the summit. Whilst digging a bivouac cave on the descent they both fell 50m into a concealed crevasse, sustaining serious injuries. They waited hopefully for four days but when no rescue came Ohmiya managed to tunnel through the snow ridge forming the outer wall of the crevasse. After twelve hours digging he escaped and began to crawl down the mountain, dragging his broken leg. Once alerted, members of the British Uzun Brakk expedition came to help with the rescue, eventually hauling Okano out of the crevasse after eight days incarceration.

The first ascent of Latok III (6949m) was less dramatic, but it did involve some very hard climbing. Makoto Hara led the first attempt, by the South-West Ridge, in 1978. The following year another Japanese team, led by Yoji Teranishi, was successful on the same route, reaching the summit on 15 July, after three weeks' work on the ridge, placing four camps and fixing 1600m of rope. With a height gain of 2300m from the glacier and rock climbing difficulties up to VI+/A2, this was a remarkably hard route for the first ascent of a peak.

Nine years later Latok III was climbed again by three Italians. When Marco Forcatura and Marco Marciano from Rome invited Enrico Rosso, a well-known alpinist from Biella, to join their 1988 attempt, Rosso decided that, 'the project was exactly in line with my idea of alpinism – an aesthetically beautiful peak, attempted by a lightweight expedition in alpine-style. There was no reason not to accept!' The Italians hoped to try the unclimbed West Face but, arriving in early June with heavy precipitation threatening avalanches, they decided, after much wading around in deep snow, to repeat the safer Japanese line up the South-West Ridge. Even this route had its dangers. On the lower mixed plinth they had to contend with unconsolidated snow as steep as 70° and higher up many of the rock cracks were choked with ice. The route was virtually in winter condition and it took seven days to reach the final crux rock wall, which took another full day to climb. After reaching the summit at 7.30 pm they had a worrying abseil descent in the dark to regain their tent, followed by two more days abseiling back down the ridge.

The Italians admitted that they were helped in places by the old Japanese ropes. Nevertheless, their ten-day self-supported push in very hard conditions was a fine achievement. After numerous official and unofficial attempts in the massif, this was the first time that one of the Latok peaks had had a second ascent. Now that they have confirmed the quality of the Latok III route it may have further repeats. The line tends to follow the right-hand (south) side of the South-West Ridge. Initial couloirs lead to the start of the ridge proper at 5100m. The Japanese placed their Camp 2 here and Camp 3 at 6500m. From Camp 3 they took the rightmost of three prominent icy grooves to a prominent snow terrace below the final wall. Camp 4 was placed here at 6700m. The 300m wall above was the crux of the climb, with steep technical rock climbing up the central crack system leading to the final snow ridge and summit.

SUMMARY STATISTICS AND INFORMATION

Mountain	Latok III
Height	6949m
Location	Panmah Muztagh, Central Karakoram, Pakistan.
Route	South-West Ridge. 2300m of ascent from the glacier, 1850m on the ridge itself. Difficult mixed climbing and rock difficulties to VI+/A2.
First ascent of mountain	Summit reached on 15 July 1979 by Sakae Mori, Kazushige Takami and Yoji Teranishi (Jap).
First ascent of route	As above.
First alpine-style ascent of route	12-20 June 1988 by Marco Forcatura, Marco Marciano & Enrico Rosso (Italy), helped partially by old Japanese ropes.
Height of b/c	4300m on south bank of Baintha Lukpar Glacier.
Roadhead	Thongl, 2km before Askole.
Length of walk-in	Approx 4 days as for Ogre.
Season	The heavy snow conditions found by the Italians are not uncommon in June. July and August are probably better months, although increasing heat will bring the risk of stonefall, necessitating some very early starts up the initial couloirs.
Permission	Ministry of Tourism, Islamabad.
Success rate	Three known attempts and two ascents to date on this route. In the Latok group as a whole the success rate has been quite low – they are not easy mountains.
Bibliography	Very little has been published on the Latok peaks. However, anyone interested in the famous North Ridge of Latok I should study Michael Kennedy's account in *AAJ* 1979. The first ascent of Latok III was recorded in *Iwa to Yuki* and the Italian repeat was written up in *Rivista della Montagna* 107.

Marco Forcatura stepping up into the crack line which is the key to the steep headwall. During the 1988 ascent many of the cracks were choked with snow and ice. The three Italians took eight days to climb to the summit in a single alpine-style push. As can be seen from the picture, route-finding was aided by old Japanese ropes. (*Enrico Rosso*)

ULI BIAHO TOWER 6109m

East Face

In 1937 Eric Shipton led an expedition to explore some of the world's greatest glacier systems at the heart of the Karakoram. After stocking up with supplies in Skardu, the team set off with a hundred Balti porters up the Braldu river, through Askole, over the Panmah river and on up the Biaho river to the black tongue of the Baltoro Glacier. Then a short way up the Baltoro they took a sharp turn left on to the Trango Glacier, following the advice of the Italian explorer, Professor Desio, who had recommended this route as the best way of crossing the Karakoram watershed to the Shaksgam. Desio's hunch was vindicated when the British team succeeded in cajoling its work force over the previously unexplored Sarpo Laggo Pass and descended the far side to the remote Shaksgam valley.

Shipton had already experienced some of the most dramatic scenery in Asia, but he was thrilled by his 1937 journey up the Trango Glacier. Describing the

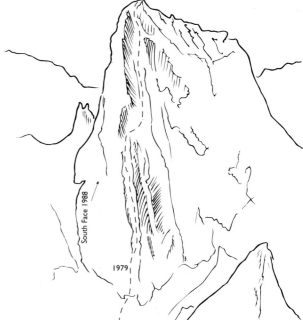

South Face 1988

1979

Uli Biaho from Great Trango. The slender East Face of Uli Biaho Tower rises at centre from the long, dirty glacier gully approach. The American route starts from the snow tongue just left of the lowest point of the face. Behind, on the left, is Paiju Peak (6610m) first climbed by Manzoor Hussain's Pakistani army expedition, with the famous Yosemite climber, Allen Steck, as technical adviser. On the right is the pointed summit of Choricho (6756m) first climbed by its South-West Face, by Ian Wade's Anglo-American team the same year as Uli Biaho's first ascent, 1979. (*Andy Selters*)

scene in *Blank on the Map*, he wrote of 'immense columns of granite supporting graceful summits, so remotely inaccessible that they seemed hardly to be part of the same colossal structures. The flanks of these peaks were frosted over with ice and powder snow sparkling like a million diamonds in the morning sunlight.' Nearly forty years passed before a new generation of mountaineers set foot on these fairytale granite spires – the Trango group on the north

bank of the glacier and, on the south side, a maze of pinnacles, turrets and minarets dominated by the unmistakable monolith of Uli Biaho.

Uli Biaho Tower (to use the full name, distinguishing the rock monolith from the higher Uli Biaho Peak) was nearly climbed in 1974 by a six-man French team, led by Jean Fréhel, attempting the North-West Pillar. Amongst the three climbers turned back by a storm 100m from the top of the pillar was Pierre Béghin, later to become one of the great international names in Himalayan mountaineering. It was another well-known star, the American John Roskelley, who arrived on the Trango Glacier in 1979 to attempt the first ascent. For Roskelley the route was everything. Uli Biaho was a wonderful unclimbed summit, but the line had to be superlative too. Whereas the French had tried what was probably the shortest, easiest route, round the back door, Roskelley chose the obvious front flank of the tower overlooking the Trango Glacier – the tall, elegant, tapered East Face which rises 1100m direct to the summit. His companions were Kim Schmitz, Bill Forrest and Ron Kauk, who was then one of the very best rock climbers in the world. In Roskelley's words, 'Success on Uli Biaho

began and ended with the selection of the team. It was their attitude that proved bigger and stronger than the obstacles and risk.'

The most obvious risk was the approach. Like some of the routes in the Trango group, the East Face of Uli Biaho can only be reached practically by a long, narrow glacier gully, which collects all the debris falling from the immense walls above. Being east-facing, it is at its most dangerous in the morning. In 1979 the Americans had to make two huge load carries up this gully to get their big-wall gear established on the face itself. Their route started just left of the lowest point on the face, at the apex of a snow bay. From there it followed the obvious crack system straight up, then trending right towards the summit. As Roskelley wrote, 'There's only one way to go and still follow the obvious crack system.'

Only two or three ledges on the entire route were suitable for one or two people to sleep on; with four climbers portaledges were essential. Even on the snowy Bat Ledge, nine pitches up the route, the bivouac was suspended. The team moved as a self-contained unit all the way up the wall, totally committed for ten days, each pair alternating the excitement of leading with the drudgery of hauling up 150kg of equipment. For the leaders there was continual interest and difficulty. For instance the first pitch above Bat Ledge used aid to surmount thin cracks in the left wall of a huge left-facing corner. The third pitch was 'an angry off-width corner' which slowed even Ron Kauk to a crawl. At the next bivouac the portaledges had to be stacked in four storeys, suspended from bolts above an immense drop. For two nights the team was pinned down here by a storm, before continuing up an overhanging corner, aided on alternate rock pins and tied-off ice screws.

A beautiful Karakoram morning at the four-tier bivouac, halfway up the East Face in 1979. (*John Roskelley*)

▲

And so it continued, almost entirely aid climbing, up to A4 difficulty. In those days no one carried friction rock boots on Himalayan walls, but even if they had, the water and ice in the cracks would have deterred them from extensive free climbing. In big boots, they climbed no free sections harder than American 5.8. In the upper section, as the route traverses right beneath snowy ledges, then heads up a right-facing corner to the summit, the climbing became increasingly mixed,

demanding skill, ingenuity and nerve.

The final dramatic obstacle was a house-sized ice mushroom on the summit ridge, perched 'like a kiwi bird on two skinny legs'. Roskelley had to crawl between its legs, before bringing the rest of the team up to the summit.

Two days later the Americans completed their thirty-fourth abseil from the summit and reached the foot of the wall. Their route remains unrepeated but in 1988 a very strong Italian team climbed the slightly shorter South Face of Uli Biaho from the same glacier cirque. Maurizio Giordani, Rosanna Manfrini, Maurizio Venzo and Kurt Walde spent four days on the 800m wall. Wearing rock boots, they managed to free over half of the twenty pitches, rating the difficulty VI to VII; the aid sections were A2 and A3. Like the Americans on the East Face, they found much of the rock encrusted with ice. However, they did climb the route in June and

perhaps it would be drier later in the summer.

The Italian route was particularly noteworthy because it was almost certainly the hardest technical route pioneered in the Himalaya by a woman. The expedition was also remarkable because the team leader, Maurizio Giordani, went on, just three days after descending from Uli Biaho, to solo a new route up the North Face of Great Trango in nine hours, showing what is possible in this granite wonderland for those with skill and stamina.

▲

SUMMARY STATISTICS AND INFORMATION

Mountain	Uli Biaho Tower
Height	6109m
Location	Baltoro Muztagh, Central Karakoram, Pakistan. (The Tower lies 3km east of the main summit of Uli Biaho Peak.)
Route	East Face. 1100m of continuously steep climbing on rock, frequently ice-encrusted. Grade VI- and A4. Difficult mixed and ice climbing on the upper pitches.
First ascent of mountain	Summit reached 3 July 1979 by Bill Forrest, Ron Kauk, John Roskelley & Kim Schmitz (USA) after ten-day alpine-style push.
First ascent of route	As above.
Height of b/c	Trango base camp on the north-east bank of the Trango Glacier at c.4000m.
Roadhead	Thongl, 2km before Askole.
Length of walk-in	3 to 5 days and about 6 porter-stages from the roadhead.
Season	The original ascent was made at the end of June. Later in the season the rock might be less encrusted with ice and snow, but there could well be greater stonefall danger in the approach gully.
Permission	Ministry of Tourism, Islamabad.
Success Rate	There have only been three official attempts on the tower, each by a different route. Two – the East Face and South Pillar – were successful; both were by exceptionally strong teams.
Bibliography	The Italian route on the South Pillar is reported briefly in *AAJ* 1989. The East Face is described in John Roskelley's article in *AAJ* 1980.

(*Above right*) Amidst the austere desert scenery of the Karakoram there are enchanting pockets of greenery. Here rhubarb and aconitums nestle amongst granite boulders at Trango Base Camp. (*Andy Selters*)

(*Above left*) A young, lean Roskelley on an earlier Baltoro expedition, en route for Trango, carrying expedition meat-on-the-hoof. (*Galen Rowell*)

TRANGO TOWER 6251m

South Pillar — Eternal Flame

It is probably the largest rock needle in the world. The early explorers marvelled at it on their way to the giant peaks of the Upper Baltoro Glacier but it was only in 1956 that Joe Brown, the legendary British climber, returning from the first ascent of the comparatively gentle Muztagh Tower, dreamed of actually climbing Trango. Nineteen years later he returned to attempt the monolith. That attempt failed but on a second expedition in 1976 he reached the dream summit with Mo Anthoine, Martin Boysen and Malcolm Howells.

That first ascent of the Trango Tower was a break-through in Himalayan big-wall climbing, yet subsequent progress was so fast that by 1992 there were no less than eight routes to the summit. Our chosen line is Eternal Flame, the route completed in 1989 by two of the world's most talented rock climbers, Kurt Albert and the late Wolfgang Güllich. It is a rock climber's dream – sustained free climbing at the highest standard on immaculate granite that reminded

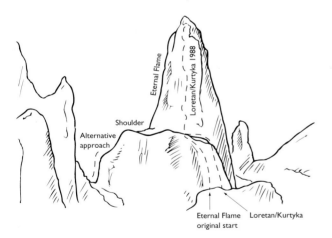

(*Far Left*) Trango Tower photographed in 1992 from the Dunge Glacier base camp. The Kurtyka/Loretan route climbs the upper tower by the right-facing dièdres in the middle of the face. Further left lie the Child/Wilford (1992) and Slovenian (1987) routes. Eternal Flame follows the left-hand profile of the upper tower. Clearly visible halfway up the left side of the upper tower is a long grey scar, site of the gigantic rockfall in 1992. It is now probably safer to approach all these routes from the other side, reaching the obvious notch to the left of the tower, then following the lower pitches of the Slovenian route to Sun Terrace. (*Greg Child*)

Albert of California's famous Joshua Tree. It is probably the hardest and most beautiful route up the tower and the position, amidst the greatest concentration of high mountains on earth, is stunning.

The Trango Tower, sometimes referred to as

(*Below*) Karakoram granite at its most immaculate. Kurt Albert leading the crux pitch of Eternal Flame, 'Say my name' (grade IX-). Although he equipped the route with double bolt anchors at each belay, Albert protected individual pitches almost entirely with natural removable gear. (*Wolfgang Güllich/Kurt Albert Collection*)

Nameless Tower, forms only a small part of the overall Trango Group which harbours more granite than the whole of Yosemite. Indeed, neighbouring Great Trango, 6286m, is an even bigger if less well defined bastion of rock than the Tower. An American party led by Galen Rowell made the first ascent of Great Trango's Central Summit in 1977 following a series of

icy ramps linked by rock steps on the South Face. Their 1000m route is graded A1 and VI; the Andy Selters/Scott Woolums 1984 route up the North-West Face is rather easier. Altogether more serious are the two routes to the East Summit of Great Trango from the Dunge Glacier. The Norwegian Pillar of 1984 is 1500m high (40 pitches), sees little sun and is ferociously hard – grade VII and A4 climbing with considerable use of sky/bat hooking and copperheads. The summit pair, Hans Christian Doseth and Finn Daelhi, were killed on the descent, presumably in an abseil accident. Perhaps even harder than the Norwegian Pillar is the parallel line, Grande Voyage, climbed in 1992 by Swiss climbers, Xaver Bongard, Ueli Bühler and François Studiman with Yosemite veteran, John Middendorf.

The Norwegian Pillar and Grande Voyage are perhaps the hardest big-wall climbs in the world. The smaller Trango Tower will probably remain more popular. It is more elegant, more symmetrical — the quintessential, isolated, surreal aiguille – a Himalayan version, on a grander scale, of Chamonix's famous Dru.

The first attempt in 1975 was led by Mo Anthoine. His British team approached the base of the South-West Face by a long couloir from the Trango Glacier. A hidden ramp, slanting from left to right, took them through the Tower's lower plinth to a snow ledge at about one third height. The route then climbed steeply rightwards toward an obvious chimney system. Disaster almost struck while Martin Boysen was leading a typically vicious pitch. As he remarked with characteristic acerbity, 'Americans would call it an off-width crack; I called it something else.' This was before Friends came on the market and Boysen led the pitch with just one five-inch bong for protection. He had nearly completed the pitch when his knee jammed

(*Above*) Kurt Albert lacing up his rock slippers during a perfect day on the Tower. (*Wolfgang Güllich/Kurt Albert Collection*)
(*Right*) Mark Wilford dressed up for the alternative reality of Karakoram weather whilst climbing a new route on the South-East Face with Greg Child in 1992. (*Greg Child*)

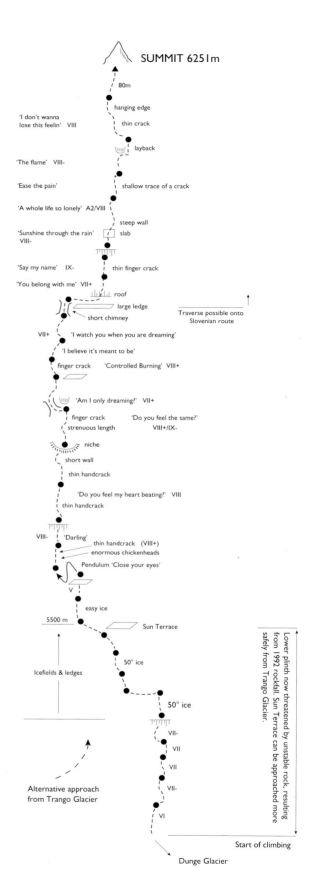

SUMMIT 6251m

80m
hanging edge
'I don't wanna
lose this feelin' VIII   thin crack
layback
'The flame' VIII-
'Ease the pain'   shallow trace of a crack
'A whole life so lonely' A2/VIII
steep wall
'Sunshine through the rain'   slab
VIII-
'Say my name' IX-   thin finger crack
'You belong with me' VII+
roof
large ledge   Traverse possible onto
short chimney   Slovenian route
VII+   'I watch you when you are dreaming'
'I believe it's meant to be'
finger crack   'Controlled Burning' VIII+
'Am I only dreaming?'   VII+
finger crack   'Do you feel the same?'
strenuous length   VIII+/IX-
niche
short wall
thin handcrack
'Do you feel my heart beating?'   VIII
thin handcrack
VIII-   'Darling'
thin handcrack   (VIII+)
enormous chickenheads
Pendulum 'Close your eyes'
V
easy ice
5500 m
Sun Terrace
50° ice
Icefields & ledges
50° ice
VII-
VII
VII
VII-
Alternative approach
from Trango Glacier
VI
Start of climbing
Dunge Glacier

Lower plinth now threatened by unstable rock, resulting from 1992 rockfall. Sun Terrace can be approached more safely from Trango Glacier.

tight in the crack. After three hours of terror he finally freed his knee by cutting through his breeches with a piton. Out of supplies, they abandoned the climb.

The following year they returned and Boysen settled his score with the offending Fissure Boysen, which opened the way to a series of twin-facing icy dièdres. They yielded in five hard pitches (VI+/A2) to the summit shoulder, three pitches (mixed) below the top. Boysen and Anthoine made the summit, fixing ropes, followed a day later by Joe Brown and Malcolm Howells. In all there were over twenty pitches of VI or harder on the route which was quickly recognised as a major tour de force. It waited fourteen years for a repeat, and then in fine alpine-style (single push over four days) by Japanese climbers Masanori Hoshino and Satoshi Kimoto to rescue compatriot Takeyasu Minamiura who had soloed a new route on the East Face, jumped from the summit and snagged his paraglider on the cliff face 80m from the top!

Minamiura's 1990 route was the seventh to be climbed on the Trango Tower. Although his line

required aid climbing to A4 standard, other people had now succeeded in climbing other routes free. That summer France's most marketable climbing star, Catherine Destivelle, made her Himalayan debut on the Tower, climbing the Slovenian route on the South-East Face completely free with her American guru Jeff Lowe, filmed by David Breashears and Jim Bridwell. Their effort followed the example set in 1988 when the German team of Kurt Albert, Wolfgang Güllich and Hartmut Münchenbach first freed the route. (The first ascent in 1987 by Slavko Cankar, Franc Knez and Bojan Srot, required some aid; now the route went free with sustained climbing at grade VI and above, including six pitches of VIII.)

The Germans represented a completely new outlook. They were not mountaineers of the old school, but pure rock climbers, some of the best in the world, bringing their refined art to 6000m in the Karakoram. Whereas Boysen, one of the finest climbers of his generation, had fought his way up brutal cracks in big boots, using aid where necessary, this new generation climbed entirely free in rock slippers. Quality was paramount. That is why, when they spotted a tenuous line of cracks up the elegant pillar between the British and Slovenian routes, promising a much finer and even harder climb, Albert and Güllich decided to return in 1989.

They named their new route Eternal Flame after an album by the American pop group, The Bangles, and each pitch was named after one of the album's lyrics. The route was climbed over a period of several weeks, using 400m of fixed rope and returning several times to base camp on the Dunge Glacier. Altogether, Albert, Güllich, Christof Stiegler and Milan Sykora dragged 180kg of food and gear up the long glacier couloir to the base of the Tower. The lower plinth gave five rock pitches and six on ice, leading to the Sun Terrace, where they placed Shoulder Camp

beneath the main headwall. (In 1992, just as Greg Child and Mark Wilford completed another new route up the South-East Face, a large section of it collapsed behind them. This gigantic rockfall swept the whole of the Dunge approach and a lot of unstable rock is now poised above the couloir. It is now probably safer to approach the Sun Terrace from the other side – from the Trango Glacier base camp – missing out the lower section of the German route.)

The real meat of the climb is the 700m headwall

(*Above*) The South-East Face towers above Sun Terrace. Despite massive foreshortening, scale is given by the tiny figure of Mark Wilford descending the Slovenian route, near the bottom centre of the picture. The huge white blotches on the rock are not giant bird droppings, but the impact marks of the massive rockfall which fell two days earlier from the huge grey scar high on the right. The chimneys of the original British route are just visible on the left. Eternal Flame starts up the left-facing corner system to the left of Wilford, then up thin cracks in the smooth red wall to the great stepped arête above. (*Greg Child*)

(*Left*) The Trango Tower photographed from Great Trango. From the snowpatch at the foot of the upper tower Eternal Flame follows almost precisely the dividing line between light and shade. The Slovenian route follows the chimney system immediately right; the original British route lies deep in shadow, immediately left. The 1987 Franco/Swiss South-West Buttress lies close to the left profile of the tower and the Kurtyka/Loretan route is close to the right-hand skyline. (*Andy Selters*)

above Shoulder Camp. The Germans climbed it in stages, using fixed ropes to return each night to the comfort of the Sun Terrace. Albert had hoped to climb the route totally free but had to resort to a pendulum on the blank third pitch above the camp and one section of A2 near the top of the route. Otherwise, the route was climbed wholly free. Both Albert and Güllich pushed themselves to the limit. Fairly early in the climb Güllich fell on the 'Am I only dreaming?' pitch, twisting an ankle ligament and being forced to descend to base camp. When he eventually returned for the final summit push he had to manage on aspirins for pain and a plastic boot to support his ankle. By now the other two climbers had left for home and Albert was doing all the leading, completing the hardest pitches above a large ledge which he had reached on the earlier attempt. He succeeded on the immaculate finger crack of the crux pitch 'Say my name' (grade IX-), but became increasingly exhausted over six days continuous climbing. He took several falls from the

minimalist crack of 'Ease the pain' and had some worrying moments on 'Don't wanna lose this feeling' as his runners fell out and he found himself facing a potential 10m fall on to the belay. Despite cramped, skinned fingers, he managed to hang on and complete the pitch safely.

A final brilliant section led right up the edge of a wild pillar, hanging 2000m above the glacier, and then Albert and Güllich joined the old fixed ropes of the Boysen route coming in from the left. Another 80m of easy mixed ground and they were on the summit.

Purists may regret the fact that Kurt Albert placed double bolt anchors at all the belays on Eternal Flame. However, the result for subsequent climbers is a magnificent free route, which could now be climbed in a single alpine-style push, carrying just nuts and Friends for running belays. For those who aspire to the hardest free climbing, at altitude, in remarkable surroundings, Eternal Flame is probably the finest way to the summit of the Karakoram's most famous tower.

SUMMARY STATISTICS AND INFORMATION

Mountain	Trango Tower
Height	6251m
Location	Baltoro Glacier region, Central Karakoram, Pakistan.
Route	South Pillar – German route (Eternal Flame). 1000m of mixed and granite rock climbing. 700m from the Shoulder – 22 pitches including 8 at grade VIII and one at IX-.
First ascent of mountain	8 July 1976, via South-West Face, by Mo Anthoine & Martin Boysen (UK), followed one day later by Joe Brown & Malcolm Howells.
First ascent of route	20 September 1989, by Kurt Albert and Wolfgang Güllich(Ger). (Christof Stiegler and Milan Sykora involved on lower pitches).
Height of b/c	c.4100m beside Dunge Glacier. However, since 1992 rockfall on South-East Face, it is probably safer to approach from the old British base camp on the Trango Glacier.
Roadhead	Dassu (road under construction to Askole).
Length of walk-in	Approx 90km and 9 days from Dassu or 40km and 6 days from Askole.
Season	Best conditions on the South Face appear in late summer and autumn (August – October).
Permission	Ministry of Tourism, Islamabad, Pakistan.
Success rate	The majority of expeditions to the Tower have succeeded. All three attempts on the Slovenian route from 1987-90 were successful. Eternal Flame (1989) had still not been attempted again in 1994.
Bibliography	First ascent of mountain chronicled in Trango – The Nameless Tower by Jim Curran (Dark Peak, 1977) and Martin Boysen's article 'Last Trango', in Mountain 52. The following AAJ references detail all ascents of the Trango Tower up to 1992: 1977 pp 266-8; 1988 pp 250-1; 1989 pp 45-9 and 250-2; 1990 pp 285-8; 1991 pp 271-2; 1993 pp 258-66. First ascent of Eternal Flame described in Rotpunkt, 1990 No.1.

4.30 pm, 21 July 1977. Dennis Hennek, belayed by John Roskelley, is the first person to stand on the summit of Great Trango. In the background the massive Baltoro Glacier snakes 40km east to the giant peaks beyond Concordia. Immediately right of Trango's summit is Broad Peak. Right of that is the flat-topped pyramid of Gasherbrum IV, the sharper summit of Hidden Peak, then the great snow masses of Sia Kangri and Baltoro Kangri. (*Galen Rowell*)

BROAD PEAK 8047m

West Spur / North Ridge

In the summer of 1994 no fewer than eleven teams attempted Broad Peak. It is an increasingly popular mountain and cynics might dismiss it as an easy 8000m tick for peak-baggers, yet Broad Peak has seen many of the most exciting developments in Himalayan mountaineering, starting with its dramatic first ascent in 1957.

Falchan Kangri is the mountain's official Balti title, but even the locals use the name coined in 1892 by the British explorer Martin Conway. Steeped in the alpine tradition,

Broad Peak from K2 Base Camp, across the Godwin-Austen Glacier.
(Jean Troillet)

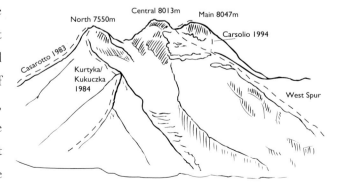

the first European to witness the stupendous glacier junction at the head of the Baltoro called it 'Concordia', after the similar but much smaller feature on Switzerland's Aletsch Glacier. And, staring up at the three-summited giant opposite K2 he recalled Zermatt's Breithorn, or 'Broad Peak'. The leader of the 1934 International Karakoram expedition, Gunther Dyhrenfurth, examined Broad Peak in more detail, concluding that the West Spur offered the best chance of a route to the summit. He can never have

guessed that when this route was finally attempted in 1957 it would be by a team of just four climbers.

The 1957 Austrian expedition was led by Marcus Schmuck. Both he and Fritz Wintersteller were extremely fit and competent. Hermann Buhl's legendary powers of endurance had been stretched to the limit four years earlier when he reached the summit of Nanga Parbat alone and survived a standing bivouac at almost 8000m, in jersey and shirt sleeves. The youngest member of the team, Kurt Diemberger, who had a string of hard alpine ice faces to his credit, was an innovator by nature and was delighted when Hermann Buhl proposed to tackle Broad Peak unsupported, in 'Westalpinstil'. Modern critics who question how 'alpine-style' the ascent really was (the team relayed loads to three fixed camps) should remember the sheer weight of equipment in 1957 – and the weight of established preconceptions about Himalayan climbing. Schmuck's team achieved nothing short of a dramatic breakthrough: four people utterly alone in the then deserted Baltoro basin, carrying their own loads, without any help from high-altitude porters, up an unknown route on one of the world's very highest mountains, placing just three camps in over 3000m of ascent.

The Austrians were incredibly determined. After weeks of work on the West Spur, Schmuck and Wintersteller eventually reached the col between the Central and Main Summit, and continued up the summit ridge, only to be stopped by darkness at about 8000m. Undeterred, the whole team returned after a week's recuperation at base camp. This time they left their top camp at 3.30 am. Even so, Schmuck and Wintersteller did not reach the col until 1.30 pm and, after a long rest there, only got to the summit at 5 pm. Meanwhile Diemberger had been waiting for Buhl, who was suffering from his Nanga Parbat frostbite injuries. Eventually, late that afternoon, Buhl persuaded the younger man to continue alone to the summit. On the way back from the summit, Diemberger discovered Buhl still struggling doggedly upward. In a moment perhaps unique on the highest peaks, Diemberger then turned round and climbed back up with his mentor, reaching the summit a second time just as the sun's last rays dwindled over the immensity of the Karakoram.

Most people would be satisfied with that unique achievement, but this team had grandiose plans. Two weeks later Schmuck and Wintersteller climbed Skilbrum (7360m) in pure alpine-style. Buhl and

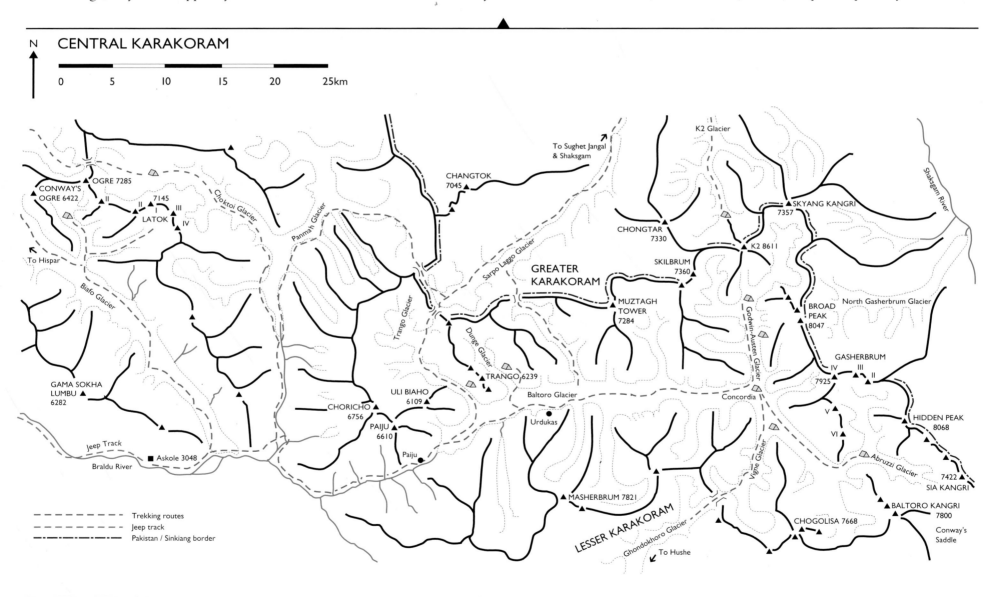

CENTRAL KARAKORAM

Diemberger almost achieved the same on Chogolisa but were turned back by a sudden storm. Whilst descending unroped through the whiteout, Buhl fell through a cornice and was never seen again. So tragedy ended one of the most successful Himalayan expeditions of all time.

Disaster also marred the next expedition to Broad Peak in 1975, when five Polish climbers repeated the Austrian route as far as the col, then headed left, up difficult terrain, to the virgin Central Summit

of Broad Peak Central. Oscar Cadiach, Enric Dalmau, Lluis Rafols and Alberto Soncini made a daring push on this final section, bivouacking without sleeping bags just short of the summit, which they reached the next morning.

The North Summit of Broad Peak (7550m) lacks eight-thousander status and was neglected until 1982, when Renato Casarotto tried its arrow-straight North Ridge. That attempt failed but he returned in 1983 to complete the route in a fantastic solo push: seven days

(*Below*) Three tiny figures are nearing the top of the final tricky ridge from the col to fore-summit. On the first attempt in 1957 Schmuck and Wintersteller were forced to turn back, tantalisingly close to success, from the foresummit. However, as they discovered a week later, it is at least another hour from there to the distant summit proper, which appears lower. (*Steve Bell*)

(8013m). They were caught by a sudden storm as darkness fell, and only two of them returned alive. One of the victims fell down the huge precipice of the North-East Face. It was from this side, from the Shaksgam valley, that a Spanish/Italian team made a remarkable ascent in 1992. It was an extended route, up the huge North Gasherbrum Glacier, through complex icefalls to a snow spur, then more icefall leading to a high plateau and, at last, the steep ice headwall

of technical ascent on rock, ice and mixed terrain, with a standing bivouac in the Buhl tradition at 7500m, and another three days for the descent. The North Summit was climbed again in 1984 by its West Ridge, as part of a greater project, the first complete traverse of the North, Central and Main Summits. As Wojciech Kurtyka remarked, a fast alpine-style ascent was probably the only feasible method on that long, long ridge at extreme altitude. No one was better qualified to try

(*Left*) Julie-Ann Clyma on the long slog up the West Spur at about 6800m. Immediately behind her is the confluence of the Godwin-Austen and Savoia Glaciers; the latter curves left then right. The distant summit appearing just above Clyma's head is Skilbrum (7360m) which Schmuck and Wintersteller climbed in pure alpine-style almost immediately after their ascent of Broad Peak in 1957. The unmistakable profile of K2 is on the right. (*Roger Payne*)

it than he and another outstanding Polish climber, Jerzy Kukuczka; together they spent six days committed on their 'sky-high ridge', returning from the Main Summit by way of the original route.

A repeat of the Kurtyka/Kukuczka traverse (perhaps taking in the additional neglected South Summit of Broad Peak) would be an inspiring challenge for the strongest and most ambitious alpinists. Other possibilities beckon. The Main Summit has still

The route follows essentially the crest of the West Spur, flanked on either side by dangerous ice cliffs. Snow on the lower section usually melts during the summer to reveal bare rubble, with some rockfall danger and the first really safe campsite is on a projecting platform at about 5600m. On the upper spur the 1957 team made quite a wide detour across the glacier slopes to the right. Nowadays most parties stick to the crest, passing rocky pinnacles, then over

(*Above*) Sunset on 9 June 1957. After a desperate battle of will Hermann Buhl stands on the summit of Broad Peak, fulfilling his dream of climbing an eight-thousander with a small team, unsupported by porters or oxygen equipment. Beyond and below him gleams the summit of Gasherbrum IV. (*Kurt Diemberger*)
(*Right*) Twenty-seven years later, Kurt Diemberger stood again on the summit of Broad Peak, this time with Julie Tullis, late in the evening as a storm brewed. On the right cloud boils around the West Face of Gasherbrum IV, delineating precisely the line of the North-West Ridge.

not been climbed from the Shaksgam side. However, the original Austrian route remains an interesting challenge in its own right and ideal acclimatisation for K2. Krzystof Wielicki showed what was possible in 1984 when he climbed the route up and down in twenty-two hours — the first one day ascent of an eight-thousander. Others have emulated him, but most prefer to stage their ascent over at least three camps, as the Austrians did in 1957.

a broader glacier hump, right up to the base of the rocky summit block. The first ascencionists made their last camp here at about 7100m, leaving a very long summit day. The summit block has been climbed direct from here by the Mexican Carlos Carsolio, during his solo ascent of the South-West Spur in 1994 (grade V rock and 70° ice). The normal route makes a long rising traverse to the left on avalanche-prone snow slopes, leading to an area of séracs at about

▲

7500m where it is usually possible to find a comparatively safe campsite. There is usually a steep ice wall just beneath the col at 7800m.

And so to the summit ridge. Opinions differ about the actual technical difficulty of this last section. Suffice it to say that more than one experienced mountaineer has died up here. There are awkward, almost knife-edged, sections where climate changes since 1957 have exposed increasing amounts of rock. There is also the

The magical experience is described in his book *The Endless Knot*, which also records the pair's desperate, avalanche-battered retreat down the West Spur as the weather broke hours later. That chapter and Greg Child's moving account in *Thin Air* of Pete Thexton's sudden death on Broad Peak from cerebral oedema, are both required reading for anyone who doubts that this magnificent and historic summit should, for all its popularity, be approached with respect.

ever-constant danger of straying left on to the immense cornices which overhang the Shaksgam side. And there is the sheer distance to be covered at an altitude where, for most people, every step requires a huge effort. Many opt for the marginally lower foresummit, but to avoid later regrets, it is necessary to force oneself on, for another half hour or so, to the distant summit proper.

Diemberger returned to the summit of Broad Peak in 1984 with Julie Tullis, arriving once again at sunset.

A similar view to Diemberger's, but taken lower down from the col, on a perfect evening. Beyond the Gasherbrums, mountain after mountain marches into the far distance of the East Karakoram. (*Greg Child*)

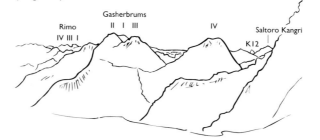

Mountain	Broad Peak (Falchan Kangri)
Height	8047m
Location	Baltoro Muztagh, Central Karakoram, Pakistan.
Route	West Spur and North Ridge. 3150m of ascent from A b/c on the Godwin-Austen Glacier at the foot of the spur. Snow and or rock scrambling weaves through the lower slopes onto the crest of the spur. Higher up the route is entirely on glacier slopes, with occasional ice walls above 7500m. A well-defined ridge leads from the col at 7800m to the summit. In good conditions the route is comparatively safe but the big snow slopes can be lethal after heavy snowfalls.
First ascent of mountain	9 June 1957 by Marcus Schmuck, Fritz Wintersteller, Hermann Buhl & Kurt Diemberger (Aus).
First ascent of route	As above.
First alpine-style ascent of route	As above, unless one is a pedantic purist. Krzystof Wielicki made the first one-day ascent in 1984.
Height of b/c	4900m on the Godwin-Austen Glacier medial moraine, about 3 hours above Concordia and just before the foot of Broad Peak's West Spur.
Roadhead	Thongl, 2km before Askole.
Length of walk-in	7 or 8 days, depending on state of *jhola* across Panmah river. The actual charge will be for at least 12 (maybe 15) porter-stages. Check government regulations.
Season	Has been climbed from June to September. July is probably the best month in an average year. The Main Summit has been climbed in winter, solo, by Maciej Berbeka (Pol) in March 1988.
Permission	Ministry of Tourism, Islamabad.
Success rate	The normal route was first repeated in 1977, then again in 1982. Since then it has been climbed every year except 1989, some years by many teams. With every increasing blurring of distinctions between different expeditions it is difficult to be statistically accurate, but approximately 40 per cent of teams have succeeded over the years.
Bibliography	Recent attempts and ascents have been well documented in the *AAJ* and *HJ*. Particularly interesting is Kurtyka's account of the three-summit traverse in the 1985 *AAJ* and the pictures of the North-East Face route from Shaksgam, in the 1993 *AAJ*. For a general introduction to the mountain and an account of the 1975 Central Summit ascent, see the Dyhrenfurth feature in *Mountain* 55. The first ascent of the Main Summit is described vividly in Kurt Diemberger's *Summits and Secrets* (Hodder & Stoughton, 1991) and again with his repeat ascent in *The Endless Knot* (Grafton, 1991). The 1983 British expedition is written up in Greg Child's *Thin Air* (Mountaineers/Oxford Illustrated Press, 1988)

GASHERBRUM IV 7925m

North-West Ridge

Of all the peaks that encircle the amphitheatre of Concordia the most immediate and imposing is Gasherbrum IV. It is one of the very highest peaks in the world, yet still by the start of 1995 only two parties had ever reached the summit. This tells us something about the severity of the mountain, but also about the attraction of the figure 8000. Gasherbrum IV falls 75m short of this arbitrary credential and for this reason may never gain the attention lavished on neighbouring Broad Peak, Gasherbrum II and Hidden Peak, which have seen almost a hundred ascents between them.

Gasherbrum IV was first climbed in 1958 by the Italians Walter Bonatti and Carlo Mauri via the North-East Ridge. Mauri was extremely experienced and Bonatti was perhaps the outstanding mountaineer of the immediate post-war generation. The expedition, led by another legendary Italian alpinist, Riccardo Cassin, approached the mountain obliquely, from the South Gasherbrum Glacier, negotiating two difficult icefalls to reach the upper cwm leading to the North-East Col. From the col a series of advances was made up the North-East Ridge in mixed weather and conditions before the expedition managed to place Camp 6 at 7350m. From here Bonatti and Mauri reached the summit on their second attempt on 6 August, commenting that the long traverse from the North to the Main Summit, with its marble gendarmes, gave the hardest test of the entire climb.

The Italian route is one of the least accessible of all Karakoram ridges and remains unrepeated. It is technically the easiest route up the mountain but still involves some very hard climbing at high altitude. It is also long and circuitous, hidden away round the back of the mountain. When a new generation of climbers came to the Baltoro in the late 'seventies, they were drawn inevitably to the immense West Face which on a fine evening glows with such luminosity above Concordia. Starting in 1978, a succession of teams came to try this great 2500m Shining Wall, trying to overcome the obvious spur just left of centre. Others, put off by tales of hideously shattered rock, tried their luck on the safer North-West Ridge, where an American expedition reached about 7300m in 1984.

That same summer two Europeans also made a foray on to the ridge as a reconnaissance for their designs on the West Face. They were two of the world's finest Himalayan mountaineers – Robert Schauer from Austria and Wojciech Kurtyka from Poland. The following year, 1985, they returned to attempt the face itself. Unlike previous parties, they ignored the obvious spur with its shattered Black Towers and took a canny diagonal line, starting on the right of the face up a couloir slicing through the lower walls, continued leftward through a wasteland of fragile marble and eventually emerged, a week later, in the top left corner at the North Summit. On the wall they faced very difficult conditions. Bivouacs were poor and on two occasions the pair slept 20m apart, each sitting on tiny rock pinnacles. Kurtyka reported three rock sections of grade V or harder on either completely rotten or completely compact marble with very little protection. A storm at the top of the face pinned them down for two days. By now they were out of food and gas and were seriously weakened. Both climbers were hallucinating wildly and Schauer later described his vivid sensation of being a raven, hovering above the wall, looking down at his own shrivelled body. When the storm ended they had to abandon the traverse to the Main Summit. Instead they set off immediately down the North-West Ridge, descending it to base camp in another three days, with a refuelling stop at the 7100m food cache they had previously left whilst acclimatising.

For many people, the West Face of Gasherbrum IV was the Himalayan climb of the 'eighties, epitomising bold commitment on tenuous mixed terrain, up a logical, compelling line on the most photographed face in the Karakoram. Schauer, who was actually there,

(*Right*) The upper part of Gasherbrum IV's West Face glowing at sunset. The upper steps of the North-West Ridge are profiled on the left, leading to the North Summit. The Main Summit is on the right. (*Greg Child*)

viewed his achievement more soberly, emphasising the danger and the sense of bordering on the edge of control; since 1985 he has spent more time with his family and has stuck to gentler climbs. Ten years on,

Dry conditions on the West Face - one of the most sought-after prizes in the 'seventies and 'eighties. Early attempts were focused on the prominent rib descending towards the camera from the North Summit. Then in 1985 Wojciech Kurtyka and Robert Schauer finally climbed the 2500m Shining Wall, starting up the couloir on the right. From very near the top of the couloir they broke out left, through chimneys to a snow patch, then continued diagonally left up the immense marble slabs to the huge snowfield and the North Summit. The demarcation between marble and black diorite is very marked on the North-West Ridge, as is the prominent black pinnacle where the ridge drops out of the picture. (*Wojciech Kurtyka*)

no one else has set foot on the West Face of Gasherbrum IV.

The Shining Wall was an outstanding achievement, but perhaps more people will be attracted in future to the less extreme route which was finally climbed in 1986 – the North-West Ridge. As Greg Child observed when he came to lead the 1986 American/Australian expedition, most of the North-West Ridge had already been climbed and the whole ridge had been descended. However, what ought to have been a pushover proved to be a very taxing climb which the other Australian team member, Tim Macartney-Snape, described as more demanding than his recent new route on the North Face of Everest.

The other climbing members on the ridge, all American, were Tom Hargis, Geoff Radford, Andy Tuthill and Randy Leavitt, the famous rock climber who had the previous summer with Child pioneered a wild new aid route on El Capitan, Lost in America. Tactics were a mixture of siege and alpine-style, with ropes fixed to the third camp, a snowcave at 7000m, before a final committing push with an unplanned bivouac on the North Summit at almost 8000m. The team followed earlier attempts up the corridor of the West Gasherbrum Glacier to a 1000m snow couloir which gives access to the col at the start of the ridge. Camp 2 was placed here at 6700m.

In the classic view from Concordia the col and the start of the North-West Ridge are hidden. However, where the ridge appears higher up, you can see clearly the black diorite rock rising for several hundred metres before changing suddenly to pink-grey marble. The lower diorite sections gave a lot of trouble in 1983 and 1984, so the 1986 team chose whenever possible to move left on to the Chinese side of the ridge, i.e. the North Face, which tends to be easier snow.

Above Camp 3, at about 7200m, séracs forced them on to a rock step, marked at its top by a black pinnacle which can be seen clearly from the valley.

Five of the climbers were now on their final push. They made Camp 4 on a snow ledge at 7350m and continued at dawn with light loads, carrying just four sleeping bags, two stoves, two 100m 7mm ropes, a few pitons and a movie camera, hoping to reach the summit that day. Windslab conditions on the North Face forced the climbers once again on to the crest,

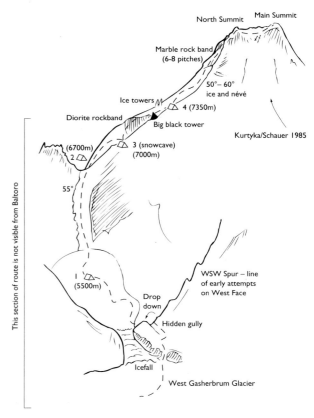

where névé and steep ice led to the foot of the final marble rockband at about 7650m. Here Radford turned back; Child, Hargis, Macartney-Snape and Tuthill decided to continue and discover whether the line of cracks and ramps that Child had spotted from Broad Peak four years earlier would prove climbable at that altitude.

The rockband was climbable but it was precarious

work, starting with a hard fist crack. The rock was brittle, with hard grade V moves during the eight or so pitches to the top of the band. By the time the four climbers reached the North Summit it was 4 pm, too late to continue across the 450m horizontal traverse to the Main Summit. To save weight, they had left the stoves and sleeping bags at the foot of the rockband that morning; if they wanted to wait here until the morning they were going to have to bivouac in just the clothes they wore, with nothing to drink. Tuthill decided the

risk of frostbite was too great and set off down with one of the ropes. The other three, in one of those special moments when everything is gambled for a great prize, started to scratch out a little snowcave on the North Summit and settled down for a long shivering night.

Another brilliant but windy day greeted them when they crawled out of the cave the next morning. Now for the first time since Bonatti and Mauri twenty-eight years earlier, human feet trod the connecting ridge to the summit of Gasherbrum IV. Whereas the Italians had stuck to the pinnacled crest, the 1986 trio traversed the upper concave basin of the West Face, which Bonatti had called the Shining Shell. At one point, Child climbed up to a false summit and had to retreat. Eventually at 10 am, after climbing up a 60° rock slab sprinkled with large holds, the three men

(*Top*) Avalanches falling from Gasherbrum V present some threat to the approach up the West Gasherbrum Glacier. (*Greg Child*)
(*Above*) Tom Hargis and Geoff Radford soloing confidently above Camp 2 on the North-West Ridge. (*Tim Macartney-Snape*)
(*Above left*) 1000m higher, at about 7700m, Andy Tuthill follows up hard, delicate terrain on the final marble rockband. (*Tim Macartney-Snape*)

▲

arrived on the summit – 'a small dome of snow clinging to a narrow rocky fin'. It was only as they were about to descend that they found Bonatti's summit abseil piton, ten metres away at the other end of the fin; the snow dome was clearly a new addition to the summit or had moved ten metres north!

On the return traverse to the North Summit, Macartney-Snape lost his balance removing a piton on a delicate verglassed traverse and took a nosedive down the 2500m West Face. Luckily Child held him on a boot belay and the other Australian lived to tell the tale. From the North Summit, the three abseiled the top rockband, taking great pains to fix good anchors in the marble. Desperate for liquid, they lit the cached stove at the bottom, only to have it explode on them. As Child later recalled in the *AAJ*, '"This is like a pub with no beer. Let's go," I said, and we continued rappelling, into the night.' They used up every single piece of gear and made their last abseil into Camp 4 from an old sling left two years earlier by Kurtyka. A day later they were all safely down, concluding the elusive second ascent of Gasherbrum IV.

Since 1986 there have been several unsuccessful attempts on the South-East Pillar, from the South Gasherbrum Glacier and a solo attempt on the East Face. The former line, when complete, will have the advantage of going direct to the summit. However, in that famous view from Concordia, which has now been entrancing mountaineers for over a hundred years, it is the symmetry of the West Face which will always appeal. The Kurtyka/Schauer route is the logical line and its one ascent was achieved in perfect alpine-style. The longer North-West Ridge has not yet been climbed in pure alpine-style but with the knowledge gained during the 'eighties, and the many abseil points now in place, such an ascent is now a possibility for a strong experienced team.

Tom Hargis, in front, smiling and fresh on a brilliant morning at 7200m during the final push to the summit, with a sea of peaks, including the prominent Muztagh Tower, stretching out to the west. (*Greg Child*) (*Below*) Three days later, back down at the Camp 3 snowcave after a totally committing journey to the summit and back, Hargis (centre) shows all the strain of climbing at extreme altitude. Macartney-Snape (left) and Child (right) also look a touch weary. (*Randy Leavitt*)

SUMMARY STATISTICS AND INFORMATION

Mountain	Gasherbrum IV
Height	7925m
Location	Baltoro Muztagh, Central Karakoram, Pakistan.
Route	North-West Ridge. 2400m of ascent from the upper basin of the West Gasherbrum Glacier. A 1000m snow couloir leads to the ridge. Thereafter the difficulties are on snow, ice and rock, first black diorite then marble. The crux is on the final rockband beneath the North Summit, with difficulties up to grade V. A long and serious high-altitude route.
First ascent of mountain	Summit reached 6 August 1958, by Walter Bonatti and Carlo Mauri (Italian) via the North-East Ridge.
First ascent of route	Summit reached on 22 June 1986, by Tom Hargis (USA), Greg Child & Tim Macartney-Snape (Australia). The North-West Ridge had been descended the previous year by Wojciech Kurtyka (Pol) & Robert Schauer (Austria) after their ascent of the West Face.
Height of b/c	Numerous sites around Concordia at c.4700m.
Roadhead	Thongl, 2km before Askole.
Length of walk-in	Approximately 70km, taking 6 or 7 days, depending on state of *jhola* across Panmah river. The actual charge will be for at least 11 (maybe 14) porter-stages. Check government regulations.
Season	June to August.
Permission	Ministry of Tourism, Islamabad.
Success rate	The North-East Ridge was climbed on the first attempt by a large and well-organised expedition. The North-West Ridge only succumbed on the third attempt. The West Face, despite at least five attempts, has only had one ascent. The Main Summit has still had just two ascents – it is probably a much harder proposition than Gasherbrum I and II.
Bibliography	The definitive book on the mountain is Fosco Mariani's evocative and beautifully illustrated *Karakoram: the Ascent of Gasherbrum IV* (Hutchinson 1961), the official account of the first ascent. Subsequent attempts on the mountain are well documented in the *AAJ*. Articles on the West Face appear in *HJ* 42 (Kurtyka's – 'The Abseil and the Ascent') and *Climbing Magazine* 95 (Schauer's – 'The Shining Wall'). The North-West Ridge ascent is described in detail in Greg Child's *Thin Air* (Mountaineers/Oxford Illustrated Press, 1988)

HIDDEN PEAK 8068m

North-West Face

Like Broad Peak, it was named by Conway. The official title is of course Gasherbrum I but, despite being the highest peak in the Gasherbrum group, it lies tucked away behind the imposing front of Gasherbrum IV, hence the name Hidden Peak. It is the world's eleventh highest summit and was the twelfth eight-thousander to be climbed.

Nick Clinch led the successful 1958 American expedition. His team, with the exception of Pete Schoening who had climbed on K2, was made up of old friends with relatively little altitude experience. Schoening, Clinch explains, was drafted in at a late hour to 'assure success'. In fact it was the shared effort between all climbing members and high-altitude Balti porters that really put Schoening and Andy Kauffman on the summit on 5 July. They established five camps on the mountain, finding the climbing technically easy but strenuous in the deep snow that characterised the middle portion of their ascent. From the Abruzzi Glacier their route followed a prominent South-West Spur, the Roch Ridge reconnoitred by Hans Ertl and André Roch in 1934, to an upper snow plateau at c.6500m, then makes a long rising north-west traverse to the summit pyramid.

Clinch himself did not reach the summit of Hidden Peak but masterminded the first ascent, two years later, of Masherbrum and was a member of that expedition's second successful summit party. His contribution to American mountaineering is thus profound, though he was never to gain the same

Reinhold Messner (left) and Peter Habeler, both looking very fit and very relaxed after their ten-hour ascent of the Eigerwand in 1974. That success cemented the climbing partnership which was to prove so effective a year later on Hidden Peak. (*John Cleare/Mountain Camera*)

acclaim as his countrymen who were to climb Everest and K2 in the following decades.

Hidden Peak was climbed for the second time in 1975, by a route that Clinch's team had considered and almost chosen in 1958 – the North-West Face. What

was remarkable about this ascent was its style. The famous Tyrolean ace, Reinhold Messner, and Austrian partner Peter Habeler climbed the mountain in pure alpine-style, the first time a two-man expedition had succeeded on an 8000m peak. Although other (Austrian) climbers shared their base camp and themselves climbed Hidden Peak, they chose to do so via the American route, quite detached from Messner and Habeler, thus making that route's second ascent and the mountain's third.

Messner and Habeler's climb coincided with other significant alpine-style ascents in the Himalaya, such as Dick Renshaw and Joe Tasker's magnificent route on the South-East Ridge of Dunagiri in Garhwal. It was inevitably contrasted with the large successful Everest South-West Face climb of the same year using siege tactics including the bottled oxygen, fixed ropes and camps. The Everest route was bigger and harder, with its crux well above 8000m, so the comparison is invidious, but Habeler and Messner's bold tactics at less extreme altitude on Hidden Peak were certainly a revolutionary pointer to the future.

The North-West Face is approached from the

Looking from the summit of Gasherbrum IV across the South Gasherbrum Glacier to the North-West Face of Hidden Peak, where Peter Habeler and Reinhold Messner made their historic climb in 1975. Although the mountaineering world was astonished by their boldness, Habeler remarked soon after the climb that, in his opinion, it was nowhere near the limit of possibility. How prophetic his words have proved to be! (*Tim Macartney-Snape*)

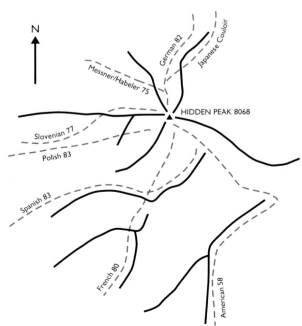

secluded South Gasherbrum Glacier. For a lightweight party this glacier appears a daunting proposition but it is rarely necessary to fix ropes at any point on it, though route finding may be tortuous; it caused enormous trouble to the earliest expeditions to Gasherbrum II and IV. The easiest line is on the true left bank beneath the West Flank of the mountain but there will be serious avalanche risk there; the safer option is a meandering line toward the centre of the glacier, for which marker wands may be useful. Once

through the most crevassed sections, the glacier levels off and becomes kinder.

Habeler and Messner made two recces to this glacier bowl beneath the Gasherbrum La before embarking on their remarkable climb. Building on the success of their recent partnership on the Matterhorn and Eiger North Faces, they climbed fast and light. On the first day they climbed the entire lower face, unroped, totally confident in each other's ability. Messner even had the strength and confidence to film

Habeler with a 16mm movie camera on the final delicate rockband, which he compared to the North Face
of the Matterhorn. By afternoon they had completed
1200m of ascent and pitched their tiny tent at 7100m
on the shoulder of the North-West Flank. Habeler
suffered appalling headaches that night but recovered
by the morning, enabling both men to continue, without rucksacks up the 1000m upper slopes to the
summit, which they reached after just six hours. By
the afternoon of that second day they were back in
their tent. Violent winds destroyed the tent that night
and on the third day the two men drained themselves
to the limit, reversing their steps down the inter-

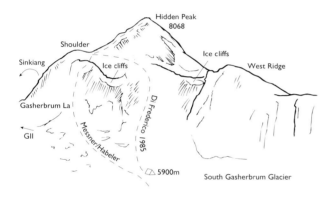

minable steep ice slopes of the lower face. Five days
after leaving base camp they were safely back, having
opened a new chapter in Himalayan climbing.

Hidden Peak continued to attract futuristic ascents
(and descents). In 1982, Sylvan Saudan (Swiss) skied
from the summit – the first complete ski-descent of
an eight-thousander. The following year Wojciech
Kurtyka and Jerzy Kukuczka, on sight, climbed a new
route up the huge triangular South-West Face, just
three weeks after completing a new route on
Gasherbrum II. Then in 1984 Messner returned to
complete what he has often referred to as his proud-
est achievement – a continuous traverse of both
Gasherbrum II and Hidden Peak.

Messner's companion this time was the fellow
Tyrolean Hans Kammerlander. In a remarkable seven-
day push, without returning to base camp, the two
men climbed Gasherbrum II, descended a new variation route to the South Gasherbrum Glacier, climbed
up to the Gasherbrum La (6500m), then continued up
Hidden Peak, following the North Face route
pioneered by Michl Dacher's 1982 expedition.
Spurred on by the deteriorating weather, Messner
continued past his 1975 campsite on the shoulder, and
this time bivouacked much higher, at 7400m. Despite
stormy weather the next day, Kammerlander and
Messner, determined to complete their dream, pushed
on to the summit, turned straight round, and the same
day started to descend the long West Ridge, first
climbed by the Slovenians Andrjez Stremfelj and N.
Zaplotnik in 1977.

Messner was forty, at the very peak of his form,
when he and Kammerlander completed that wild
traverse of Hidden Peak in stormy weather at the end
of a week's continuous high-altitude climbing. Those
aspiring to emulate their climb should take note of
Messner's comment that in 1975 he never would have
dreamed of pulling off such a feat. Then it was enough
of a breakthrough just to climb the North-West Face
straight up and down.

The original American route on Hidden Peak is
now closed to expeditions, because it lies close to the
front line between Pakistani and Indian troops fighting
for control of the Siachen. Most parties now climb the
mountain from the Gasherbrum La, taking the Japanese
Couloir well to the left, on the Sinkiang side of the
mountain. However, the harder rocks (up to grade IV)
taken by the German route straight above the col are
less threatened by avalanche. On the upper slopes all
routes converge on the Habeler/Messner line. The

SUMMARY STATISTICS AND INFORMATION

Mountain	Hidden Peak (Gasherbrum.1)
Height	8068m
Location	Baltoro Muztagh, Central Karakoram, Pakistan.
Route	North-West Face (Habeler/Messner route). 2400m of ascent, first on a steep snow/ice slopes and a mixed rockband (grade IV) then on easier angled snow and mixed slopes above the shoulder.
First ascent of mountain	5 July 1958, by Pete Schoening and Andy Kauffman (USA) via the South-East Ridge
First ascent of route	Peter Habeler (Aus) and Reinhold Messner (South Tyrol), 9-10 August 1975.
Height of b/c	5200m, on medial moraine at the junction of the Abruzzi and South Gasherbrum Glaciers.
Roadhead	Thongl, 2km before Askole.
Length of walk-in	8 or 9 days, depending on state of *jhola* across Panmah river. The actual charge will be for at least 12 (maybe up to 16) porter-stages. Check government regulations.
Season	Best conditions generally appear in late July and early August.
Permission	Ministry of Tourism, Islamabad.
Success rate	Quite high on the various routes on this side of the mountain. A few teams have been stopped by deep, fresh snow blanketing the loose rocks, others by typically poor Karakoram weather.
Bibliography	With regard to the North-West Face, the following *AAJ* references are worth reading: 1976 pp 541-2; 1983 pp 268-9; 1986 pp 269-272. The 1975 expedition is vividly described by Reinhold Messner in *The Challenge* (Kaye & Ward, London 1977) and by Peter Habeler in his section of *Great Climbs* (ed. Chris Bonington, Mitchell Beazeley, London 1994). See also Messner's account of the 1984 traverse in *All 14 Eight-Thousanders* (Crowood Press, 1988). For the first ascent of the mountain see Nick Clinch's *A Walk in the Sky*.

lower North-West Face proper has been climbed on
the right side, but the original Habeler/Messner line is
probably the most direct and elegant. Above all, it has
historical appeal, for it was on this route that Messner
first really proved what minimalist teams could achieve
on the world's highest peaks.

▲
___

K2 8611m
___

South-East (Abruzzi) Spur

K2 is the centrepiece of the Karakoram — its highest and most impressive peak. In the opinion of Reinhold Messner, K2, even by its easiest routes, is the most difficult peak in the world to climb and this view is shared by many modern alpinists. For 'easiest routes', read Abruzzi Spur and North Ridge. It is these routes, one from Pakistan and one from China, that we detail in this book.

The North Ridge, in particular, is a compellingly direct line. The Abruzzi, although less elegant, appears from Concordia to be the most obvious route, but the first attempt to climb K2 was made by the much longer North-East Ridge. The 1902 team of Austrian, British and Swiss climbers was led by Oscar Eckenstein. They reached around 6500m, barely getting to grips with the long, complex of knife-edge and corniced arêtes which eventually merge with the upper East Face, and seventy-four years were to pass before a team of Polish climbers would try this route again.

It was the famous Italian explorer, Duke Luigi Amedeo di Savoia, the Duke of the Abruzzi, on the second ever climbing expedition to visit K2 in 1909, who first identified and attempted the South-East Spur which now bears his name and it was another Italian expedition which eventually climbed the route right to the summit in 1954, but not before three American expeditions had done most of the groundwork.

Charles Houston's 1938 expedition was a light-weight affair, he being of the opinion that small self-contained groups had the best chance of success, a view reinforced by his experience with Bill Tilman two years earlier on the first ascent of Nanda Devi. Now, on the harder terrain of the Abruzzi, his American team made steady progress up the line of snowfields and rock ribs that leads eventually to the Shoulder. One key rock-band at about 6700m was led by William House and to this day House's Chimney inspires respect from the best modern alpinists. Above 7000m there was more hard climbing through the Black Pyramid, before an exposed ice traverse took them out on to the lower slopes of the Shoulder where they made Camp 7 at about 7600m. Despite their successful progress, there was still a great distance and height to be covered and, with dwindling supplies and fear of the onset of colder and unsettled weather, the whole party withdrew just days before a sustained storm swept the peak. Houston gave a prophetic warning, then, about the difficulty of retreat from the Shoulder in poor weather.

The following year saw another American expedition, this time led by the German emigré Fritz Wiessner, who had been a member of Willy Merkl's 1932 Nanga Parbat expedition. K2 proved traumatic, with a largely inexperienced team failing to keep up with their leader, who was one of the best and most driven climbers of his day. The final disaster was a cata-logue of misunderstandings and wrong decisions which culminated in three Sherpas dying in a heroic attempt to rescue Dudley Wolfe, who was stranded high on the mountain, collapsed in the last stages of high-altitude sickness. The blame for the four deaths was put squarely on Wiessner, detracting from his extraordinary performance before the disaster, when he had come within a whisker of success.

From Camp 9 at 8000m Wiessner led Pasang Dawa Lama up very difficult rocks and would have continued by night to the summit if Pasang had not forced him to turn back at 6 pm from 8400m. Undeterred, Wiessner tried to climb back up two days later, this time taking the easier line further right followed by all subsequent parties, the icy Bottleneck. However, because both men had lost their crampons, Wiessner had to abandon the attempt and descend, concluding a performance on difficult terrain above 8000m which any climber, blessed with today's state-of-the-art equipment and high-altitude knowledge, might feel proud of.

Houston returned to K2 in 1953 with seven other climbers but no high-altitude porters. Making excellent progress, all eight climbers were established at Camp 8 on the Shoulder on 2 August. But by cruel chance the weather broke, trapping the men in their tents for five days. After five days at nearly 8000m, Art

The view which draws hundreds to Concordia every year. K2 fills the sky, 10km to the north, with the characteristic step of the Shoulder profiled on the right. The immense South Face, first climbed in 1986 by Jerzy Kukuczka and Tadeusz Piotrowski faces the camera. Left of that is the South-West Ridge or Magic Line, with its prominent hanging glacier shelf halfway up. The left skyline is the West Ridge. (*Galen Rowell*)

Gilkey became ill and was then paralysed by a thrombosis. In a heroic bid to save him, the other six started to lower him rope-length by rope-length, all the way down the Abruzzi. The storm had resumed and the descent gained epic proportions when five climbers fell in a tangle of ropes and were checked miraculously by Pete Schoening's ice axe belay. Gilkey was then lost in an avalanche and the others, frostbitten, shocked and exhausted, fought against furious storms to reach Camp 2 where their Hunza porters helped them down.

After three epic near-misses by the Americans, success came in 1954 to Ardito Desio's lavishly prepared Italian expedition. Thanks to a heroic effort by Walter Bonatti and the Hunza porter Mahdi, oxygen was carried up to the Shoulder to support Achille Compagnoni and Lino Lacedelli on their successful push to the summit – a summit which then remained untrodden until 1977, when a huge Japanese expedition repeated the Abruzzi. In 1978 the mountain was climbed for the first time without oxygen by Americans John Roskelley, Rick Ridgeway and Lou Reichardt (Jim Wickwire used some oxygen but ran out on the summit and survived a solo open bivouac at 8460m). The Americans finished up the top section of the Abruzzi after traversing on to the Shoulder from the high plateau on the North-East Ridge. A year later Michl Dacher and Reinhold Messner repeated the Abruzzi in lightweight-style, also without oxygen.

Despite the successes of the late 'seventies the Abruzzi's reputation for tragedy was not to lessen. In 1986, in the worst incident in recent mountaineering history, a sustained storm again claimed more lives. Five out of seven climbers, trapped on the Shoulder in bad weather, perished in a desperate and tragically delayed bid to retreat, bringing the total number of deaths on the mountain that summer to thirteen. Paradoxically, during that same summer, Benoît Chamoux made a twenty-three-hour ascent of the Abruzzi Spur. Although he was no doubt helped by the activities of others on the route, not least their trail and fixed ropes, his was a singular achievement, made just a few days after a sixteen-hour solo of Broad Peak. It was an advertisement for the expediency of speed, for Chamoux needed only two good days' weather to climb the mountain and descend safely. Given the superb fitness of the climber, his ascent was probably the one most likely to succeed and least likely to meet with disaster.

Since 1986 there have been further disasters on the Abruzzi and the majority of teams have not reached the summit, confirming Messner's sobriquet 'hardest mountain in the world'. However, the climbers still come, because K2 is such a stunning peak and the Abruzzi is probably the most feasible route on the Pakistan side.

The most popular base camp site for an ascent of the Abruzzi is on a section of lateral moraine beneath the South Face known as the Strip near the junction of the Filippi and Upper Godwin-Austen Glaciers. As many as a hundred tents can gather here some years; a scene more reminiscent of Chamonix than the Himalaya. From here it is a

climb of about two hours through a short sharp icefall to advance base at about 5400m, right at the foot of the Spur.

These days, despite a big clean-up effort in 1990, the detritus of past expeditions is one of the best pointers to the route, which initially weaves its way up rocky ribs,

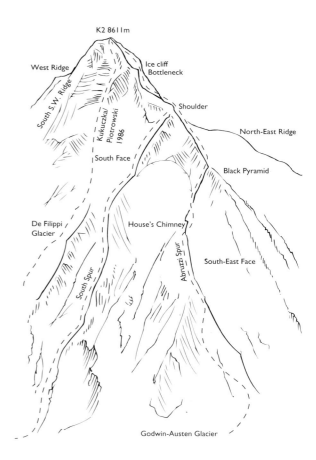

(*Left*) Wojciech Kurtyka took this photo in 1984 during his extraordinary traverse of Broad Peak with Kukuczka, looking from the Central Summit, across the North Summit, to K2. From this angle the colossal scale and steep angle of the Abruzzi Spur are quite apparent. (*Wojciech Kurtyka*)

(*Right*) Lou Reichardt above 8000m, heading up from the Shoulder into the Bottleneck, during the third ascent of K2 in 1978. After climbing the main part of the long, difficult North-East Ridge, the Americans, like the Poles in 1976, found the final headwall impossible, so they traversed round on to the Shoulder, to finish up the Abruzzi route. After a long summit day, Wickwire bivouacked alone at 8460m, a record at that time. The following morning, as he descended, Rick Ridgeway and John Roskelley passed him on their way to the summit. (*Jim Wickwire*)

bounded on the right by a huge snow/icefield. Most parties place Camp 1 at c.6150m and Camp 2 at c.6750m, just above the left-slanting cleft of House's Chimney. From there easier climbing up a reddish spur leads to the harder rocks of the Black Pyramid. Houston's party climbed virtually all this section with-

Camp 3 is usually at c.7400m and Camp 4 at 7900, on the Shoulder.

The crux is saved for the last 700m. It is a long summit day and for most parties only a very early start will avoid benightment on the return. The Shoulder steepens into a couloir, the Bottleneck, running directly up beneath the massive summit séracs, until one is forced left on an icy traverse, exposed above a 3000m drop. Several people have come to grief here, exhausted on their descent from the summit. Beyond the traverse easier snow slopes are gained, but it is still a long long way to the top.

However there is perhaps a better route to the Shoulder, a prominent rib left of the Abruzzi Spur, slanting across the South Face. On his last expedition in 1983, the wily Himalayan veteran Don Whillans suggested this line and it was attempted a few days later, in pure alpine-style, by his companions, Doug Scott, Andy Parkin and Jean Afanassieff. Parkin had virtually set foot on the Shoulder when Afanassieff's sudden attack of oedema forced the team to make a rapid retreat. Subsequent attempts by various Spanish teams culminated in a successful ascent of this route to the summit by Juanito Oiarsabal's Basques in 1994. Sadly, the adventurous example set by Scott's 1983 team was ignored, and the Basques fixed ropes up the Spur.

Jumping on the Basque bandwagon, several other parties repeated the South Spur in 1994, confirming that it may well be better and safer than the traditional Abruzzi line. It is more direct and in descent it avoids the dangerous slopes between the Shoulder and Black Pyramid, which in a storm are avalanche-prone and extremely difficult to navigate. However, whichever line is taken, the crux remains above the Shoulder, where even the best alpinists will always find their skill and stamina stretched to the full.

out fixed ropes; today a sorry mess of old perlon provides dubious security to so-called alpine-style climbers. However, above the Black Pyramid the safety line ends and it is up here, on the thinly featured snow and ice terrain leading to the Shoulder, that parties are at most risk, particularly retreating in poor weather.

K2 8611m

North Ridge

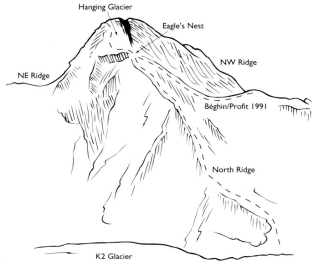

The southern side of K2, comparatively accessible from Kashmir, now Pakistan, has become increasingly familiar over the last hundred years, but the northern flank, overlooking the desert valleys of Sinkiang, still retains an air of remote mystery. Francis Younghusband was the first white man to see the North Face, in 1887, during his astounding journey from the Gobi Desert to Kashmir via the Shaksgam valley, Sarpo Laggo Glacier and Muztagh Pass. Fifty years later another great explorer, Eric Shipton, saw this face. Unlike Younghusband, he walked right up the K2 Glacier almost to the base of the mountain. Describing that moment afterwards in *Blank on the Map*, he wrote:

'The afternoon was fine and nothing interrupted my view of the great amphitheatre about me. The cliffs and ridges of K2 rose out of the glacier in one stupendous sweep to the summit of the mountain, 12,000 feet above. The sight was beyond my comprehension and I sat gazing at it, with a kind of timid fascination, watching wreaths of mist creep in and out of corries utterly remote... [it] was an experience I shall not forget; no mountain scene has impressed me more deeply.'

Shipton and his team approached this Shaksgam side of the mountain from the south, by the Sarpo Laggo Pass. After the tightening of Chinese rule in Sinkiang and the creation of Pakistan to the south, the

The North Ridge drops in a single sweep of over 3500m from the summit to the K2 Glacier. (*Greg Child*)

whole northern side of the Karakoram was closed to foreigners. Only in the 'eighties did it open again, and then only to expeditions approaching from the north, and sufficiently well financed to pay the draconian charges imposed by the Chinese authorities. It is still a very expensive area to visit but, for those lucky enough to go, the long camel journey over the Aghil

Pass to the surreal landscape of the Shaksgam valley is an unforgettable experience. As for K2 itself, the North Face is stupendous. Bounded on the left by the icy undulations of the North-East Ridge and on the right by the rocky North-West Ridge, the, North Face is really two faces – the North-North-East and the North-North-West – separated by a single line soaring from base to summit, the North Ridge.

Like so many of the great Himalayan prizes of recent years, the North Ridge of K2 was snapped up by the Mountaineering Association of Japan. In 1982 Isao Shinkai and Masatsugo Konishi led a fourteen-member climbing team to a 'home base' near the snout of the K2 Glacier, the end of the road for camels in this porterless area. From here, twenty-nine

(*Above*) Above Camp 4 old fixed ropes lead on to the hanging glacier. A short way above the climber the route traverses the snowslope to the far side, which is followed until the snow ramp leading out left at the top of the picture. (*Greg Child*)

(*Above left*) Juanjo San Sebastián climbing steep rock just below Camp 4 on the North Ridge. (*Alan Hinkes*)

(*Left*) The Eagle's Nest, site of Camp 4, with the ice pinnacles of the K2 Glacier nearly 3000m below. (*Greg Child*)

Japanese volunteers ferried four tons of supplies 13km up the glacier to base camp. (Other nationalities, less disciplined, have tried this wheeze without much success, but nowadays it is possible to take Hunza or Balti porters up the Karakoram Highway from Pakistan, and employ them to ease the load-carrying.)

The climbers now set to work on the mountain, fixing ropes most of the way up the ridge, generally following the right-hand flank, to Camp 4 at 7900m. From this spectacular promontory, the Eagle's Nest, the ridge rears up in a series of fierce towers. The obvious climbing line draws the climber inexorably left on to a huge hanging glacier. After fixing ropes across the concave snowslope, the first summit team cut loose, unroped and without oxygen, for the final push to the top. Takashi Ozaki had to turn back but the other three, Naoe Sakashita, Yukihiro Yanagisawa and Hiroshi Yoshino, continued up the hanging glacier, finally reaching the summit twelve hours after setting out. On the descent they were caught out by darkness. Bivouacking at 8350m without a duvet, Yanagisawa

▲

had to be hugged and massaged all night by Sakashita. Yoshino shivered alone, about 100m higher.

They survived their ordeal but in the morning, just as the second summit team was bringing up a spare rope and hot tea, Yanagisawa suddenly lost his balance and fell 3000m to his death. Despite the disaster, and despite being delayed by their generous rescue attempt, the second team of four climbers all reached the summit, concluding a brilliant exercise in concerted teamwork.

In 1982 a Polish/Mexican team also appeared on the North Ridge, while ostensibly attempting the North-West Ridge from Pakistan. The upper section of that ridge (still unclimbed) is ill-defined and the rock formations tend to force climbers left, into Sinkiang. Having reached the North Ridge near the Japanese Camp 4, two famously tough Poles, Leszek Cichy and Wojciech Wröz, tried to push on up the direct line of the ridge, but were stopped by bitter autumn cold on 6 September. In 1989 the brilliant French team of Pierre Béghin and Christophe Profit, unsupported, repeated the Polish ramp from the North-West Ridge to the North Ridge to the Eagle's Nest. Béghin had long had his eye on the direct finish of the North Ridge (in 1988 he had soloed the Japanese route to 8000m) but, faced with the reality of those complex towers and pinnacles, he and Profit followed the obvious line left on to the frightening windslab of the hanging glacier. They reached the summit at nightfall and their torch lights were visible right down at Concordia.

The Frenchmen's spiralling route from Pakistan into

▲

Sinkiang was a brilliant achievement but the most appealing line must be the original Japanese route from the K2 Glacier. It is harder than the Abruzzi and although it has been climbed by small lightweight parties, they have relied heavily on the fixed ropes left by others. The route starts up to the right of the toe of the ridge, traversing right on snow and ice slopes to avoid an obvious slanting sérac band, then back left above

(*Above*) For some climbers the greatest attraction on expeditions to the north side of K2, is the sense of remoteness at the heart of a huge desert landscape. Without camels the complex, fast-flowing channels of the Shaksgam and its tributaries would not be crossable during the summer months. (*Greg Child*)

(*Left*) A bewitchingly calm evening on K2, with the North Ridge in sharp relief. The snow hump on the left is the upper part of the North-East Ridge, seen from the other side on page 62. (*Greg Child*)

it towards the ridge crest. There is a Camp 1 site on the snowslope here at c.6000m but even tents dug into the slope are at great risk from avalanches. The route now diagonals right again, with some steep smooth ice, past a rock island to the bottom right end of a rockband. This is climbed at about grade III before a diagonal traverse left leads to Camp 2 on the ridge at c.6700m. From here mixed climbing up the ridge leads to Camp 3 at 7500m, almost level with the huge ice cliff at the bottom edge of the hanging glacier on the left. From Camp 3 a gully

leads right on to the face before one moves back left and up mixed and rock terrain (grade III/IV) to the Eagle's Nest. Just above Camp 4 there is an obvious traverse line out left on to the hanging glacier. After crossing the snow and ice slopes, the route follows its far side, finally breaking out left along a snow ramp to the ridge one hour below the summit.

As on the Abruzzi, the summit day on this route is a very long one and most parties seem to end up either bivouacking on the way down or descending in the dark. Immediately after a big snowfall the couloir will always be lethal; even in settled weather it is unnerving, as it seems to be permanent windslab. As Greg Child put it, after climbing the route with a small team in 1990, 'If that slope was lower down on the mountain you probably wouldn't consider crossing it.' The summit of K2 is a very special prize and to complete this route there is an uncomfortable element of gambling; several people, deciding that the risk is too great, have abandoned the prize. Others have been lucky, but in 1994, descending after a very high unplanned bivouac, the Basque climber Juanjo San Sebastián was avalanched 400m, miraculously coming to a halt just 50m above the giant ice cliff. After another night in the open, and a further night at Camp 4, he then climbed heroically back up to help his seriously ill companion Atxo Apellaniz, who was still struggling down the snowslope. With two other companions, San Sebastián managed eventually to get Apellaniz down to Camp 2, but there, pinned down and delayed by a storm, he finally succumbed to pulmonary oedema and died.

San Sebastián's horrific epic and his heroic efforts to save his friend illustrate just how serious this route is. For all its beautiful symmetry, K2 will always be a dangerous mountain. The North Ridge is one of the

Mountain	K2
Height	8611m
Location	Baltoro Muztagh, Central Karakoram, Sinkiang.
Route	North Ridge.
First ascent of mountain	1954. See Abruzzi Spur.
First ascent of route	Summit reached by Naoe Sakashita, Yukihiro Yanagisawa & Hiroshi Yoshino (Jap), 14 August 1982.
First alpine-style ascent of route	Solo attempt to 8000m by Pierre Béghin in 1988. Climbed in lightweight style in 1990 by Greg Child, Greg Mortimer (Austr) & Steve Swenson (USA), but greatly benefiting from ropes fixed by a Japanese expedition earlier that summer.
Height of b/c	Sughet Jangal is a delightful base at 3900m. However, the real base of operations need to be at c.5000m at the head of the K2 Glacier.
Roadhead	Maza in the Yarkand valley, approached from Urumchi.
Length of walk-in	6-8 days via the Aghil Pass, with camel transport.
Season	June to August. It is best to approach early in the summer while camels can still wade the rivers safely and leave in September when the waters have started to subside. Several climbers have nearly died in the Shaksgam and its tributaries.
Permission	Sinkiang Mountaineering Association, Urumchi or Chinese Mountaineering Association, Beijing, usually through an agent.
Success rate	Surprisingly high. About 35 per cent of expeditions have succeeded, perhaps because the route tends to attract strong and well-motivated teams. However, some successes have been achieved at a high price.
Bibliography	Eric Shipton's *Blank on the Map* in *The Six Mountain-Travel Books* (Diadem, 1985) is one of the most evocative accounts of the area. No one has spent more time here than Kurt Diemberger who describes his journeys and climbs in *The Endless Knot* (Grafton, 1991). See also Greg Child's account of the 1990 ascent in *AAJ* 1991, reproduced in *Mixed Emotions* (Mountaineers, 1993). The Japanese first ascent is well documented in *Iwa To Yuki*. 85, 87, 91 & 92. The Béghin/Profit variation is recorded in *Mountain* 143.

world's great climbing lines but, like so many great lines, it is marred by remains of fixed ropes. A pure alpine-style ascent is a fine ideal, but the reality is that most people seek a degree of security on this long difficult route where retreat is never easy.

CHOGOLISA 7665m

South-West Ridge and Traverse

Chogolisa is one of the highest mountains in the Central Karakoram: an impressive and elegant snow fluted peak rising to 7665m. Its trapezium shape accommodates two distinct summits and four ridges, three of which have been climbed. By any of these routes, the peak is a relatively straightforward proposition, certainly one of the easier summits of over 7500m anywhere in the world, yet it has been climbed only a handful of times.

Like many great peaks, Chogolisa achieved both fame and notoriety before it was ascended. As early as 1892, Martin Conway, on his epic crossing of the Karakoram, was drawn by the mountain's fluted white form and christened it Bride Peak. It seemed to Conway that the North-East Summit was the higher of the two tops, and this was the goal of the first three attempts on the mountain. The Duke of the Abruzzi's 1909 expedition reached over 7400m on the North-East Ridge, an altitude record that was to stand for thirteen years, until the early attempts on Everest. But Chogolisa is perhaps best known as the place where Hermann Buhl died in 1957, while attempting the peak with Kurt Diemberger, just two weeks after their success on Broad Peak. Bad weather threatened, so they had called off their bid at 7100m on the North-East Ridge and were descending unroped when, in a moment of poor

visibility, Buhl strayed from the ridge and plunged through a cornice to his death. Diemberger completed the descent alone and stricken by the loss of his partner – one of the greatest mountaineers of a generation. His chilling photograph showing Buhl's tracks leading over the edge is a powerful reminder that even the best climbers can make errors in the high mountains.

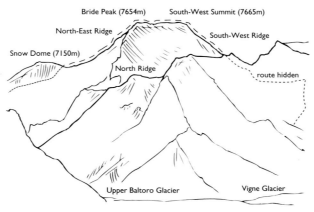

(*Right*) Chogolisa reposes in stately elegance behind a retinue of satellites, the Vigne peaks, in this view from Concordia on the Baltoro Glacier. (*Andy Fanshawe*)

The following year a Japanese team from Kyoto University completed the North-East Ridge. After an exhausting wade through chest-deep snow, M. Fujihira and K. Hirai reached the spectacular rock pinnacle of the North-East Summit late in the afternoon, only to learn later that it was 11m lower than the South-

West Summit, nearly a kilometre distant. Their route remains unrepeated in ascent.

The only other route to the North-East Summit is the North Ridge. First climbed in 1986 by a Spanish party, it has the advantage that it ascends directly from the Upper Baltoro, though it is threatened in its lower section by séracs overhanging the initial 60° ice slopes.

The higher South-West Summit was finally reached by Erich Lackner's Austrian party in 1975. Their line, the South-West Ridge, is probably the best route for those wishing to climb Chogolisa and return by the same way. It is accessible, direct and route-finding is obvious. Graced by calm weather, climbers on the upper portion of this route are ideally positioned to enjoy stunning views of the Karakoram giants – K2, Broad Peak and the Gasherbrums – and even Nanga Parbat, 130 km to the west in the Himalaya.

To reach the ridge, one must first negotiate a snow and ice face either from the north (Vigne Glacier) or south (Kaberi Glacier). On the first ascent in 1975, approaching from the Kaberi, the Austrians used 3km of fixed rope to reach the start of the ridge, the 6500m col between Prupoo Burahka and Chogolisa. However, in 1983, a German party under Heinz Fischer showed it was easier to reach this point from the Vigne. Three years later, Andy Fanshawe's British party repeated the German route, traversed the one-kilometre ridge to

Bride Peak and then descended the Japanese (1958) North-East Ridge route and the Upper Chogolisa Glacier, thus making the first traverse of the mountain.

Both the German and British parties made their base camp on the Upper Baltoro Glacier, though it should be possible to negotiate for porters to carry expedition equipment the extra 5km to the base of the North-West Face at the head of the Vigne Glacier. The British party chose a base camp on the Baltoro because it was more convenient for their traversing plan of descending the North-East Ridge, and it allowed them to make a reconnaissance of the descent route which in turn was a useful acclimatisation exercise.

The 1100m high North-West Face, of mostly 45° or 50° snow and ice interrupted by séracs, leads from the Vigne basin to the South-West Ridge at about 6500m. No obvious line beckons, but by starting on the left and climbing diagonally right the British party avoided the main dangers. Fischer's party took a line even further to the left.

At the top of the face, which a reasonably fast party

could climb in a day, one joins the South-West Ridge at the site of the Austrian (1975) Camp 4. Easier climbing on the crest of the ridge then leads in a few hours to séracs at about 7000m, above which the upper arête rises more steeply to the summit. The German party, who travelled light, reached the summit and returned in a day from below these séracs.

This upper arête enjoys superb views of the Western

The ridge grows thinner and thinner the higher one climbs until, finally, a knife-edged arête leads on to the broader, horizontal summit ridge. The summit itself, like that of Nuptse, is rather ill-defined and is situated about 100m along a long flat ridge that leads on to the North-East summit. This ridge between the summits is relatively straightforward to traverse, though it is committing for, in the event of an emer-

composed of very unstable rocks giving the only section of rock climbing on the entire expedition. Belays are poor but the climbing is never harder than II or III. In early morning, the steep snow that bounds the rock on one side may be secure enough for a climber to kick steps straight to the summit – a tiny perch with room for just one person.

The British party descended rapidly to a col on the

Karakoram. It is also very exposed to winds and one characteristic feature of this ridge is its deep snow flutings and cornices which most dangerously overhang the Kaberi (south-east) side of the ridge. There is no respite in the angle of these snow slopes and after ten hours of strenuously breaking trail, the British party, carrying full bivouac gear, were forced to dig platforms for their tents at about 7400m for a third camp.

gency, losing height from the middle of this traverse would involve descending unexplored slopes with no realistic means of ever regaining one of the established routes on the mountain. Nevertheless, with no obstacles on the ridge, the British Party took just two hours to make the 900m long connection to Bride Peak.

The 40m pinnacle of the North-East Summit is

North-East Ridge (heavily corniced) at about 7000m before Snow Dome (7150m). After bivouacking here, they descended directly south, crossing the bergschrund and then following the basin west and north, around Snow Dome to the North Chogolisa Glacier. This route is preferable to continuing along the North-East Ridge over the summit of Snow Dome to gain the same point.

Negotiating a safe route from here to the Upper Baltoro (first achieved by Conway when he climbed Pioneer Peak, 6550m, in 1892) is difficult and for this reason a recce/acclimatisation climb is desirable. In 1986 the key to the descent was a steep ice slope on the side of a large rognon in the Upper Chogolisa Glacier, but conditions may change yearly.

The South-West Ridge which received its sixth ascent (again from the Baltoro) in 1987, is surely destined to become a classic Himalayan climb, as it gains high altitude without great technical difficulty amid some of the most spectacular mountain scenery on earth. The traverse of the mountain, though more serious, is even more attractive, as it gives continuous interest and is at its least demanding at the highest altitude.

(*Opposite page left*) Glorious skywalking on the ridge between Chogolisa's South-West Summit and the North-East Summit (Bride Peak). The twin pyramids on the far left are Gasherbrum III (left) and Gasherbrum II. The peak immediately left of the climber's arm is Gasherbrum I (Hidden Peak). The big triangular face in shade was climbed by Kurtyka and Kukuczka in 1983; the upper part of the Messner/Habeler route is in profile on the left. (*Ulric Jessop*)

(*Opposite page right*) Hermann Buhl, the phenomenal Austrian mountaineer whose Himalayan ideas were twenty years ahead of his time, photographed after the Broad Peak triumph and few days before his untimely death on Chogolisa. (*Kurt Diemberger*)

(*Left*) Hamish Irvine choosing the sensible way to tackle a spectacular knife-edge near the South-West Summit of Chogolisa. Almost immediately behind him, 25km to the south-west, is the gleaming pyramid of Drifika, with K6 on the extreme left. (*Liam Elliot*)

SUMMARY STATISTICS AND INFORMATION

Mountain	Chogolisa
Height	South-West Summit: 7665m; North-East Summit (Bride Peak): 7654m.
Location	Masherbrum range, Central Karakoram, Pakistan.
Routes	South-West Ridge and Traverse (incorporating North-East Ridge). 2300m of ascent, mostly on snow with some ice.
First ascent of mountain	North-East Summit: reached by North-East Ridge by M. Fujihara & K. Hirai (Jap) on 4 August 1958; South-West Summit: reached by South-West Ridge by G. Ammerer & F. Pressl (Aus) on 3 August 1975.
First ascent routes	South-West Ridge from Kaberi: as above; from Vigne: 1983, by Adi Fischer, Georg Brosig & Hubert Wendlinger (Ger); first traverse: 10-16 August 1986 by Andy Fanshawe, Liam Elliot, Hamish Irvine, Simon Lamb & Ulric Jessop (UK).
First alpine-style ascent of routes	German party 1983 and British 1986.
Height of b/c	5000m, on junction of Vigne and Upper Baltoro Glaciers.
Roadhead	Askole.
Length of walk-in	Approx 70km and 7 days from Askole.
Season	Best conditions are usually in late July or August.
Permission	Ministry of Tourism, Islamabad.
Success Rate	Of the eight expeditions attempting the South-West Ridge, six have reached the summit. Two French climbers were killed in 1984 attempting to ski from the summit.
Bibliography	The 1909 attempt is described in Filippo de Filippi's classic account of the Abruzzi expedition, *Karakoram and Western Himalaya 1909* (Constable, 1912). The ill-fated alpine-style attempt by Buhl and Diemberger in 1957 is described movingly by Kurt Diemberger in his *Summits and Secrets* (Hodder & Stoughton, 1991). *Coming Through* (Hodder & Stoughton, 1990) by Andy Fanshawe has a full account of the first traverse of Chogolisa. This and other ascents mentioned here are chronicled in the *AAJ* and *HJ*.

Chogolisa (left) with its South-West Ridge dropping to the 6500m col at the head of the Vigne Glacier. The ascent to the col leads up diagonally from the left. (*Andy Fanshawe*)

DRIFIKA 6447m

North Ridge

Ambition draws climbers year after year to the giant peaks at the head of the Baltoro, but for many people the real joy of the Karakoram lies on smaller, more intimate peaks at an altitude where body and mind are still in harmony with their surroundings. In recent years the Hushe valley has attracted an increasing number of hedonists, intent on enjoying the wealth of varied climbing at comparatively reasonable altitudes.

From Skardu the jeep road runs east to Kaphalu on the Shyok river. From Kaphalu, valleys branch out to the Kondus and Kaberi Glaciers, round the back of Chogolisa, and the Bilafond La, from where Tom Longstaff in 1909 first realised the huge extent of the mighty Siachen. Since 1984 the whole area has been a war zone, disputed by India and Pakistan. However, immediately north of Kaphalu, the Hushe valley and its five major glacier systems are open to foreigners.

The Aling Glacier gives arduous trekking with no ablation valley. The Masherbrum Glacier is gentler and it

The classical spire of Drifika, photographed from Poro. The North Ridge descends towards the camera. The route approaches from the left, through a gap behind the climber, up on to the sunlit shoulder on the right and thence back left to the main ridge. (*Datsu Hakimoto*)

was from the Sérac Glacier branch, that Masherbrum's magnificent Main Summit (7821m) was first climbed by Nick Clinch's 1960 expedition, building on the experience of British 1938 and 1957 expeditions on the South-East Face. The mountain has still had only a handful of ascents and the slightly lower South-West Summit has only been climbed once, in 1981. This was one of many first ascents throughout the Karakoram and Himalaya made by the Polish alpinist Zygmunt Heinrich, but success came at a huge price, when his two companions died from hypothermia during a bivouac on the summit ridge, leaving him to make a harrowing solo descent.

From the Ghondokhoro Glacier two high glacier passes, the Masherbrum La and the Ghondokhoro La, lead over to the Baltoro basin. In mid to late summer the latter is being used increasingly as a fast alternative to the traditional Askole route for expeditions returning from Concordia. On the watershed between the Ghondokhoro and Chogolisa Glaciers

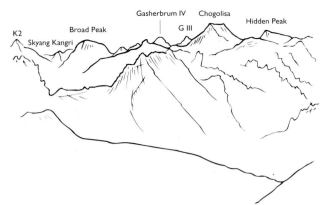

lie the shapely summits of Trinity Peak or Tasa and the lower Ghondokhoro Peak, popular with trekking parties, but perhaps the most spectacular peaks are those rising from the Charakusa Glacier.

This is granite country and the Charakusa bristles with stunning towers and spires. The head of the glacier is dominated by two strangely neglected peaks, K6 and K7. The North Face of K6 is as spectacular as

made from the Nangmah Glacier, crossing a col beneath the West Summit and traversing round to the South Ridge of the higher Main Summit (7281m). K7 (6934m), has also had just one ascent, from the Charakusa Glacier. The 1984 Japanese expedition led by Toichiro Nagata took no chances, fixing 450 pitons and bolts and 6500m of rope on the South-West Ridge! In rather more sporting style, Dai Lampard recently

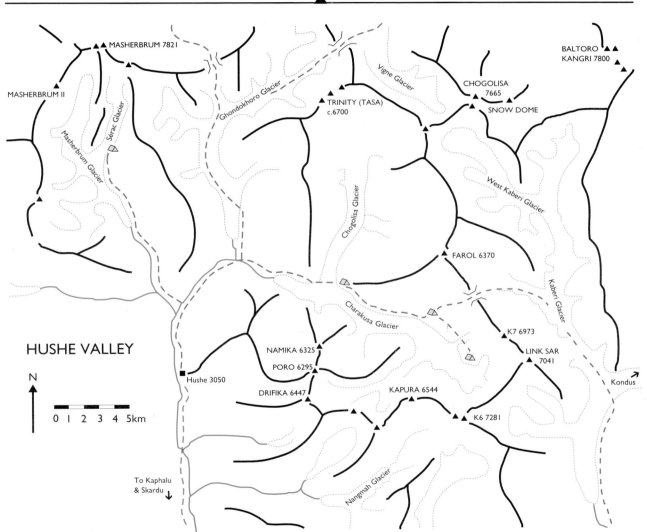

(*Above*) Alpine ambience on the North Ridge of Drifika, with a backdrop of Karakoram giants. (*Michel Sèvres*)

the Ogre and Latok walls further west, but has never been attempted, and the one ascent of the mountain, by E. Koblmüller's 1971 Austrian expedition, was

led two British attempts on a more direct line, avoiding a dangerous couloir. On the first attempt in 1990 they climbed eighty-eight difficult pitches (up to grade

VII) in one continuous unsupported push before retreating; three years later they returned and in thirty-two continuous days climbed slightly further, to the top of the Fortress at c.6300m, before turning back.

In contrast to that extraordinary marathon on K7, there are literally hundreds of small peaks and spires in the Chogolisa/Charakusa basin. Many are below 6000m so do not require a climbing expedition permit. On the north bank of the Charakusa a few granite spires have been climbed, like the shapely Naysa and The Dog's Knob (sometimes referred to

coyly as TDK Peak; no Urdu translation has been forthcoming), but many are still untouched. Of the more mixed peaks, Layla is rumoured to have been climbed, as is Namika. Immediately south of Namika lies our selected peak, Drifika.

The mountain was climbed in 1978 by an eight-man Japanese expedition led by Akiya Ishimura, with six of the team reaching the summit. Their brief report in the *Iwa To Yuki* mentions that local inhabitants call the peak Drefekal, meaning the House of Ghosts, but it has also been referred to as Angel Peak,

perhaps because it resembles the Angelus by K2. It is a beautiful white pyramid with a single perfect line to the summit – the North Ridge. The first ascent team used some fixed rope on the ridge, but this is very definitely a route where pure alpine-style is the only sensible option. The climb is short and straightforward and it lies at a comparatively low altitude.

The ridge is approached by a long walk up the major south-western tributary of the Charakusa Glacier, just west of Kapura (see map). From the head of the glacier one has to climb round to the right of a prominent

▲

shoulder to get established on the North Ridge of Drifika. There is a wonderful campsite on the shoulder and the ridge above is not very long (the total height gain from the head of the glacier is not much over 1000m). However, it is corniced and the climbing on the West

climb more than one peak and the choice is huge. The wealth of good climbing, the fantastic surroundings, the delightful campsites and the hospitality of the local people, who are amongst the most friendly in Pakistan, make this area perfect for a Himalayan climbing holiday.

Mountain	Drifika
Height	6447m
Location	Masherbrum Range, Central Karakoram, Pakistan.
Route	North Ridge.
First ascent mountain	Six climbers led by Akiya Ishimura (Jap) reached of summit on 17 August 1978.
First ascent of route	As above.
Height of bc	There are several good sites between 4000-4500m on the north bank of the Charakusa Glacier, but the best is the K7 base camp, situated in a delightful ablation valley which boasts a Japanese volley ball court.
Roadhead	Hushe village.
Length of walk-in	3 days and 4 porter-stages to K7 base camp.
Season	June to September, but in recent summers extreme heat has become a problem on lower peaks from mid-July onward.
Permission	Ministry of Tourism, Islamabad. Drifika, like many of the most tempting peaks, is well above 6000m so requires an expeditions permit and liaison officer; however there is also much good climbing, particularly rock climbing, to be had below 6000m, for which no permit is necessary
Success rate	One successful ascent and one unsuccessful attempt recorded.
Bibliography	This is one of the least well documented areas of the Karakoram and therein lies its charm. There have been occasional articles in various climbing magazines. British climbers can also consult individual reports in the Alpine Club Library, such as those of the British K7 Reconnaissance Expedition (1975) and the British South-East Karakoram Expedition (1986).

Flank can be icy; the summit, inevitably, is not the obvious point in the picture, but is set further back to the south. A very fit party might climb up and down the ridge in the early morning, before snow and ice conditions deteriorate in the fierce Karakoram heat, but most parties will probably decide to bivouac high on the route and descend the next morning.

Drifika is a beautiful objective with magical views north to the giants of the Baltoro but most parties will probably want to combine it with other peaks. Even with just three weeks in the area it should be possible to

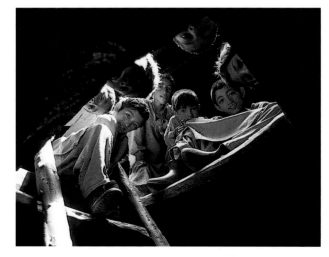

(*Facing*) The stupendous North Face of K6 from the north side of the Charakusa Glacier. The Main Summit on the left was climbed from the south in 1971. The West Summit on the right is unclimbed. The glacier branch at the bottom right leads up past Kapura to Drifika. (*Simon Yates*)
(*Above left*) Looking further round to the west from a slightly different viewpoint. The rubble-strewn glacier in the foreground leads down to the main Charakusa. On the left is Kapura. Drifika is the snow spire in the centre, with Namika to the right. The dark rock tower on the extreme right is TDK Peak. (*Stephen Jones*)
(*Left*) The next generation of farmer-porters, boys at home in Hushe. The people in this valley have always been particularly friendly to trekkers and mountaineers. (*Stephen Jones*)

NANGA PARBAT 8125m

Diamir Face (Kinshofer route)

Nanga Parbat is one of the most sought after of all Himalayan mountains. It stands as a huge monolith, a sentinel at the western end of the Himalayan chain, separated from the Karakoram ranges to the north and east by the Indus river which has carved a deep gorge around the mountain, just as the Brahmaputra has done around Namche Barwa over 2000km to the east. This means that the ascent of Nanga Parbat from its various base camp sites represents an altitude gain of over 4000m, much more, for instance, than Everest from its Rongbuk base. And Nanga Parbat's northern latitude brings colder weather, more snow and ferocious storms, although there is less monsoon effect in the warmest months of July and August.

Nanga Parbat was first attempted in 1895 by a team of British mountaineers, led by Fred Mummery and including the Gurkha officer Charles Bruce, who was later to lead the first attempt on Everest. The expedition was beset by illnesses; nevertheless, Mummery and the Gurkha Raghobir Thapa reached nearly 7000m, climbing a rocky spur in the centre of the Diamir Face – a remarkable feat of alpine-style climbing, way ahead of its time. Seventy-five year later the young Reinhold Messner was to descend this way in a desperate retreat with his brother Günther, after climbing the Rupal Face.

Mummery and the two Gurkhas died later on the

The immense massif of Nanga Parbat seen from the north, towering over the great gorge of the Indus river. The Diamir Face is in shadow on the right. Facing the camera is the Rakhiot Face, scene of so many dramas and tragedies during the 'thirties and route of the first ascent in 1953. Hermann Buhl's final solo marathon was made by the long ridge on the left. (*Ulric Jessop*)

1895 expedition trying to negotiate a route around to the Rakhiot Glacier for a recce on that side of the mountain. They were to be the first of thirty-one men who would be killed on Nanga Parbat before it was eventually climbed in 1953.

After Mummery's futuristic reconnaissance Nanga Parbat became a German domain. Throughout the 'thirties, five expeditions laid siege to the Rakhiot Flank on the north side of the mountain and another to the Diamir Face. The accounts of their efforts do not make cheerful reading, though they demonstrate the depth of experience these German climbers possessed: in 1932, under the leadership of Willy Merkl, a practical route was found for future attempts on the Rakhiot side, over Rakhiot Peak to the East Ridge at 6950m. In 1934, again under Merkl, the route was pushed yet further, as far as the Silver Saddle at 7451m. Indeed, Peter Aschenbrenner and Erwin Schneider, travelling unladen, continued across the plateau and reached an altitude of about 7700m before returning to their camp on the Saddle. Then, with Merkl, Aschenbrenner, Schneider, Welzenbach, Wieland and eleven porters camped on the col, a storm swept Nanga Parbat. To continue was impossible. They descended as soon as they dared, in two groups. Of the sixteen men, nine perished in a relentless blizzard, among them Wieland, Welzenbach and

the leader, Merkl. Three years later, sixteen more men were lost on the mountain when a single avalanche engulfed Camp 4 at 6200m on the Rakhiot Face. The expedition leader Paul Bauer, veteran of Siniolchu and Kangchenjunga, returned to Nanga Parbat in 1938 to conduct a cautious though determined attempt, but failed to reach a new high point, due largely to poor weather. In 1939 a party under Peter Aufschnaiter switched attention to the Diamir Face, reaching about

6000m on a rocky rib to the left of Mummery's.

The war intervened and the Germans did not return to Nanga Parbat until 1953, when at last a German/Austrian expedition claimed the elusive summit. The leaders of this expedition, Karl Herrligkoffer and Peter Aschenbrenner, had ironically abandoned the attempt and ordered the four climbers at Camp 3, no higher than 6100m, to descend. The climbers refused and moved up to Camp 4 on 1 July; the following day Hermann

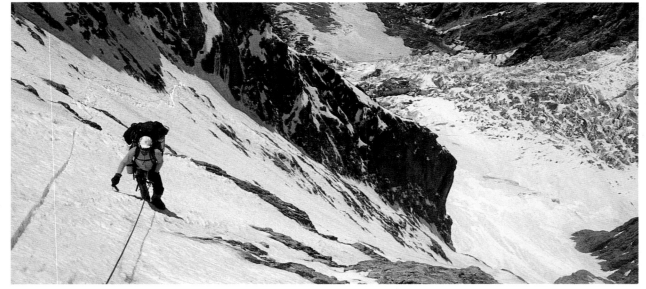

(Above) Dave Walsh on the initial couloir of the Kinshofer route, heavily laden with supplies for a week. (Roger Mear)
(Far Left) The messy reality of popular routes on eight-thousanders: ropes and ladders draped over the 60m step at 5900m. (Roger Mear)
(Left) Ghazala Mear surveys the detritus of past expeditions at the Diamir base camp. (Roger Mear)

Buhl and Otto Kempter reached Camp 5. After a stormy night, Buhl set off early on the morning of the 3rd, with Otto Kempter a few hours behind. Kempter reached the Silver Saddle before returning to Camp 5. Buhl however made the summit, on hands and knees after seventeen hours of desperate climbing, then survived an open bivouac on the descent, standing up all night in just two thin layers of clothing. It was a feat equal to anything that had been achieved on Everest that

year, or on Annapurna three years earlier. Buhl used no bottled oxygen on his final bid and drove himself way beyond normal human limits. It was his moment of exaltation – a justification for life itself.

This 1953 Rakhiot route to the summit of Nanga Parbat is a difficult one with very real avalanche danger, as the 1936 disaster bears out. Although it has been repeated, most parties nowadays attempt either the gigantic Rupal precipice or the line of the second ascent, the Kinshofer route on the Diamir Face.

Toni Kinshofer made the first winter ascent of the Eiger North Face in 1961 and was a member of Herrligkoffer's reconnaissance to the Diamir Face later that year. They concentrated their efforts on a couloir between the Aufschnaiter and Mummery Ribs and succeeded in climbing the face right up to the plateau (the Bazhin Hollow) below the summit block at 7100m.

Austrian team repeated the Kinshofer route. Rather than joining Buhl's route above the Bazhin Gap, they traversed the Bazhin Hollow rightwards below the summit block and ascended directly to the summit (see right). This has become the preferred route of ascent on Nanga Parbat from the north.

On the southern side, the most rapid route is that taken by Hanns Schell's four-man party in 1976 – a

Peter Scholz and the Messner brothers reaching the summit; the South-East Pillar was climbed by a Polish expedition in 1985, more or less following a line taken by Ueli Bühler in 1982 when he reached the South Summit (8042m) during yet another expedition organised by Herrligkoffer.

One final route has to be mentioned. During the desperate unplanned descent of the Diamir Face in

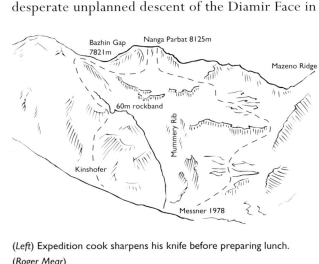

(*Left*) Expedition cook sharpens his knife before preparing lunch. (*Roger Mear*)

(*Above right*) The Diamir Face. Mummery and Raghobir Thapa were way ahead of their time when they climbed the central rib as far as the huge séracs at nearly 7000m. Seventy-five years later, Günther and Reinhold Messner made a desperate on-sight descent of the rib, unable, according to Reinhold, to reverse their ascent route on the Rupal Face. Günther was lost at the bottom of the face, annihilated by an avalanche falling from one of the sérac barriers which make the main face so unpredictable. The Kinshofer route on the left avoids most of that danger. (*Roger Mear*)

(*Right*) Dave Walsh on the rocky summit of Nanga Parbat in 1991, after completing a continuous alpine-style ascent of the Kinshofer route. (*Roger Mear*)

The team returned the following year, this time installing a cable-hoist at the top of the initial couloir. Kinshofer, Löw and Maanhardt were among the climbers who again reached the Bazhin Hollow. This time, however, they continued, to join Buhl's route at the Bazhin Gap at 7821m and then follow the ridge to the summit. The main difficulties of their climb appeared to be in its upper section, on the summit ridge, though these were largely avoided when in 1978 a small

curving ridge on the left-hand side of the Rupal Face that leads to the Mazeno Gap at 6940m and from there on the South-West Ridge to the top. It is marginally less direct than the modern version of the Kinshofer route and more difficult in its upper ridge section. Nevertheless it has been repeated several times. The Rupal Face has two other routes. Both are direct and very hard. Herrligkoffer's 1970 expedition climbed the direct route (still unrepeated), with Felix Kuen,

1970, Reinhold Messner lost his brother. He returned twice to the face, finally, in 1978, climbing it solo by a new route up the right-hand side. For Messner this cathartic first solo of an eight-thousander was more important than his oxygenless ascent of Everest two months earlier. It was a milestone in Himalayan history but the route was dangerous and we shall concentrate now on the better line of the Kinshofer route.

Base camp for an attempt on the Kinshofer is best

SUMMARY STATISTICS AND INFORMATION

Mountain	Nanga Parbat
Height	8125m
Route	Diamir Face (Kinshofer Route). 4025m of ascent, mostly on snow and ice.
First ascent of mountain	Summit reached solo by Hermann Buhl (Aus), 3 July 1953
First ascent of route	T. Kinshofer, S. Löw and A. Mannhardt (Ger), 21 June 1962. Variation on summit block by lightweight Austrian expedition, 1978.
First alpine-style ascent of route	Roger Mear and David Walsh (UK) 1991.
Height of b/c	4080m, on north bank of Diamir Glacier.
Roadhead	Bunar, on the Karakoram Highway.
Length of walk-in	Approx 30km, 3-4 days.
Season	Best conditions appear historically to be in late June and July.
Permission	Ministry of Tourism, Islamabad.
Success rate	Low. Fewer than 30 of the 80 expeditions to Nanga Parbat have put anyone on the summit. In the past Nanga Parbat had a casualty record second to none, but that was mainly on the Rakhiot Flank and in recent years the mountain has seen fewer tragedies than many other eight-thousanders.
Bibliography	Hermann Buhl's classic *Nanga Parbat Pilgrimage* (Hodder & Stoughton, 1981) concludes with a personal record of the legendary first ascent of the mountain, whilst Kenneth Mason's *Abode of Snow* (Diadem/Mountaineers, 1987) summarises the early attempts on the mountain. Reinhold Messner knows more about the Diamir Face than anyone; his involvement with it is detailed in his autobiography *Reinhold Messner, Free Spirit* (Hodder & Stoughton, 1991) and *All 14 Eight-Thousanders* (Crowood, 1988). There is an excellent 1:50,000 contour map of the mountain published by the German and Austrian Alpine Clubs.

sited on the true right bank of the Diamir Glacier at 4280m, after a three- or four-day walk from the road-head at Bunar above the Indus. The climb begins with a steep snow couloir, capped by a vertical 60m rock step adorned with old fixed ropes at 5900m. After this, mixed ground leads up the front of a buttress to its top at 6150m. A rising leftward traverse on snow and ice is followed by a large sweep back right to break through rocks and séracs (6800m) to the lower

slopes of the Bazhin Hollow. The climber is now faced with two obvious options. By ascending to the left of the summit block, one can pick up the Buhl route below the subsidiary summit at 7910m and then follow the ridge southwards, on to the Shoulder at 8070m and finally the summit. Much easier is to cross the Hollow to wide snow slopes running up into the summit block. These give way to broken, mixed ground, although at least one recent party has climbed directly to the summit by way of a wide snowy gully.

From Nanga Parbat it is possible to see into three distinct mountain ranges: the Karakoram to the north-east, with its unmistakable pyramid of K2; to the north-west, the Hindu Kush; and further north in the very distance, the Pamirs. Nanga Parbat itself, spreads out beneath your feet, has seen more deaths than any of the world's great mountains. Why do climbers return again and again? What compels us to place

ourselves at such blatant risk? Whatever the answer, it lies too deep in our psyche to erase. We must channel, control and ultimately feed our passion. To deny it is to dilute the experience of living. To let it run riot is to risk losing everything.

To ascend Nanga Parbat, the ninth highest mountain in the world, is to achieve a great deal.

A Hindu pilgrim heading up the Bhagirathi river to Gangotri. *(John Cleare/Mountain Camera)*

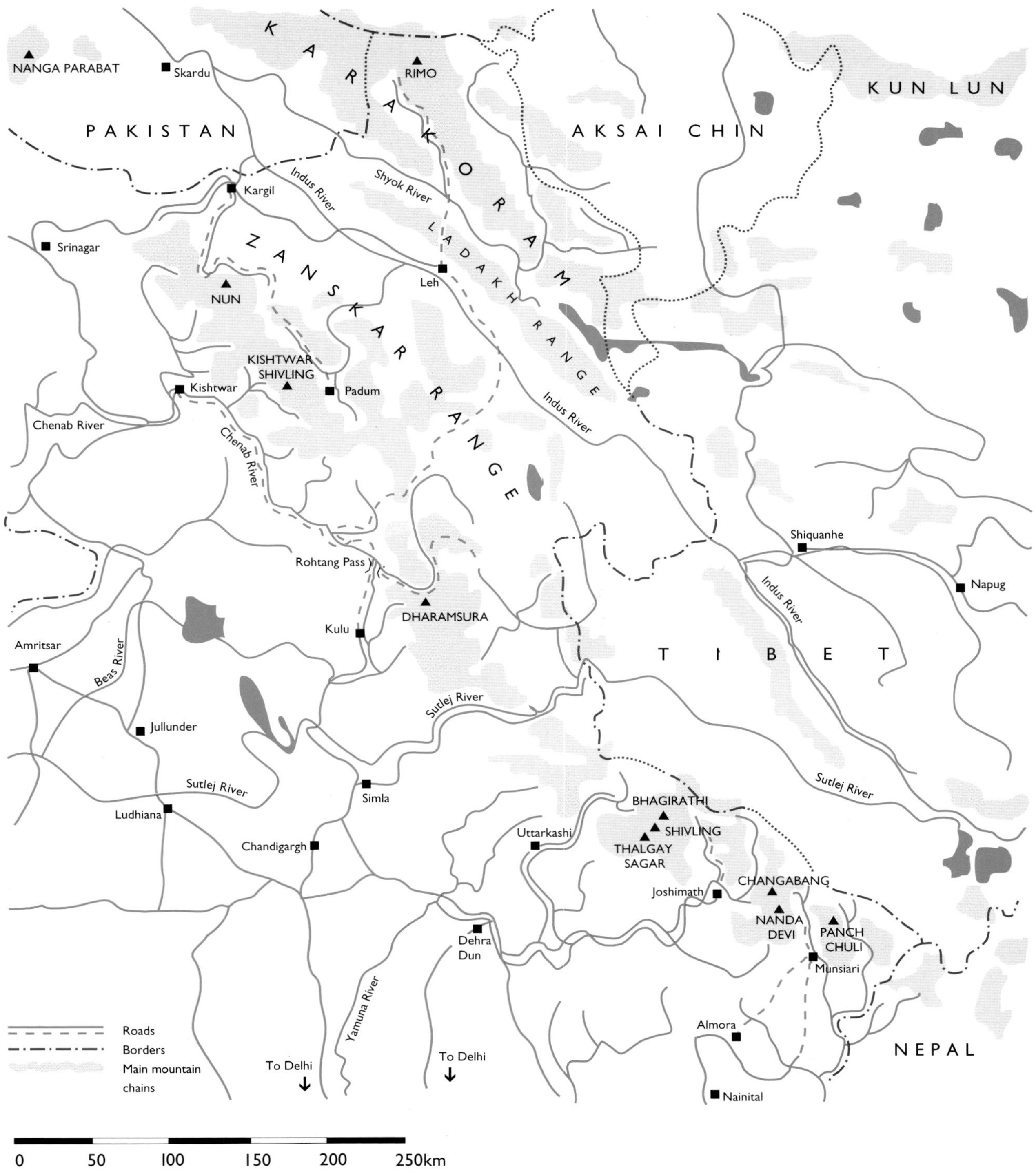

INDIA

KUN LUN

AKSAI CHIN

PAKISTAN

NANGA PARABAT

Skardu

KARAKORAM

RIMO

Kargil

Shyok River

Indus River

Srinagar

ZANSKAR RANGE

LADAKH RANGE

Leh

NUN

KISHTWAR SHIVLING

Kishtwar

Padum

Chenab River

Chenab River

Indus River

Shiquanhe

Rohtang Pass

Napug

Amritsar

Beas River

Kulu

DHARAMSURA

Jullunder

Sutlej River

TIBET

Indus River

Sutlej River

Ludhiana

Sutlej River

Simla

BHAGIRATHI

Chandigargh

Uttarkashi

SHIVLING

THALGAY SAGAR

Joshimath

CHANGABANG

NANDA DEVI

PANCH CHULI

Dehra Dun

Munsiari

Yamuna River

Almora

NEPAL

To Delhi

To Delhi

Nainital

Roads
Borders
Main mountain chains

0   50   100   150   200   250km

RIMO I 7385m

South Face / South-West Ridge

For many years it remained a mystery mountain, hidden away at the heart of a remote ice wilderness. Early travellers on the Central Asian trade route must have glimpsed its summit on their way to the desolate Karakoram Pass, but it was only in 1914 that the Italian explorer Filippo de Filippi surveyed and photographed the north side of the mountain. In 1929 the famous Dutch couple, Dr Philip and Jenny Visser, led the first ever party into the Terong valley and glimpsed the south side of Rimo but no photos were published.

After the second world war politics put a virtual stop to mountaineering in the Eastern Karakoram, whose central ice highway, the immense Siachen Glacier, remained an unresolved issue in the India-Pakistan Kashmir dispute. Occasional foreign expeditions visited the upper glacier, but the eastern approaches, up the Nubra valley, were closely guarded by India.

Saser Kangri (7672m) was climbed by an Indian military expedition in 1973, but other neighbouring 7000m peaks remained untouched. The only attempt on the Rimo massif was a Japanese foray in 1978. A small team crossed the Siachen from Pakistan and reached the Terong valley, only to be stopped

by the fierce glacial river. That same river was to cause more problems seven years later when an Indian/British expedition finally set foot on Rimo.

It was 1985. The Indian army now controlled the entire Siachen glacier and was allowing joint Indian/foreign expeditions to visit the area. Arriving in early June, before significant glacial melt, the Indian/British expedition, led by Harish Kapadia, was

Rimo, the mystery mountain. Dr Visser saw this view in from the North Terong Glacier in 1929 but published no photographs, so no one else knew what the mountain looked like from this side until Harish Kapadia's Indo-British expedition visited the valley in 1985. Rimo III (left) was climbed by Jim Fotheringham and Dave Wilkinson, from the Rimo Glacier on the far side. Rimo I (right) was attempted unsuccessfully by the South-West Ridge descending towards the camera. The mountain was finally climbed by the Indo-Japanese expedition of 1988. Rimo II was climbed in 1989. (*Stephen Venables*)

able to cross the Terong river easily and become the first party since the Vissers in 1929 to reach the Terong Glacier system. During the next four weeks eleven climbers enjoyed a feast of exploration, roaming wide, climbing peaks and crossing passes.

The major success was Dave Wilkinson and Jim Fotheringham's first ascent, on sight, of Rimo III (7233m) by its North-East Ridge after a committing journey over the Ibex Col. The highest peak, Rimo I, proved an even more magnificent chal-

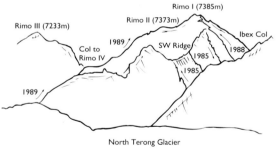

lenge, shapely and inspiring on every side. Victor Saunders and Stephen Venables, also climbing alpine-style, spent six days on the South-West Ridge but had to retreat from 6850m after Venables dropped a rucksack full of bivouac gear. There was no time for a second attempt.

After that bitter disappointment Venables redeemed himself by securing the expedition's exit from the Terong valley. It was now mid-

Victor Saunders following one
of the excellent mixed pitches
through the Pinnacles on the
South-West Ridge of Rimo I,
still heavily snowed-up in early
July during the 1985 attempt.
(*Stephen Venables*)

July and the river was in full flood, raging against cliffs on both sides of the valley. By fixing ropes across cliffs on the right bank, Venables and Saunders created a safe route back to the Siachen, avoiding the lethal river crossing and concluding a memorable expedition.

The successful 1988 expedition climbed directly up the South Face, fixing ropes all the way. This is the crux rockband at about 6600m. Just visible top right is the big sérac which overhangs this route. In 1988 it was judged safe, but future parties may need to study it carefully. (*Yoshio Ogata*)

Rimo I was now recognised as one of the Karakoram's great unclaimed prizes. In 1986 another international expedition, led by Col. Prem Chand, attempted the peak, this time from the north-east,

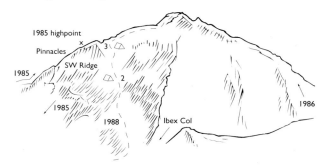

taking the long harsh approach over the Saser La to the South Rimo Glacier and a line on to the North-East Ridge. Desperately short of time and hampered by poor weather and dangerous snow conditions, this expedition was also turned back at about 6850m.

Success came finally in 1988 to a superbly organised eighteen-man Indian/Japanese team, led by Hukam Singh and another distinguished Himalayan veteran Yoshio Ogata. They chose the shorter southern approach, building on the experiences of Kapadia's expedition and learning from the tactical mistakes of Saunders and Venables on the mountain. As so often happens in the Himalaya, the obvious ridge line had actually proved very awkward. Ogata and Singh chose a much more direct line, starting very high at the Ibex Col and heading straight up the South Face to reach the final section of the South-West Ridge above the 1985 highpoint.

The Indian/Japanese team took no chances. From Camp 1 at 6100m, just below the Ibex Col, they fixed over 2000m of rope and established two more camps, one on the face at 6750m and one on the crest of the ridge at about 7000m. On 28 July Ogata and three companions left Camp 3 just before dawn, reaching the summit of Rimo I at 2 pm. Later that day two more

climbers reached the summit, racing up the ropes all the way from Camp 1. Over the next two days another six climbers reached the summit, bringing this outstanding international effort to a successful conclusion.

The following year's international expedition was very different. Led by Col. Prem Chand, the party split into small groups. From the North Terong Glacier Indian climbers Tsewang Smanla, Kanhaiwa Lal and Mohan Singh crossed a new col between Rimo III and Rimo II, to make the second ascent of Rimo IV (first climbed by the Indian army in 1984). Meanwhile Nick Kekus and Stephen Sustad, supported by Doug Scott and Sharu Prabhu, made the first ascent of Rimo II by its North Ridge. After that fine alpine-style coup, the British climbers hoped to go on to the inspiring South-West Face of Rimo III, but at that stage the leader brought the expedition to a close. No one was quite sure why this happened and the incident showed how misunderstandings can easily arise on joint expeditions to this sensitive area.

The South-West Face of Rimo III remains a fine unclimbed objective, as do numerous other potential routes in the Terong basin. However, we shall now concentrate on the Indian/Japanese route on Rimo I.

Although it was first climbed by a rather ponder-

(*Left*) A face-on view of the South Face taken during the first ascent of Sundbrar. (*Dhiren Toolsidas*)
(*Right*) A glorious evening high on the South-West Ridge of Rimo I, looking south to a sea of peaks beyond the Nubra valley, virtually all of them unnamed and unclimbed. (*Stephen Venables*)

ous siege it is the perfect route for a rapid alpine-style ascent. The line is interesting, direct and comparatively short, with a height rise of less than 1500m from the start of the difficulties. From advance base camp on the North Terong Glacier, a side glacier (quite crevassed) leads east to the Ibex Col. The climb starts just below the col at 6100m, taking a broad couloir up the South Face. Rock barriers give pitches of grade IV/V, with some difficult mixed climbing. The first ascent party placed a rather precarious Camp 2 at 6750m, below the hanging glacier, which was deemed safe in 1988 but might in future become threatening – all the more reason for speed. A very fit, competent party could probably climb the whole face in one day to the top camp at 7000m. From here 100m of knife-edge ridge leads north-east on to the broad back of the hanging

glacier. From there onwards the climbing is straightforward, but the first ascent party found deep snow and took ten hours to reach the summit from Camp 3.

If the hanging glacier does look threatening, a safe alternative project would be to complete the 1985 British route, starting left of the Indian/Japanese route, up the big icefield which Venables and Saunders descended in 1985. Once on the crest of the ridge, twelve superb pitches of hard mixed climbing, then five easier snow pitches, lead to a prominent shoulder. From here one final unclimbed knife-edged gap would join up with the Indian/Japanese route at 7000m.

Rimo I is a magnificent peak. Any route to its summit will give some testing climbing in the most dramatic surroundings. The Eastern Karakoram has a feeling of limitless space, with dramatic views north

SUMMARY STATISTICS AND INFORMATION

Mountain	Rimo I
Height	7385m
Location	Rimo Muztagh, Eastern Karakoram, India.
Route	South Face/South-West Ridge. 1500m of ascent, including steep mixed ground, snow/ice to 60° and rock to V.
First ascent of mountain	28 July 1988. Nima Dorje Sherpa & Tsewang Smanla (India), Yoshio Ogata & Hideki Yoshida (Japan). Eight more climbers reached the summit during the next day.
First ascent of route	As above.
Height of b/c	Most effective is an advance b/c at 5000m on North Terong Glacier which has dry ice and rock from late June.
Roadhead	Siachen Glacier snout, Nubra valley, reached in 2 days' hard driving from Leh.
Length of walk-in	4 days minimum from roadhead, but allow extra time for river complications.
Season	Best snow conditions in July and August.
Permission	Indian Mountaineering Federation. Only joint Indian/foreign expeditions are allowed in this militarily sensitive area. Delays common in Leh.
Success rate	Now that approaches have been well reconnoitred, future teams should have a good chance of success.
Bibliography	Early exploration is covered in Filippo de Filippi's *The Italian Expedition to the Himalaya, Karakoram and Eastern Turkestan* (1913-14), and Dr P. C. Visser's *The Karakoram and Turkistan Expedition of 1929-1930, Geographical Journal* 84. More recent journeys are described in *Painted Mountains* by Stephen Venables (Hodder & Stoughton, 1986), account of 1985 expedition; *Rimo, Mountain on the Silk Road* by Peter Hillary (Hodder & Stoughton, 1988), controversial account of 1986 attempt from north-east; and *Himalayan Climber* by Doug Scott (Diadem, 1992) has excellent photos of Rimo massif. *HJ*: vols 42 and 46 for comprehensive articles and maps; vol. 45 for account and photos of first ascent.

to the wide skies of Sinkiang, east to Saser Kangri, south to a sea of unclimbed peaks around the Nubra valley and west across the velvet expanse of the Teram Shehr plateau to the distant Baltoro giants, dominated

NUN 7135m

East Ridge

Nun, with its twin peak Kun, is the only 7000m massif in the Himalaya between Nanga Parbat and the Garhwal. The two peaks and their satellites, Barmal, White Needle and Pinnacle Peak, form a horseshoe rising above a great bend in the Suru river, on the border of Kashmir and Zanskar. The whole area is wonderful trekking country, with a profusion of peaks to climb, nowadays made more accessible by the summer road which follows the Suru south from Kargil, past the famous monastery, Ringdom Gompa, and over the Pensi La to the Doda valley and Padum, gateway to the Kishtwar mountains.

For the first European explorers, of course, it was very different. Early visitors included Hunter and Fanny Bullock Workman, who climbed Pinnacle Peak (6962m) in 1906, approaching it from the beautiful Snow Plateau at the head of the Parktik Glacier. Kun was climbed in 1913 by the Italian Count Piacenza. The first attempt to climb the harder summit of Nun, in 1934, focused on its East Ridge, reached more easily from the Shafat Glacier further east, outside the horseshoe; James Waller and J.B. Harrison climbed White Needle (6600m), but could make no further progress along the connecting ridge towards Nun itself.

Waller later confirmed the West Ridge as a simpler option and this was the route chosen by a strong French-Swiss-Indian team in 1953. Like the earlier Nun explorers, Arthur and Ernest Neve, the Swiss leader Pierre Vittoz was a missionary. In the words of his French co-leader Bernard Pierre, 'Having lived for three years at Leh, 100km from Nun, Vittoz converted souls while occasionally tormenting the six-thousanders.' This time it was the turn of Kashmir's virgin seven-thousander. Pierre's French contingent comprised Michel Désorbay, Jean Guillemin and Claude Kogan; India was represented by Nalni Jayal and K.C. Johorey. In keeping with the times a team of imported Sherpas gave the expedition added strength and their sirdar was the great Angtharkay who had played such a crucial role in Shipton and Tilman's pre-war expeditions.

Looking south-east from Nun, past Z1 (6181m) and other Zanskar peaks to the distant summits of Kishtwar. The Shafat Glacier curves up from extreme left. Although this picture was taken in July, conditions are more like winter. Some wonderful ski tours have been done through this area in spring but it is big, remote country, usually requiring pre-placed caches of food and fuel. (*Steven Berry*)

▲

The intended northern approach was closed in 1953, so the team marched from about 200km to the south, in the Chenab valley. It was an enchanting approach, through the hill station of Kishtwar, up the verdant Maru valley and eventually up the Krishnai river, through progressively drier country to the southern foot of Nun. From base camp they climbed up the edge of an unnamed glacier to a col on the West Ridge. On the ridge itself the team had some narrow escapes with avalanches. From Camp 3, at 6400m, Pierre Vittoz and Claude Kogan made the final push to the summit, taking turns to lead arduously up deep, rotten snow, steepening at one stage to 55°.

Claude Kogan remains one of the few women to have made the first ascent of a major peak. Her route has now, to invert Mummery's famous quip, become

The 1953 Nun expedition. At the back, in glasses, is the Swiss missionary leader, Pierre Vittoz with the well-known French climber, Bernard Pierre, next to him. In the middle row is Claude Kogan, one of the few women to have made the first ascent of a major Himalayan peak. On her left is the legendary Sherpa, Angtharkay, looking rather respectable and no longer sporting the traditional pigtail which graced the Shipton/Tilman expeditions of the 'thirties. (*Bernard Pierre Collection*)

an easy day for a gentleman, ascended by numerous teams, usually these days from the north. However, the Indian climbers who made the second ascent of Nun, chose a new route up the steeper-flanked East Ridge, reaching it from the Snow Plateau. In 1978 a Japanese team also climbed the East Ridge, but approached it by James Waller's White Needle route from the Shafat Glacier. Since 1978 this route has been repeated several times, with a consensus that it offers more interesting climbing than the West Ridge.

More typical summer conditions in a view looking more to the south-west. The valley below (just visible extreme right in the picture opposite) is the head of the Krishnai river, the route by which the 1953 expedition approached the West Ridge. (*Andy Selters*)

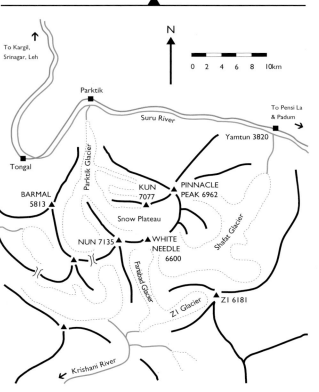

Other routes on the mountain include the North-West Ridge, climbed by a Czech team in 1976 and a variation traversing on to the West Face, climbed by Americans in 1977. These routes have the attraction of being approached from the spectacular Snow Plateau. However, the Japanese East Ridge route is perhaps more scenic, with tremendous views south over the Zanskar peaks to the distant Kishtwar range. The route climbs steadily west up the Shafat Glacier, crossing a spur by a rabbit-shaped rock at 5700m, then continuing across an upper branch of the glacier to the spur descending from White Needle. The route climbs over White Needle and onto the final East Ridge of Nun. One knife-edged section of the ridge, studded with rock pinnacles, is avoided by a detour on to the South Face, before one regains the crest for classic snow and ice climbing to the summit.

From Camp 2 on the east side of White Needle, Steven Berry looks out past his cramponed feet at the East Ridge leading to Nun's summit. Tracks show the detour beneath the difficult pinnacles. (*Steven Berry*)

SUMMARY STATISTICS AND INFORMATION

Mountain	Nun
Height	7135m
Location	Nun Kun massif, Zanskar, India.
Route	East Ridge. A moderate snow and ice route from the Shafat Glacier.
First ascent of mountain	28 August 1953 by Claude Kogan (Fra) and Pierre Vittoz (Swi), by West Ridge.
First ascent of route	East Ridge from the north: summit reached 20 July 1971 by M.S. Gill, Phenjo, K.S. Rawal & S.S. Singh (India). Route from south climbed in 1978, summit reached 25 October by Ken Takahashi & S. Saito (Japan).
Height of b/c	Good sites near the snout of the Shafat Glacier at about 4000m, but a well-stocked ABC further up the glacier is a great advantage.
Roadhead	Yamtun, if the Kargil-Padum road is open this far. (The natural road approach to Kargil is over the Zoji La from Srinagar. However, recurring political trouble has frequently kept this closed to foreigners. The alternative is to reach Kargil from Leh, first either flying to Leh or driving up the spectacular road from Manali.)
Length of walk-in	4 km from Yamtun to the glacier snout.
Season	Pierre and Vittoz chose Nun in 1953 because it was feasible during the monsoon, the only time they were free. The peak lies quite far north and climbing is possible throughout the summer. However, autumn probably offers the best chance of fine weather and open roads.
Permission	Indian Mountaineering Foundation, New Delhi.
Success rate	High. This is the probably the most frequently climbed seven-thousander in the Himalaya.
Bibliography	The first ascent of Nun is written up in Bernard Pierre's delightful *Nun – Une Victoire sur l'Himalaya* (Éditions Amiot-Dumont, 1954). Pierre Vittoz's account appears in English in *Mountain World* 1954. Anyone interested in the area should read Arthur Neve's *Thirty Years in Kashmir* (Edward Arnold, 1913). Recent ascents of the various routes on Nun and Kun are recorded in the *HJ* and *AJ*.

KISHTWAR-SHIVLING 6040m

North Face

Kishtwar Shivling is not a particularly high mountain. It is not even marked on most maps and there is some doubt about the authenticity of its name. Shivling means the lingam, or phallus of Shiva, the god of Creation and Destruction. There are several famous shrines in the Himalaya – freak pillars of ice inside caves, revered by pilgrims – called Shivling; and there are also mountains, the most famous being in Garhwal. The Kishtwar Shivling has also been called Talangana and some maps refer to a peak called Sibspahar. Whatever its correct name, it is a stunning peak and the route up its North Face is a good example of the excellent climbing to be found in Kishtwar, one of the most enchanting regions of the Himalaya.

The area was strangely neglected by mountaineers until quite recently. The first recorded expedition was Fritz Kolb's visit in 1947 and the first major ascent did not happen until 1974 when British climbers Chris Bonington and Nick Estcourt, attached to an Indian expedition, made the first ascent of Brammah I (6416m) by its South-East Ridge. Brammah, like the highest Kishtwar peak, Sickle Moon (6574m – first ascent 1975 by Indian High-Altitude Warfare School), lies in the western part of the range, approached from the Maru valley north of Kishtwar town. Most recent expeditions have concentrated on the eastern area, following the Chenab river to Atholi, then heading north-east up the Bhut nullah to the village of Machail.

It is beautiful country, reminiscent of the Swiss or Austrian Alps, until one remembers the sheer size of the deodar cedars, the volume of glacier meltwater in the huge river gorges and the complexity and altitude of the mountains themselves. There are few easy peaks in Kishtwar and many are defended by chaotic glaciers. So although the ambience is idyllic, the actual climbing can be very serious. Despite several attempts in the 'seventies, the highest summits of Barnaj remain unclimbed. On the same

There are no dull mountains in Kishtwar! This picture was taken from a summit called Consolation Peak above the East Donali Glacier, looking south-south-east to the distant summits of Arjuna (left) and Brammah II (right), and the closer summit of Dreikant (extreme right). (*Rob Collister*)

watershed between Kishtwar and Zanskar, Hagshu Peak resisted several attempts before it was climbed from the north in 1988. Cerro Kishtwar, so named because of its monolithic, Patagonian character, gave Mick Fowler and Stephen Sustad one of the hardest technical climbs they (or anyone else) had ever done in the

would be graded TD or ED if they were in the Alps; here they are the easiest routes up the peaks.

Until recent political tensions in Kashmir closed off the western approach, foreign expeditions usually reached Atholi from Jammu, via Kishtwar. The longer alternative is to approach from the east, via Manali and

south-east towards Lahul; the other is the shorter Bujwas river, fed by four main glaciers, one of which is the improbable trade route over the Umasi La (5330m) to Zanskar. Every pilgrim, merchant and mountaineer who travels this route passes beneath the North Face of Kishtwar-Shivling which rises up in a single sweep of 2500m from the Bujwas river.

When Dick Renshaw and Stephen Venables made the first ascent of Kishtwar-Shivling in 1983 they did not necessarily take the easiest line. The South Face would have given a much shorter, albeit steep, rock climb, approached by a long slog up scree slopes from the Darlang nullah. That would have been the most efficient option, but the point was to reach a virgin summit *and* to climb a beautiful technical mixed route up a stunningly architectural face; so they chose the North Face. If one wanted an alpine comparison, the North Face of the Droites is vaguely similar, but this Kishtwar face rises above steep dramatic icefalls and culminates in the kind of vertiginous snow flutings one never finds in Europe. The summit is also finer, for the peak stands proud and detached from its surroundings.

The 1983 base camp was in a flowery meadow, fringed by stands of *Betula utilis*, the Himalayan birch, whose bark peels in great papery wads of gleaming white. The nearest village is Sumcham, home to a handful of Buddhist families, ethnically identical to the people of Zanskar over the watershed. In the summer the valley is also inhabited by the Gujahs, wealthy Muslims who come up each summer from Jammu with their flocks of sheep and goats. Both they and the locals treat the other migrants, the white-skinned mountaineers, with refreshing detachment, friendly but undemanding.

Above this idyllic valley looms the face. To get on to it, Renshaw and Venables followed a spur which bypasses the steep sérac-threatened glacier. Advance

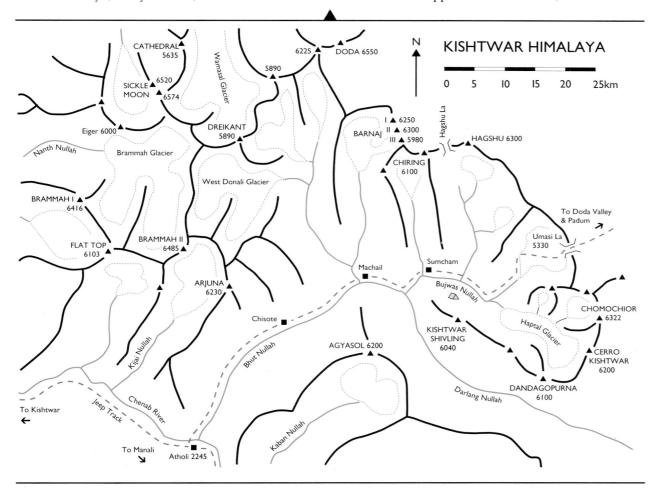

Himalaya, when they made the first ascent in 1993. Further west, approached by the precipitous Kijai nullah, Arjuna, another spectacular six-thousander, defeated several attempts before B. Slarno's Polish team climbed it in 1983 by its West Face. All these climbs

Dick Renshaw leading the first ice cliff on Kishtwar Shivling. The main face looms above, very foreshortened, with the Runnel, just right of Renshaw, leading almost directly to the summit. Renshaw and Venables eventually climbed the dark rocks immediately left of the Runnel, before traversing back right to the summit. (*Stephen Venables*)

the Rohtang Pass, a route which should be motorable all the way by 1996. Coming this way, just before Atholi one passes a side valley leading up to the three-summited Agyasol, first climbed by Simon Richardson's British expedition in 1981. From Atholi the Bhut nullah leads up round Agyasol to the village of Machail, where tempting valleys branch off in three directions. The eastern valley splits after a few kilometres. One branch is the long Darlang river heading

base was at c.4500m on the crest of the spur, approached by a scramble up gullies and scree slopes. The real climbing started soon after Advance Base, with snow arêtes and rock steps leading to the vertical First Ice Cliff. Above that a snow arête led in seven pitches to a rock rib which abuts against the prominent hanging glacier of the upper face. Here they bivouacked before tackling two more vertical ice pitches to get on to the snowy shelf of the hanging glacier, the start of the face proper.

The terrain now became increasingly interesting. From the bergschrund, three pitches up the 65° icefield led to a bivouac from the ice just beneath the rock headwall which bounds the left side of the face. In the morning Renshaw and Venables traversed right on snow and ice for four pitches to reach the central ice runnel descending from the summit. This was the

logical route but after one pitch, deterred by increasingly thin ice, limited protection and doubts (probably unnecessary) about the stability of the huge summit cornice overhanging the runnel, the pair decided to move left on to the comforting granite of the headwall. It was a move worth making, for the climbing was brilliant.

That afternoon four mixed pitches took the climbers diagonally into the centre of the headwall, where they settled for a character-building half-buttock bivouac ledge. After an uncomfortable night, day 4 brought huge rewards, eight pitches of superlative rock and mixed climbing to the snow mushrooms of the East Shoulder. The line trended steadily back right, following a series of cracks and corners. Perhaps the highlight was the Renshaw Dièdre on pitch 3, an immaculate left-facing corner formed by a 30m high

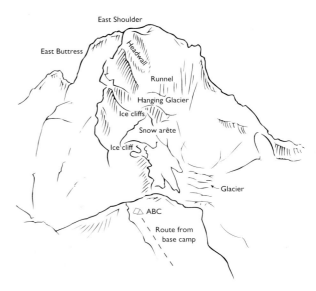

pillar leaning against the wall, but every pitch offered sustained entertainment in a tremendous position, poised above an immense drop.

The final day to the summit involved some hard work on snow and ice. The ridge from the East

A perfect Himalayan day looking north-east from the summit of Agyasol, across the Darlang nullah to the South Face of Kishtwar-Shivling and the main chain of peaks on the Kishtwar/Zanskar watershed. (*Simon Richardson*)

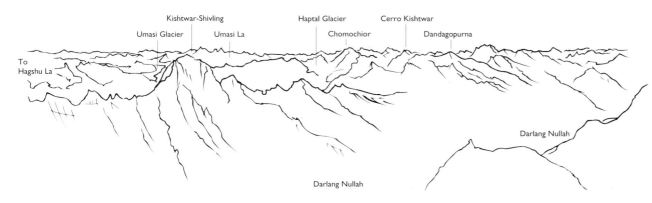

Shoulder looked rotten, so Renshaw and Venables traversed back on to the North Face, crab-crawling diagonally across a succession of fragile flutings until three 70° ice pitches took them straight up to the broad snowy summit. They regained the East Shoulder bivouac at midnight and it took another two days of down climbing and abseiling to reverse the rest of the route back down to base camp.

Kishtwar-Shivling has not had a second ascent. Few Kishtwar peaks have, for there is still so much

Kishtwar-Shivling with a fresh coat of autumn snow, photographed from the Hagshu nullah, looking across the hidden Bujwas nullah. The rock spur, snow arête and ice cliffs leading on to the North Face are highlighted in the sunlight. The East Face on the left promises some very hard rock climbing. (*Stephen Venables*)

new ground to cover. However, now that most of the main summits have been reached, people may well be attracted to previously climbed peaks. The hardest climbs by far in the Bujwas cirque have been on Cerro Kishtwar. In 1991 Brendan Murphy and Andy Perkins almost reached the summit after seventeen days tenuous climbing up a line of thin cracks and flakes on

(*Above*) Brilliant but cold rock climbing early in the morning on the headwall, with the previous night's bivouac ledge 25m below. (*Stephen Venables*)
(*Left*) Two pitches higher, Renshaw leads his Dièdre, one of the finest pitches on the climb. (*Stephen Venables*)

the monolithic East Face; the 1993 Fowler/Sustad route takes a snow and ice ramp up the left side of the face, until a ferocious chimney leads out on to a brèche from where the pair climbed out on to the precarious mixed terrain of the North Face. The neighbouring peak of Chomochior, was climbed in 1988 by Roger Everett and Simon Richardson, whose route up the South-West Ridge was a gentler, more traditionally alpine, affair. The North Face of Kishtwar-Shivling is harder, but nowhere near as extreme as Cerro Kishtwar. It is certainly a route worth repeating, perhaps with a bolder more logical finish up the runnel (although this would miss out the beautiful rock of the

(*Right*) Gujah shepherds visiting base camp. (*Stephen Venables*)

(*Far right*) Temple near Atholi. In this region Hindus, Muslims and Buddhists live side by side, with older religions also evident in the beautifully carved deodar cedar. (*Stephen Venables*)

headwall). The West Buttress to the right would be excellent but the approach looks dangerous. The East Face sports a tremendous rock buttress which will give someone, some day, some wonderful climbing.

There is no shortage of good climbs to do in Kishtwar. The only concern is that future expeditions continue to climb in the spirit of Fritz Kolb's 1947 reconnaissance, working in small teams, making minimal impact. All the climbs in this chapter were achieved alpine-style, without resorting to fixed ropes or a single bolt. Long may this tradition continue.

Mountain	Kishtwar-Shivling
Height	6040m
Location	Kishtwar Himalaya, Kashmir, India.
Route	North Face. 1500m from advance b/c, on varied terrain, including vertical ice, steep mixed ground (up to 70°) and rock climbing to VI.
First ascent of mountain	Summit reached 12 September 1983 by Dick Renshaw and Stephen Venables (UK).
First ascent of route	As above.
Height of b/c	3500m, on a grassy meadow in the Bujwas valley near the snout of the glacier descending from the peak.
Roadhead	Atholi, on the Chenab river. The road comes from the west and may be closed at times of political tension in Kashmir, in which case there are two options: 1. Approach by foot from Ating on the north side of the watershed, crossing the Umasi La. (In summer there is usually a road open from Kargil to Ating). 2. Approach Atholi from the east, via Manali and the Rohtang Pass. Recently this involved walking the last section from Purthi, but by 1996 the road should be open all the way to Atholi, linking up with the Kishtwar road.
Length of walk-in	Three days from Atholi.
Season	Lying south of the watershed, this area gets heavy winter snowfalls and is much more affected by the monsoon than Zanskar. Best conditions seem usually to occur in September and early October.
Permission	Indian Mountaineering Foundation, New Delhi.
Success rate	There was one brief attempt on the mountain before the 1983 ascent and there have been none since. Of the other Kishtwar peaks, Brammah I has been climbed at least three times, so has Sickle Moon, but the majority have had just one ascent.
Bibliography	This climb is recorded in detail in Stephen Venables' *Painted Mountains* (Hodder & Stoughton, 1986), which also has a useful historical survey up to 1985. Also useful is Simon Richardson's article 'A Peak-bagger's Guide to the Eastern Kishtwar' in *AJ* 1989/90. The first ascent of Cerro Kishtwar is described in Mick Fowler's autobiography, *Vertical Pleasure* (Hodder & Stoughton, 1995).

A foreshortened view of Kishtwar-Shivling from amongst the Himalayan birches at base camp. (*Stephen Venables*)

DHARAMSURA 6446m / PAPSURA 6451m

South-West Ridges

Dharamsura, previously known as White Sail, is an elegant ice steeple first climbed in 1941 by a British expedition led by Jimmy Roberts. Three kilometres to the west and marginally higher is the broader bulk of Papsura, first climbed in 1967. Kulu provides wonderful opportunities for small expeditions to climb several peaks up to 6600m, all accessible from rough but motorable roads.

The main centre, Manali, has been a popular resort for over century and is a delightful place to start an expedition. A few kilometres to the north, the Rohtang Pass now carries a road over to the Chandra valley. North of that rise the mountains of Lahul, of which the most famous is Mulkila. Further east, over the Kunzum La, lies the harsh desert landscape of Spiti. Closer to Manali, immediately to the east are the Kulu mountains, which are perhaps the most interesting to the technical climber. Many of the finest peaks are clustered round two glacier systems – the Malana and the Tos, which flow south into the Parvati valley. Indrasan (6221m) and Deo Tibba are the best known peaks in the Malana cirque; Ali Ratni Tibba, several hundred metres lower, is an impressive spire. The Tos Glacier basin is ringed by a fantastic wall of peaks, of which perhaps the finest are Dharamsura (Peak of Good) and Papsura (Peak of Evil).

Dharamsura was climbed for the second time in 1961 by another British expedition, led by Bob Pettigrew. Like Roberts, Pettigrew's team approached by the East Tos Glacier, placing their base camp at the most obvious site at about 4350m below an impressive icefall. From there they reached a col on the

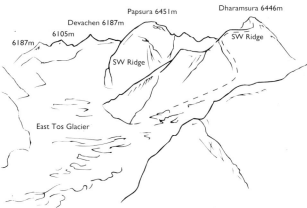

The east wall of the East Tos Glacier is a great line of peaks linked by slender snow ridges. In this shot the South-West Ridges of Dharamsura and Papsura are the dominant features in the landscape. (*Nick Groves*)
(*Far right*) An unnamed peak on the west wall of the Tos Glacier, above the Sara Umga Pass. (*Bob Pettigrew*)

Tos/Bara Shigri divide and continued up Dharamsura by its South-East Ridge. On a later Pettigrew expedition to the area, in 1967, Geoff Hill and Colin Pritchard made the first ascent of Papsura by a snow couloir on the South Face, leading to the col on the South-East Ridge. In 1977 another British party led by Paul Bean made alpine-style ascents of the South-West Ridges of both Papsura and Dharamsura, both new routes. Visually these are the most elegant and impressive lines in the massif and they provide the most direct and attractive climbs on each peak.

Dharamsura's prominent shoulder at c.6000m is reached by an obvious 800m couloir/ramp (c.50°) on the east side of the ridge. Thereafter the beautiful crest is followed, on snow throughout, to the top; in places the route is narrow and delicate. From the summit the reciprocal ridge of Papsura will be in profile on the left. This route negotiates the 300m high rock buttress at the toe of the ridge by linking snowfields on the edge of South Face. From a shoulder at its top, icy chimneys are taken on the west side before the ridge is again met and followed on delicate slabs for several more pitches (up to VI) to mixed ground, eventually giving way to snow, about 500m above the shoulder. Thereafter the angle eases to the summit.

The best descent for Dharamsura is probably back by the South-West Ridge, whereas coming off the

▲

SUMMARY STATISTICS AND INFORMATION

Mountains	Dharamsura (White Sail); Papsura
Heights	6446m; 6451m
Location	Kulu, Himachal Pradesh, India.
Routes	South-West Ridges.
First ascent of mountains	Dharamsura: 1941, by a party led by Jimmy Roberts (UK) on the South-East Ridge; Papsura:1967 by Colin Pritchard and Geoff Hill by the South Couloir and East Ridge.
First ascent of routes	Dharamsura: 27-28 May 1977 by Rowland Perriment and George Crawford-Smith (UK); Papsura: 31 May-2 June 1977 by Perriment and Barry Needle (UK).
Height of b/c	4350m on the East Tos Glacier, below the first major icefall and a few hours above the snout of the Tos Glacier, at 3840m.
Roadhead	Kasol, by bus or jeep from Bhuntar in the Beas valley south of Manali.
Length of walk-in	40km; about 7 days from Kasol.
Season	May/June or September/October.
Permission	Indian Mountaineering Foundation, New Delhi.
Success rate	Quite high.
Bibliography	These two first ascents are reported briefly in *AAJ* 1978 and there is an illustrated article in *AJ* 1978.

more serious Papsura it is advisable either to follow the North-West Ridge to the col beneath Devachen or down the steeper East Ridge to the steep and possibly icy couloir that descends directly to the glacier — the line of the first ascent.

Some of the peaks in this area lend themselves, individually or in small groups, to traverses, usually utilising the long ridge dividing the East Tos from the Bara Shigri Glacier. In 1978 Mike Searle and Nick Groves traversed the peaks of Deception, Angdu Ri and Dharamsura, ascending the latter by its first ascent route. An intégrale traverse of Papsura and Dharamsura, starting up the South-West Ridge of Papsura and descending the South-West Ridge of Dharamsura would be a fine project.

SHIVLING 6543m

East Ridge

Of all the hundreds of magical peaks in the Garhwal Himalaya, the most dramatic must be Shivling at the western gateway of the Gangotri Glacier. The glacier snout is called Gaumukh, the Cow's Mouth, source of the Ganges' most holy tributary, the Bhagirathi river. Thousands of Hindu pilgrims trek here every year and many of the dedicated ones continue higher to the meadows of Tapovan to gaze up at the granite obelisk soaring above. To them Shivling is a symbol of the creative power of Shiva; to mountaineers it is the quintessential climber's mountain. When Colin Kirkus and Charles Warren came here in 1933 to make the first ascent of Bhagirathi III, they called Shivling 'Matterhorn Peak' and from Tapovan it certainly does present a monolithic pyramid. However, continue up the Gangotri Glacier and you see that it has two summits, each remarkably similar. Walk round the other side, on to the Meru Glacier, and you find the same mirror imaging. That symmetry heightens the peak's appeal.

The Gangotri Glacier is 30km long. Together with its tributaries it covers a vast area, ringed by six-thousanders, including many famous names, such as Chaukamba, Kedarnath, Satopanth and Sri Kailas. Together with all the glaciers and peaks on the outside of the circle, these peaks represent several lifetimes' worth of climbing possibilities, but for the purposes

of this book we are going to concentrate on three which particularly distinguish Gangotri from other areas of the Garhwal – the granite spires of Bhagirathi III, Thalay Sagar and Shivling.

Shivling, the greatest prize of all, was climbed in 1974 by an India-Tibet Border Police expedition led by the prolific peak-bagger Hukam Singh. His team worked on the only obvious weakness in the mountain's defences, the mixed spur of the West Ridge, which forms a gangway on to the col between the two summits, followed by a steep snow ice ridge to the Main Summit. The gangway is blocked just beneath the col by a sérac barrier which some years can be extremely unstable. In 1994 a large chunk broke off, demolishing an Indian camp on the ridge below and very nearly killing one of the climbers. So this original route is not at all straightforward and it may be that the corresponding route to the col on the East Face, a superb rock climb pioneered by Masaki Nakao, Kenji Ohama and Masami Yamagata in 1983, will prove to be a safer, if technically much harder, voie normale.

It was also in September 1983 that that irrepressible snatcher of unclimbed summits, Chris Bonington, made the first ascent of Shivling's South-West Summit with Jim Fotheringham. The pair climbed from the Kirti Bamak, skirting the lower rotten section of the South-East Ridge by climbing fast up a dangerous

gully, then emerged on the beautiful curving granite arête of the upper ridge, which gave a succession of brilliant pitches to the summit. The mirror image of this route – the South-West Ridge of the South-West summit – was climbed by Australians Brigitte Muir, Jon Muir and Graeme Hill in 1986. They too made their descent down to the col between the two

(Above) Sadhus, holy men, washing at Gaumaukh, the Cow's Mouth where the Bhagirathi river flows from the Gangotri Glacier.
(Far left) Shivling, one of the most beautiful summits in the whole of India. Fresh snow in early May frosts the serrated outline of the East Ridge on the left. *(Both John Cleare/Mountain Camera)*

summits and thence down the original West Ridge.

The West Summit is as dramatically pointed as any fairytale peak, but the first choice will probably always be the Main Summit, which so dominates the entrance to Gangotri. The original West Ridge has

Shivling's unique symmetry from the Kirti Bamak to the east. The East Ridge of the main summit is on the right. Highlighted on the left is the elegant curve of the South-East Ridge of the South-West Summit, climbed by Chris Bonington and Jim Fotheringham in 1983. Behind that on the left skyline is the South-West Ridge climbed by Australians Brigitte and Jon Muir and Graeme Hill in 1986. Running almost directly to the col between the two summits is the Japanese route of 1983, the South-East Face, climbed by Masaki Nakao, Kenji Ohama and Masami Yamagata in 1983. When a British party repeated the route in 1986 they reported that it was excellent, with a particularly dramatic final pitch, traversing left (on big holds) to the col. *(John Cleare/Mountain Camera)*

proved, despite the offending séracs, to be a perennially popular route. However, more direct, more aesthetic and more technical are the four routes visible from Tapovan.

The first big technical route to be climbed was the East Ridge, pioneered in 1981 by the Anglo/Australian/French team of Doug Scott, Greg Child, Rick White and Georges Bettembourg. It was a particularly remarkable achievement for Child and White, who had virtually no experience of snowy mountains. Of course the East Ridge does have sections of very hard rock climbing, but there are some thoroughly super-alpine sections of dizzy knife-edge ridge, rather more menacing than Yosemite. The route was climbed in a single thirteen-day push and was then possibly the hardest technical Himalayan climb to have been climbed alpine-style.

The North-East Face was attempted with tragic results in 1983, by British climbers, Nick Kekus and Richard Cox. Its main feature is the central 65° icefield. Reaching this involved climbing some hard mixed ground and two rockbands with difficulties VI/A1. On the fifth day the pair climbed the icefield and started to climb the rock headwall, but at the top of the first pitch Cox fell 20m when an anchor failed. He broke his ankle and, after a day's delay in stormy weather, Kekus had to start lowering him back down the face. During the lower Cox, now badly weakened, became detached from the rope and fell to his death. Kekus managed to descend alone. The face was climbed successfully three years later by Italian climbers, Paolo Bernascone, Fabrizio Manoni and Enrico Rosso. However, from the top of the icefield

they had to traverse diagonally left on to the final wall of the East Ridge, which is not quite so steep as the ferocious headwall of the North-East Face proper.

A 1700m line was climbed up the North Face by Czechs Bronislaw Adamec, Pawel Rajf and Jiri Svejda in 1987. A lower icefield and mixed slopes lead to the central funnel with rock pitches of IV+ and 70° ice. The funnel opens on to the upper icefield which merges at its top into 75-80° water ice grooves heading up to the headwall. Here, unlike the North-East Face, the headwall is split conveniently by a deep chimney. Although the rock is briefly rotten, it soon improves to give excellent mixed climbing and rock to V+, until one emerges on to the summit icefield. Because this route does not evade the headwall it seems more satisfying than the North-East Face, but the Czechs did report considerable avalanche danger in their funnelled line.

There is one final major route on the north side of the mountain, the North Ridge, which divides the North-East and North Faces. Whereas the East Ridge takes its time, with long horizontal diversions and decorative pinnacles to entertain the climber, the North Ridge is uncompromisingly direct; there is no let up in the angle here, no delay in the relentless, compulsive rush for the summit. In its direct form it is perhaps the best line on the mountain. The indirect version, climbed by a Japanese team in 1987, followed the more pinnacled right-hand spur on the lower section. At the top it evaded the final prow by a long diagonal traverse right into the final chimney of the North-West Face route. In 1993 the line was significantly straightened by the young Tyrolean guide Christoph Hainz and his elder neighbour and colleague, Hans Kammerlander, a mountaineer best known for his remarkable fast ascents of several eight-

Ten days into the climb, Georges Bettembourg, belayed by Rick White, leads the final knife-edge section to the huge headwall on the East Ridge. Over on the right is the overhanging prow at the top of the North Ridge Direct. (*Greg Child*)

thousanders with Reinhold Messner.

The direct line up the North Ridge would appear to be a fantastic climb. Most remarkable is the fact that Kammerlander and Hainz, after initial acclimatisation forays to 5700m, climbed the final 850m to the summit in just twelve hours, returning to base camp in another twelve hours, abseiling through the night to escape a storm. Unfortunately, it has been impossible to elicit any details but, if the altitudes are correctly quoted, this must have been an astounding day's work, for the pair say that, whereas the Japanese had at the top followed a ledge system way out on to the North Face, they only deviated very slightly to the right on the final prow of vertical and overhanging granite: 850m of hard mixed climbing, capped by overhanging granite at 6400m, climbed in a snowstorm, in just eleven and a half hours, on sight adds up

(*Below*) Shivling's two summits from the Shark's Fin on Meru, showing the rocky West Ridge slanting up to the sérac barrier which guards the col between the two summits. The barrier can be very problematical and, some years, dangerous. The Australian route to the South-West Summit is in the foreground. Behind Shivling, Bhagirathi II, III and I stand guard on the far side of the Gangotri Glacier. (*Paul Pritchard*)

1. East Ridge – France, Australia, UK 1981
2. North-East Face – Italian 1986
3. North Ridge Direct – Tyrolean 1993
4. North Ridge – Japanese 1987
5. North Face – Czech 1987

Shivling's 'Matterhorn' aspect rising elegantly above Tapovan on a crisp October morning. Attempting the West Ridge that month, Larry Stanier recorded dawn temperatures of -35°C. (*Larry Stanier*)

to an incredible performance, even if old Japanese ropes were used on the common sections of the route.

The North Ridge Direct is a fantastic line, which ambitious alpinists will want to investigate. However, for the purposes of this book and in the absence of hard information, we shall settle for the East Ridge. With difficulties up to A3, the 1981 team employed big-wall tactics, but the gendarmed nature of the ridge meant that this was a cumbersome exercise and only a few pitches each day were possible. However, the first ascent team believe that the route could be climbed much more quickly, particularly with better weather. Retreating from high on the route in bad weather could be very difficult, but the ridge is free of avalanche danger. The climbing remains satisfyingly on the crest of the ridge, culminating in the

(*Left*) Andy Parkin just above the col, on the final ridge of the Main Summit completing an ascent of the West Ridge. The South-West Summit rises behind the col. (*Sean Smith*)

(*Below*) Georges Bettembourg near the top of the East Ridge, jumaring the first pitch on the headwall, suspended by a thread over the North-East Face. (*Doug Scott*)

Mountain	Shivling
Location	Gangotri group, Garhwal, India.
Height	6543m
Route	East Ridge. 1200m of vertical ascent, but 60 rope-lengths, mainly on rock up to VI/A3, but with some mixed climbing, especially on the long central horizontal section.
First ascent of mountain	Summit reached 3 June 1974 by Hukam Singh, Ang Tharkey, Pemba Tharkey, Laxman Singh and Pasang Sherpa of the India-Tibet Border Police, by the West Ridge.
First ascent of route	3-15 June 1986, by Georges Bettembourg (France), Doug Scott (UK), Greg Child & Rick White (Australia).
Height of b/c	4300m, on grass at Tapovan at the junction of the Meru and Gangotri Glaciers.
Roadhead	Gangotri, just one day from New Delhi.
Length of walk-in	3 days, on easy terrain, via Gaumukh.
Season	In a good autumn, the weather will be very stable in September/October. However, temperatures can be very low at this time of year, and the spring may offer better all round conditions.
Permission	Indian Mountaineering Foundation, New Delhi
Success rate	The East Ridge is unrepeated, but the North-East Face has had at least two ascents. On the West Ridge normal route at least 50% of expeditions are successful. The South-East Ridge of the col has had two successful ascents.
Bibliography	The East Ridge is well documented in Doug Scott's *Himalayan Climber* (Hodder & Stoughton/Sierra Club, 1992) and Greg Child's *Thin Air* (Mountaineers/Oxford Illustrated Press, 1988). The Georges Bettembourg version appears in *Mountain* 84. Other routes are recorded in the *AAJ*, *HJ* and Jan Babicz's *Peaks and Passes of the Garhwal Himalaya* (Alpinistyczny Klub Eksploracyjny, u.l. Armii Krajowej 12, 81-849 Sopot, Hungary).

spectacular headwall, which took the 1983 team two full days to climb.

Descents are traditionally made down the West Ridge. However, without prior reconnaissance of the sérac barrier, this could be very difficult, particularly if the barrier's condition continues to worsen. As mentioned above, the South-East Ridge on the other side of the col, an excellent rock climb in its own right, could be the best alternative, providing a safe abseil descent.

Hans Kammerlander grits his teeth during stormy weather on the North Ridge Direct in 1993. Parts of this route have become sadly draped with rope. (*Christoph Hainz*)

BHAGIRATHI III 6454m

South-West Buttress

Bhagirathi III, is the central and lowest of the three Bhagirathi peaks viewed from the Gangotri Glacier. It is also the most spectacular. On the west side, a huge scooped amphitheatre plunges down from the summit snowfields, continuously overhanging in its upper reaches. It is flanked by bold pillars of granite, each of which can claim to be one of the greatest rock climbs in the world.

Colin Kirkus and Charles Warren were the first to reach the summit of Bhagirathi III on 18 June 1933. Their climb on the South Ridge was one of the hardest then achieved in the Himalaya, though it did not receive the acclaim it deserved, owing in part to confusion as to which peak they actually climbed. In Marco Pallis' book, *Peaks and Lamas*, Kirkus wrote of their ascent of Satopanth Central but a subsequent Austrian reconnaissance to the Gangotri Glacier determined that what he described was in fact the central Bhagirathi peak – i.e. Bhagirathi III. Their climb included rock pitches of grade IV and was made over four days in pure alpine-style.

Charles Warren described that 1933 expedition as the 'logical extension of an alpine holiday'. That approach was revived enthusiastically in the late 'seventies and 'eighties, when an increasing number of climbers aspired to alpine-style first ascents on difficult peaks of medium altitude. The newly re-opened Gangotri basin was a tempting area and the granite pillars of Bhagirathi III in particular were obvious targets. Georges Bettembourg described them evocatively as 'an El Cap with a Droites North Face on top at 6000m'.

The right-hand pillar, some 1500m high, fell to Scots Bob Barton and Allen Fyffe in 1982, this being the third serious attempt on the route. Their climb, for the most part on rock at around grade IV/VI and A2, immediately gained vogue and was attempted again in 1983 by an American party without success. It received its second ascent in September 1988 by the New Zealand team of Phil Castle and Carol McDermott who eliminated some of the aid. The route was repeated again in 1989 by a Korean team and by two Canadians in 1992.

On the first ascent Barton and Fyffe climbed in a capsule style, fixing six rope-lengths each day before abseiling back to their previous night's bivouac site. Next morning, weather permitting, they would jumar with all their equipment back up the ropes, lifting them as they went. Then they would tackle the next six rope-lengths. 'Something between big-walling and alpine-style,' commented Barton. 'It suited our purposes nicely.' Which it did, for they made steady progress, eventually reaching the top of the granite after eight days.

Suddenly the whole nature of the route changed as the Scots tackled one of Gangotri's bands of metamorphic slates. Barton described the next day of mixed climbing as 'a horror show of insecurity'. On the tenth day, still a fair way from the summit, they stashed all of their fixing rope and rock climbing rack into a haul bag and threw it down the face! It took another two days to climb the final icefield and ridge to the summit and two further days to descend the North Ridge and Chaturangi Glacier back to base camp. It only remained to collect their haul bag from the bottom of the amphitheatre!

In May 1984 the pillar on the left side of the amphitheatre, more commonly referred to as the West Face, was climbed by a Spanish (Catalan) team of Juan Aldeguer, Sergei Martinez, Jose Moreno and Juan Tomas. Again climbing in a capsule style, the two pairs of climbers spent eight days on the pillar, bivouacking in hammocks. They described their route, Impossible Star, as 'basically a free climb – beautiful, athletic and vertical, on excellent granite'. Most of the twenty-nine pitches on the rock were given grade V-/VI+, with sections of A1 and one passage of A3. On reaching the shale band, which they described as 'dangerous', they too discarded their haul bag and climbed lightweight to the summit and down the South-East Ridge a short way before abseiling directly in eight rope-lengths down the North-East Face to

difficult snowslopes that led to the Chaturangi Glacier.

The Catalan route quickly gained acclaim and was repeated four months later by Canadians Dave Lane and Scott Flavelle, who removed much of the Catalans' detritus. A third ascent was made in June 1985 by French climbers Pierre Faivre, Jeff Lemoine and Guy Mevellac Bouvet, who compared the route to Yosemite's Salathé Wall. Both parties confirmed the difficulties to be extreme – each taking nine days to complete the thirty pitches of climbing.

The amphitheatre – the evil-looking scooped wall between the two pillars – was climbed in autumn 1990 by Slovenians Silvo Karo and Janez Jeglic. This

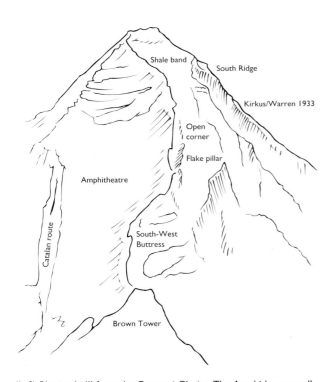

(*Left*) Bhagirathi III from the Gangotri Glacier. The Amphitheatre wall broods in shadow, flanked by the West Face route on the left and the South-West Buttress curving round on the right. The first ascent of the mountain by Colin Kirkus and Charles Warren in 1933, was made by the South Ridge on the right skyline. At the time it was one of the hardest routes to have been climbed in the Himalaya. (*John Cleare*)
(*Above right*) The Canadian climber Mark Gunlogson enjoying himself on the perfect granite of the South-West Buttress, approaching the Flake Pillar, which is above him to the right, on the skyline. (*Micha Miller*)

route, 1600m in length takes the challenge of the upper leaning wall head on and is graded at VIII and A4!

The Slovenian line is by all accounts desperate and inelegant, and on poor rock in the upper section, whereas the companion pillar routes are both excellent. The Catalan climb is harder and steeper, so sack-hauling is easier but there are no natural bivouac sites. The Scottish pillar is a little easier and has the advantage of better bivouac sites; with a more southerly aspect, it also clears more quickly after bad weather.

Our topo follows the line of the Barton/Fyffe route on the South-West Buttress. The climb proper starts at the Brown Tower, at the toe of the well defined ridge on the right-hand edge of the amphitheatre. The approach to the Brown Tower is by scree and complicated scrambling, with one pitch of IV exposed to stonefall. A fit, acclimatised party should be able to reach the Brown Tower in a day from Tapovan. From the Tower the climb moves up and right, at first on perfect granite (V), including a pendulum move to reach the ridge crest which is followed to a snowy bay beneath leftward leaning grooves. These are climbed (awkward A2) to a sentry box before the route again moves right to a crack system to the left of the Flake Pillar – the most obvi-

ous feature of the face. On the first ascent a bivouac site on the right was gained by a long swing on the rope – Pendulum Ledge. The only pitch of poor granite they encountered was above this ledge. This was followed by a hard pitch (V/A2). Above the Flake Pillar a spectacular rising traverse (V/A2) leads left into a huge open groove which, once reached, yields

(*Right*) Micha Miller leading another immaculate pitch, on aid, just above Pendulum Ledge and virtually level now with the Flake Pillar. (*Mark Gunlogson*)

(*Above*) Bhagirathi II (left) and III, seen during a ski descent of the North-West Flank of Kedarnath Dome (6831m). The route has many ascents and is becoming an increasingly popular ski ascent in spring. The first ascent of this route and of the Main Summit of Kedarnath was made in 1947 by a Swiss team including the distinguished and idiosyncratic Genevan climber, André Roch. The East Face of Kedarnath Dome, involving sixty pitches of very hard rock climbing, was climbed in 1989 by a Hungarian team led by Attila Ozsvath. (*John Cleare*)

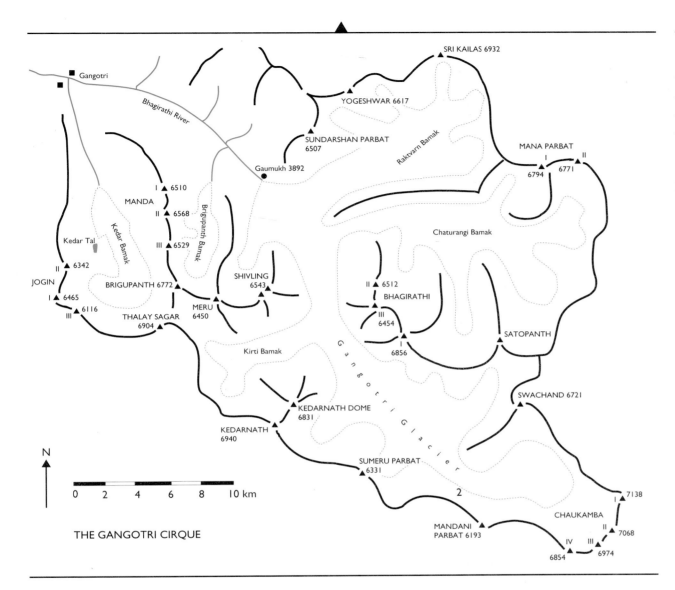

THE GANGOTRI CIRQUE

SUMMARY STATISTICS AND INFORMATION

Mountain	Bhagirathi III
Height	6454m
Location	Gangotri Group, Garhwal, India.
Route	South-West Buttress. 1400m of ascent, on steep granite up to VI and A1 (800m) and mixed ground (600m).
First ascent of mountain	Colin Kirkus & Dr Charles Warren (UK), 18 June 1933 by South Ridge. First ascent of route 28 September - 10 October 1982 by Bob Barton & Allen Fyffe (UK).
Height of b/c	4300m, on grass at Nandanvan at junction of Chaturangi and Gangotri Glaciers, or further down valley at Tapovan.
Roadhead	Lanka
Length of walk-in	3 days, on easy terrain, via Gangotri and Gaumaukh.
Season	Best conditions are in May or September. By October conditions become very cold for rock climbing.
Permission	Indian Mountaineering Foundation, New Delhi.
Success rate	Most parties who have seriously attempted this climb have reached the summit. It appears to be reasonably safe from stonefall.
Bibliography	Allen Fyffe's article,' Bhagirathi South-West Pillar', appears in *Mountain* 91. Bob Barton's account appears in the *AJ* 1983, pp 49-54. Subsequent ascents are described briefly in the *AAJ*. See also Jan Babicz's *Peaks and Passes of the Garhwal Himalaya*. (Alpinistyczny Klub Eksploracyjny, u.l. Armii Krajowej 12, 81-849 Sopot, Hungary).

to easier climbing of about grade V. Above, the route continues straight up, keeping just to the right of the crest, for about eight more pitches (IV/V). By keeping to the left, climbers can avoid the greater stonefall threats of the afternoon. Better bivouac sites are offered hereabouts, though you could never call them comfortable.

From the top of the granite, the route slants left up shale and icefields to the apex of the amphitheatre wall, then back right up the snow arête to the summit. On the fourth ascent in 1992, Mark Gunlogson and Micha Miller climbed all the way from the granite to the summit and back in a day, then abseiled back down the pillar. The alternative is to traverse the mountain. The difficult North Ridge, as descended by Barton and Fyffe, is not recommended. Better to take the Catalan option of the South-East Ridge and North-East Face. Most parties will be tempted first to jettison their heavy rock gear, like the first ascencionists, but beware: when Castle and McDermott did this in 1988 their haul bag was buried by a subsequent snow storm and was never found!

THALAY SAGAR 6904m

North-East Buttress

This is the last of our trilogy of hard, modern classics in the Gangotri group. Thalay Sagar, probably the hardest peak in the range and the fifth highest, is formidable from all sides; not until 1979 did anyone seriously think about climbing it. It was an Anglo/American team that reached the summit in June that year, by the line of least resistance, the North-West Couloir and Ridge. This first ascent route was certainly not easy, but it was inevitable that soon attention would shift to the more beautiful line of the North-East Buttress.

Mo Anthoine led three successive British attempts on the buttress between 1980-2. The third attempt was thwarted just 100m short of the summit when Joe Brown and Malcolm Howells dropped a rucksack full of bivouac gear. Brown, the great survivor, chose to retreat rather than press on up the final band of shale and risk hypothermia, and it was left to a Norwegian/Polish expedition to complete the route in 1984. This strong five-man team, including the late Andrzej Czok and Hans Christian Doseth, succeeded in a lightweight style, fixing some ropes for descent but climbing the buttress in a continuous seven-day push. As expected, the brilliant quality of the climbing immediately made it a route that future parties wished to repeat and both the third and fourth ascents of the peak were made by this route.

Soaring 1000m up the left profile of Thalay Sagar's North Face, it is perhaps the nearest thing to a Walker Spur in the Himalaya.

The North Face itself was eventually scaled, after several attempts, by the bold Hungarian duo of Attila Oszvath and Peter Dekany in 1991. Their route was extremely hard and the metamorphic slates in the upper section forced them rightwards to climb the last 500m of the North-West Ridge to the summit. Although proud to achieve the first completely new Hungarian route in the Himalaya, they were disappointed by the unattractive climbing, with its frequent sections of rotten ice and powder snow lying on rock,

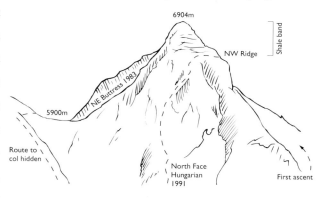

The tremendous North Face of Thalay Sagar from base camp at Kedar Tal. After several attempts the face was eventually climbed in 1991 by the formidable Hungarian team of Atilla Ozsváth and Peter Dekany, following the obvious right-slanting corner system as far as the shale band, where the team traversed precariously right on to the top part of the original North-West Ridge route. The North-East Buttress rises 900m from the col on the left. The route is partly in shadow, set back slightly from the edge of the North Face. (*Andy Selters*)

(*Above*) Randy Trover aiding up a delicious slab of white granite in the first main rock climbing section of the North-East Buttress. (*Michael Kennedy*)

(*Right*) Thalay Sagar, like Bhagirathi III, suddenly presents the climber with an alarming belt of metamorphic slates just before the summit. (*Michael Kennedy*)

swept constantly by spindrift avalanches. The following year a British team attempted the sunnier South Face, but evaded its very steep headwall by traversing out on to the North-West Ridge. The headwall remains an interesting challenge for future pioneers.

Our chosen route, the North-East Buttress, actually starts from the 5900m col separating Thalay Sagar from Brigupanth (6772m). This broad snowy col is usually approached from the west, from a base camp in the

delightful Kedar Bamak. From the glacier beneath the North Face a 40-50° couloir (usually snow not ice) cuts through the rock barrier to the col, where most parties will establish a camp. From this camp, one possibility for acclimatisation, before tackling Thalay Sagar, is to first climb Bhrigupanth, traversing quite easily to the moderate snow and mixed slopes of the South-East Face. (This was the route of the first ascent of the mountain by an American/Indian women's expedition in 1980, led by Arlene Blum). Having acclimatised on Brigupanth, the party will then be in perfect condition to turn its attention to the main objective.

In clear weather the 1000m pillar that rises above the col catches the sun early in the morning at the coldest part of the day producing warm sunlit rock and hard névé snow – perfect mixed climbing conditions. Later in the day the route is shaded and cold. The buttress falls into four main sections: first snowfields, then predominantly rock climbing on

steep band of black shale. Michael Kennedy, who led the pitch on the second ascent in 1984, described it like this: 'It was one of the most frightening leads of my life – an awkward layback/offwidth, a fist in a snowy crack, desperate mantels on to sloping debris, a final pull over the mercifully solid chockstone that capped the chimney. I felt as shattered as the rock all around. A verglassed chimney and a final headwall, climbed on aid, put us on the summit snowfields 150m from the top.'

excellent granite, then a more mixed section and, finally, the obligatory band of Gangotri metamorphic slates, which provide a sharp sting in the tail. The harder climbing starts after a huge ledge 360m up the buttress. Details will vary according to conditions but from here to the summit most parties will find several pitches of grade VI/A1, with some awkward manoeuvres to avoid blank slabs. The hardest pitch will probably be the initial groove in the

SUMMARY STATISTICS AND INFORMATION

Mountain	Thalay Sagar
Height	6904m
Location	Gangotri Group. Garhwal, India
Route	North-East Buttress. 1400m of ascent (1000m from the col), mostly on granite (up to VI and A1) but with steep mixed ground as well.
First ascent of mountain	Summit reached 24 June 1979 by Roy Kligfield, John Thackray & Pete Thexton, via the North-West Couloir and Ridge.
First ascent of route	23 August 1983 by Janusz Skorek, Andrzej Czok (Pol), Hans Christian Doseth, Havard Nesheim & Frode Guldal (Nor).
First alpine-style ascent of route	10-15 September 1984 by Michael Kennedy and Paul Trower (US).
Height of b/c	4750m, on grass at Kedar Tal (lake), 6km from the base of the route, above the true left bank of the Kedar Bamak Glacier.
Roadhead	Lanka.
Length of walk-in	3 days, steeply, up the Kedar Ganga Gorge.
Season	Best conditions are in June or September, on either side of the monsoon.
Permission	Indian Mountaineering Foundation, New Delhi.
Success rate	Remarkably high considering the difficulties; three ascents in as many serious attempts.
Bibliography	John Thackray described the first ascent of the mountain in AAJ 1980 pp 457-62. The North-East Buttress first ascent is recorded in the AAJ 1984 pp 273-5. Michael Kennedy published an illustrated article in the AAJ 1985 pp 102-8 on the second ascent. See also Jan Babicz's Peaks and Passes of the Garhwal Himalaya (Alpinistyczny Klub Eksploracyjny, u.l. Armii Krajowej 12, 81-849 Sopot, Hungary).

(Above) Randy Trover greeting a perfect morning from a bivouac two-thirds of the way up the North-East Pillar. In the background is Brigupanth, first climbed by Arlene Blum's American/Indian women's expedition in 1980. (Michael Kennedy)

(Left) In this view from Kedarnath, Brigupanth is on the right with the American/Indian route climbing the face just left of the right-hand rock buttress. Thalay Sagar is on the left with the North-East Buttress just hidden behind the right-hand profile. On the left, outside the main Gangotri cirque, is the very steep headwall of the South Face. A British team attempting the face in 1991 skirted left underneath the headwall to join the North-West Ridge near the summit. (John Cleare)

NANDA DEVI 7816m

South Ridge

One cannot mention Nanda Devi, the Bliss-Giving Goddess, highest mountain wholly in India and perhaps the most majestic of all Himalayan peaks, without considering also the vast basin in which she stands. A hundred kilometres in circumference, the outer rim of this huge amphitheatre rarely dips below 6000m and its floor is never less than 5000m, except in the west where its entire drainage cuts through the formidable Rishi Gorge. Nanda Devi does not stand detached in the basin but is connected by a narrow corniced ridge 3km long to Nanda Devi East (7434m) on the outer wall. It was from a col on the rim, just south of the east peak, that Tom Longstaff gazed down into the Sanctuary in 1905; and it was he who encouraged his natural successor, Eric Shipton, to try and force a route into the Sanctuary in 1934.

Shipton invited his friend Bill Tilman, with whom he shared a commitment to the concept of lightweight exploration and mountaineering for the sake of enjoyment, speed and success. With just three Sherpas, led by the legendary Angtharkay, this small and highly effective self-supporting unit found a precarious route up the Rishi Ganga Gorge to reach the elusive Sanctuary. They spent three weeks there in June exploring and mapping the northern aspects of Nanda Devi and made three ascents to the outer rim, including a climb of Sakram, 6254m. They left as the monsoon arrived, then returned in September to complete their exploration on the southern side of the peak, reconnoitring to about 6250m on the South Ridge and climbing Maiktoli, 6803m. After such a thorough reconnaissance, Shipton and Tilman were satisfied that the South Ridge of Nanda Devi offered the best chance of success for an eventual ascent. This remarkable journey of exploration was concluded when they exited the basin via the Sunderdhunga Khal on the southern rim.

Two years later, the South Ridge of Nanda Devi was climbed; the summiters were Tilman and Noel Odell. It was a joint American/British effort compris-

Eric Shipton (left) and Bill Tilman, despite, or perhaps because of, their strongly contrasted personalities, formed one of the most successful climbing partnerships of all time. The 1934 Nanda Devi reconnaissance was their first Himalayan venture together and it demonstrated the effectiveness of their bold, flexible, lightweight approach to mountain exploration. (*Audrey Salkeld Archive*)

(*Right*) Nanda Devi, the goddess mountain, floating above the Himalayan foothills at sunset, photographed from Nilkanta. On the left is the steep North Buttress climbed by the American 40th anniversary expedition in 1976. The original South Ridge route is just out of sight, round to the right. (*Andy Selters*)

ing just seven climbers, carried out in superb lightweight style. No ropes were fixed and there was no Sherpa support above 6200m. More remarkable was the difficulty of the terrain; nothing this steep and sustained had ever been undertaken before in the Himalaya, certainly not at these altitudes. Sixteen years were to pass before a higher summit, Annapurna, was climbed. Shipton, busy that year on Everest, was unable to join the 1936 team, but as a protagonist of their style and pioneer of the Sanctuary, he was amply qualified to remark later that 'the climbing of Nanda Devi was the finest mountaineering achievement ever performed in the Himalaya'. Sixty years on his words still ring true for many.

Polish mountaineers first made their mark in the Himalaya in 1939, when M. Karpinski's expedition made the first ascent of Nanda Devi East. They approached Longstaff Col (5910m) from the east, then climbed the South Ridge. This route was repeated by Louis Dubost and Tenzing Norgay in 1951. They were actually the support party of an ambitious Indo-French expedition which aimed to make the first traverse of the two summits; but they found no sign of Roger Duplat and Gilbert Vignes, who had last been seen eight days earlier at the top of the 1936 route, heading for the main summit and hoping to continue across the connecting ridge. Like

(*Right*) Rather like Shivling, but on a much more massive scale, Nanda Devi's two summits have a satisfying symmetry. (*Eric Roberts*)

(*Below*) Expedition porter burning live juniper in the Nanda Devi Sanctuary. Environmental damage was the reason given by the Indian authorities for re-closing the Sanctuary after a spate of expeditions in the late 'seventies and early 'eighties. (*Eric Roberts*)

(*Below right*) Overnight camp in the Rishi Gorge. (*Eric Roberts*)

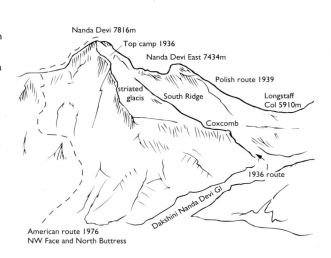

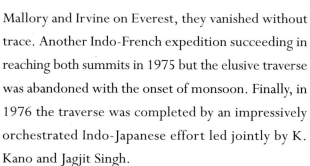

Mallory and Irvine on Everest, they vanished without trace. Another Indo-French expedition succeeding in reaching both summits in 1975 but the elusive traverse was abandoned with the onset of monsoon. Finally, in 1976 the traverse was completed by an impressively orchestrated Indo-Japanese effort led jointly by K. Kano and Jagjit Singh.

1976 also saw the return of the American Ad Carter, who had taken part in the first ascent of Nanda Devi. To celebrate the fortieth anniversary he organised

a large American team to siege a new route up the North-West Face and on to the spectacular North Buttress, which was forced during poor weather, with hard rock climbing to grade VI standard. This final section was led almost entirely by the tenacious John Roskelley, who reached the summit with Lou Reichardt and Jim States. Despite this tremendous success, the expedition was not entirely happy, and in its final stages was marred by the tragedy of Willi Unsoeld's daughter, ironically named Nanda Devi, dying high on the moun-

NANDA DEVI SANCTUARY

0   5   10km

tain. Nanda Devi Unsoeld was a beautiful and vivacious young woman, whom the porters called 'Didi', or sister; many even suspected that she was the Goddess herself returning forever to her mountain.

The main peak's most awesome challenge, the 3000m high North-East Face, was climbed by Josef Rakoncaj's ten-man Czech team in 1981. British alpinists, Terry King and Paul Lloyd had made a bold, futuristic attempt in 1978 on the obvious central spur, but had been defeated by its surreal snow mushrooms.

Even with a large team and fixed ropes, the Czechs were stretched to complete this daunting route, whose crux is the sustained summit headwall, with rock pitches up to grade VI/A3.

The 1981 expedition was the last to climb Nanda Devi before the Indian government closed the Sanctuary to all traffic. The reason stated was environmental damage. For six years a succession of expeditions had taken their toll. For example the 1976 Indo-Japanese team of twenty-one climbers needed

vast quantities of supplies ferried up the tortuous Rishi Gorge and several kilometres of ropes were fixed just to reach base camp. And there was the familiar problem of expedition porters, not equipped with paraffin stoves, burning wood. As well as climbers and trekkers, local shepherds may have contributed to the damage, grazing their herds in the fragile ecosystem. In 1993 the Sanctuary was re-opened to an Indian Army Corps of Engineers expedition which removed a ton of old rubbish, but added its own new detritus –

A climber negotiating an exposed section about halfway up the South Ridge in 1977, with two camps visible immediately below. The Coxcomb is clearly visible at the bottom of the ridge. Note the fixed ropes, which were never found necessary on the first ascent in 1936. (*Eric Roberts*)

3000m of rope in the Rishi Gorge and another 2000m on the South Ridge, which was climbed successfully to the Main Summit.

In 1994 the Indian government tentatively re-opened the Sanctuary to trekking parties. If and when climbing expeditions are lucky enough to visit this magical corner of the Himalaya, one can only hope that they will operate as small teams, with minimal equipment, emulating the fine example of the first ascent in 1936.

The choice of objectives on Nanda Devi's twin peaks is tantalising. The greatest untried challenge is the stupendous 2600m high North Face of the East

Peak. Also for the bold, the traverse awaits an alpine-style ascent. On the Main Peak three routes have been completed to the summit. The Czech route up the North-East Face is certainly the hardest. The American route on the North-West Face/North Buttress is more reasonable, but it too has its crux above 7000m and its lower traverse is dangerously exposed to avalanches. That leaves the original route up the South Ridge, which is selected here as the safest route up the mountain and as a tribute to the legendary figures who pioneered its first ascent.

The South Ridge forms a great ramp, slanting

from right to left across the South Face. From base camp on the Dakshini Nanda Devi Glacier, the route sneaks round to the right of the elaborately pinnacled Coxcomb Ridge, until it is possible to slant left on to the main ridge at about 5600m. The ridge is followed, with occasional detours on to the gentler east side. The rock is mainly rotten, and snow is followed whenever possible. At about 6500m the ridge broadens into a wide 30° snow saddle. The 1936 team placed their fourth camp at the top of this snow saddle. Above that is the most precarious section of the route, a steeper glacis of awkward striated rock

which the 1936 team bypassed by a faint gully on the left. This led to the top camp at c.7300m, where the South Ridge meets a prominent spur from the left, forming the apex of a triangle.

The Everest veteran, Noel Odell, was selected to try for the summit with the young American doctor, Charles Houston. However, severe food poisoning forced Houston to descend and his place was taken by Bill Tilman. On the morning of 29 August 1936 the two Englishmen left the top camp to negotiate a narrow ridge leading to the summit wall. The route is best described in Tilman's own words:

'This difficult ridge was about three hundred yards long, and though the general angle appeared slight it rose in a series of abrupt rock and snow steps. On the left was an almost vertical descent to a big ravine, bounded on the far side by terrific grey cliffs that supported the broad snow shelf for which we were making. The right side also fell away steeply, being part of the great rock cirque running round to Nanda Devi East. The narrow ridge we were on formed a sort of causeway between the lower south face and the upper snow shelf.

'One very important factor which, more than anything, tended to promote a happier frame of mind was that the soft crumbly rock had at last yielded to a hard rough schistose-quartzite which was a joy to handle; a change which could not fail to please us as mountaineers and, no doubt, to interest my companion as a geologist.'

Tilman then proceeds to poke his habitual fun at

Gilbert Harder on the summit day in 1977. Behind him stretches the long, difficult connecting ridge to Nanda Devi East, where Roger Duplat and Gilbert Vignes disappeared in 1951. Behind and just to the right of Nanda Devi East, 50km to the east, rises the distinctive pyramid of Panch Chuli II (see page 121) and behind that are the bigger peaks of western Nepal. (*Eric Roberts*)

Odell's geologising, before describing the continuation of the route. Once the 'causeway' was crossed, a gentle snow shelf led up to the final rock wall, which was climbed from the left. At 3 pm Tilman and Odell stood on the flat snow ridge of Nanda Devi's summit and, in Tilman's immortal words, 'so far forgot ourselves as to shake hands on it'. Success had been achieved through a harmonious team effort and when the victorious telegram was sent to Tom Longstaff no names were mentioned — just 'two reached the top August 29'.

By modern standards the South Ridge is not a difficult technical climb. However, it is a big, mixed route to one of the world's highest summits. The terrain is sometimes precarious and campsites are awkward to construct. All this suggests that a small team will operate most efficiently on the route. By acclimatising first on some of the magnificent peaks on the Sanctuary rim, it should be quite possible to climb this classic route up Nanda Devi in a pure alpine-style push.

Allen Fyffe during the ascent of a new route on the South-East Face of Kalanka in 1978. Nanda Devi dominates the Sanctuary, with the huge fluted North Spur (climbed by Josef Rakoncaj's Czech team three years later, in 1981) rising directly to the summit.. The North Face of Nanda Devi East awaits an attempt by a suitably futuristic alpinist. (*Bob Barton*)

SUMMARY STATISTICS AND INFORMATION

Mountain	Nanda Devi
Height	7816m
Location	Nanda Devi Sanctuary, Garhwal, India.
Route	South Ridge. 2600m of ascent from base camp, on mixed terrain. A good snowpack will reduce the problems of rotten rock. Above 7300m the rock changes to a solid friendly quartzite.
First ascent of mountain	29 August 1936 by Noel Odell & Bill Tilman (UK).
First ascent of route	As above.
Height of b/c	c.5200m beside Dakshini Nanda Devi Glacier.
Roadhead	Lata, in the Dhauli Ganga valley.
Length of walk-in	Approximately 120km and 7 days from Lata. However, snow on the Dharansi Pass and technical difficulties in the Rishi Gorge may cause delays.
Season	The first ascent was made during the late monsoon, in mixed but not impossible weather. Most expeditions have reached the summit earlier, in June. Post-monsoon conditions can be clear and bright, but the October fine spell often fails to materialise in this part of the Himalaya.
Permission	Indian Mountaineering Foundation, New Delhi.
Success rate	The majority of attempts on the 1936 route have been successful with at least nine ascents by 1993.
Bibliography	*Nanda Devi* by Eric Shipton (in *The Six Mountain-Travel Books*, Diadem/Mountaineers, 1985) is one of the classic stories of mountain exploration. H.W. Tilman's *Ascent of Nanda Devi* (in *The Seven Mountain-Travel Books*, Diadem/Mountaineers, 1983) describes the 1936 first ascent. John Roskelley's *Nanda Devi — The Tragic Expedition* (Stackpole Books, 1987) is the controversial account of the American 1976 ascent of the North-West Ridge. See also Lou Reichardt's and Willi Unsoeld's account in *AAJ* 1977. For accounts of the North Face see Terry King's humorous article in *HJ* vol. 36 and Josef Rakoncaj's account of the successful ascent in *Mountain* 83. Accounts of the many attempts on the original route between 1976-82 appear in the relevant volumes of the *HJ* and *AAJ*.

CHANGABANG 6864m

South Buttress

Few would argue that Nanda Devi is the most impressive mountain in Garhwal; it is also India's highest outside Sikkim. But there are equally beautiful, if lower, peaks on the outer rim of the Sanctuary. Of these, Changabang offers particularly spectacular and challenging climbing.

If Changabang was not climbed until 1974 (W.W. Graham claimed an ascent in 1914) this was in no small way due to its formidable profile and very real difficulties. The Indo/British team led by Chris Bonington and Balwant Sandhu approached the mountain via the Rishi Ganga but then branched off on to the Ramani Glacier, on the south-west side of Changabang. From this side the mountain stands as a huge granite needle with its West Face in profile, plunging steeply 1700m from the summit. Daunted, Bonington's team crossed the difficult Shipton Col to reach the snowy South-East Face and the saddle between the West Ridge of Kalanka and the East Ridge of Changabang, which provided the key to the summit. Although their route is by far the easiest option on the mountain, the final ridge is an exposed knife-edge.

A succession of expeditions followed. In the 1976 spring season a six-man Japanese team led by Naoki Toda climbed the fine architectural line of the South-West Ridge. They fixed over 2000m of rope but admirably removed it all on the descent. Then in the autumn, amidst considerable scepticism from the mountaineering establishment, two young British alpinists, Joe Tasker and Pete Boardman set out alone to try the formidable West Face. Their route, involving over twenty-five days of climbing, was mostly on rock up to VI/A2. They used big-wall tactics to overcome these difficulties, though in the upper part the climbing relented to mixed climbing and, finally, easier snowfields. This achievement was hailed as a landmark in Himalayan climbing and the route remains unrepeated.

Changabang's 1700m high South Buttress, climbed in 1978 by MacIntyre, Kurtyka, Porter and Zurek. The route cuts a line up the Central Buttress, first slanting in from the right, then following the mixed crest to the upper headwall. The most obvious feature here is the hanging snowpatch of the Cyclops' Eye, from where the route exits left, then back right through sensational rock scenery to the summit snowfield. The upper section of the South-West Buttress is on the left skyline and the original South-East Ridge on the right. (*Bob Barton*)

Two etriers hang from the first overhang on the headwall. Reaching over the bulge, Kurtyka, climbing in 'seventies-style double leather boots, was delighted to discover a single curving crack splitting the smooth shield above. *(John Porter)*

(Far right) Spectacular aid climbing on tied-off blades, above the point where the chimneys petered out. The lower arête is in the top left corner of the picture. The team are using the efficient tactic for Himalayan big walls, where one pair works on a new pitch, while the other jumars the previous pitch, carrying up all the luggage. *(John Porter)*

At the same time, another British expedition led by Colin Read attempted the South Buttress. They fixed 1000m of rope on the lower half before abandoning the route, stripping the ropes, and then completing a new ice route on the South-East Face to the summit.

Two years later, the South Buttress was climbed in a single push to the summit by a very strong Anglo/Polish team. They worked in pairs: Wojciech Kurtyka and Krystof Zurek comprising one; John Porter and Alex MacIntyre the other. Each pair alternated the leading, fixing ropes behind them

while the second pair jumared, hauled the equipment and cleaned each pitch. Eight days were spent on the face, in mixed weather, with bivouacs mostly in hammocks. From the summit it took another two days to return to base camp via the original East Ridge route.

Given good weather the South Buttress is obviously much sunnier than the West Face which, particularly in autumn, can be fiercely cold. However, the former is equally sustained and the first ascencionists report pitches of A3 skyhooking, Scottish grade 5 mixed and free climbing to VI.

With those kinds of difficulty sustained to at least 6600m, this is a very demanding climb.

Base camp for the South Buttress is best placed on the Changabang Glacier, approached from the Nanda Devi Sanctuary. The face rears up above base camp and it is possible to discern the line of the route that leads into and out of a small hanging icefield near the top of the wall, the Cyclops' Eye, a feature reminiscent of

too, after four pitches, runs out and a blank wall then provides the crux of the climb with some serious aid climbing (A3). Two pitches above, a line of ledges offers a possible bivouac site. Chimneys and dihedrals then lead to the Cyclops' Eye that provides another bivouac site and some steep ice climbing to cross it to its left edge. More chimneys and cracks splitting the final rock wall and a giant detached flake are followed

awaits a second ascent. For those seeking new ground, the smooth South-West Face left of the South Buttress remains untouched, as does the cold monolithic North Face. Few mountains in the Himalaya offer such a wealth of beautiful and demanding climbing.

▲

SUMMARY STATISTICS AND INFORMATION

Mountain	Changabang
Height	6864m
Location	Nanda Devi Group, Garhwal, India.
Route	South Buttress. 1700m of ascent, on steep granite up to VI/A3 and ice/mixed to Scottish 4.
First ascent of mountain	4 June 1974 by Tashi Chewang & Balwant Sandhu (India); Chris Bonington, Martin Boysen, Dougal Haston & Doug Scott (UK).
First ascent of route	18-29 September 1978, by Wojciech Kurtyka and Krystof Zurek (Pol); Alex MacIntyre(UK) & John Porter (USA).
Height of b/c	4500m, beside the Changabang Glacier.
Roadhead	Lata, in the Dhauli Ganga valley.
Length of walk-in	Approximately 120km and 7 days from Lata. However, snow on the Dharansi Pass and technical difficulties in the Rishi Gorge may cause delays.
Season	The old Garhwal gamble – spring or autumn? In a good year there should be a long stable spell in September or October, when low temperatures will ensure safe conditions on the ice and mixed sections.
Permission	Indian Mountaineering Foundation, Delhi. Since the early 'eighties Changabang has been out of bounds to climbers. However, rules do change and the area might well be opened again in the not too distant future.
Success rate	Only one attempt, successful, to date, by an unusually strong team.
Bibliography	John Porter's illustrated articles, 'Changabang South Buttress' and 'South Side Story' were published respectively in *Climbing* 55 and *Mountain* 65. Further details of the route appear in *AAJ* 1979. The first ascent of the mountain was recorded in a book *Changabang* (Heineman, 1975) by Bonington and his team. The West Face was described in gripping detail in both Joe Tasker's *Savage Arena* (Methuen, 1982) and Peter Boardman's *Shining Mountain* (Hodder & Stoughton, 1978).

Bob Barton took this shot from the summit of Kalanka, after completing a new route up the South-East Buttress with Allen Fyffe. On the left is Changabang, with the East Ridge of the first ascent descending towards the camera. Profiled on the left is the South Buttress with the Cyclops' Eye near the top. The peak on the right is Dunagiri (7066m), first climbed in 1947 by André Roch's Swiss team along the South-West Ridge on the left skyline. In 1975 British climbers Dick Renshaw and Joe Tasker climbed the South-East Buttress slanting up from the left, one of the hardest climbs to have been done alpine-style at that time. (*Bob Barton*)

the Eiger's Spider. The line of the climb reaches the crest of the lower buttress from the right and then follows the crest itself with increasing difficulties on both rock and mixed ground to the headwall.

Here the the climbing becomes even more sustained, starting with a spectacular overhang leading on to a shield of rock split by a single curving crack. The route then aims left for a line of promising-looking chimneys heading up to the Cyclops' Eye. However, after some demanding mixed climbing the chimneys fizzle out, leaving just a single crack heading diagonally right (V) across an unlikely wall. This

to the summit icefields and, finally, the summit ridge just below the top.

The South Buttress is a magnificent route which was climbed in an uncompromising spirit of adventure by some of the most innovative mountaineers of their day. When Changabang is again opened to mountaineers, a repeat ascent of the buttress, in the same style as the first ascencionists, will be a fine objective. Also well worth repeating is the Japanese South-West Ridge, perhaps with the direct start from the ridge of Shipton Col pioneered by an Italian team in 1981. The Boardman/Tasker route on the West Face also

PANCH CHULI II 6904m

South-West Ridge

East of Nanda Devi, separated by the immense trench of the Goriganga river, rises the Kumaon Himalaya. This region is still part of Garhwal, but the peaks have never attracted the same attention as their more famous neighbours to the west. It is an area of remote villages, luxuriantly forested valleys, flower-studded alpine meadows and some fine peaks. There are no seven-thousanders but the highest mountain reaches 6904m and is a serenely beautiful pyramid. It is called Panch Chuli II. *Chuli* means cooking hearth and in the great Hindu epic *Mahabharata* the five (*panch*) Pandava brothers rested at these *chulis* for their last earthly meal before ascending to heaven.

For the earthbound purposes of the mountaineer the five peaks are numbered from left to right, with number II as the crowning glory of the massif, dominating the whole area. Early attempts to penetrate the complex approaches to Panch Chuli II read like a *Who's Who* of European and Indian mountaineering. Hugh Ruttledge of later Everest fame made the first foray from the Sona valley to the east in 1929, followed in 1950 by Bill Murray's Scottish Himalayan expedition. Then in 1951 Heinrich Harrer and Frank Thomas found a route from the hot depths of the Goriganga valley to the west, climbing up the Balati valley, to the tortuous icefalls of the Uttari Balati Glacier and eventually the Balati Plateau. This was to be the route of

the first ascent, but not before P.N. Nikore, D.D. Joshi, A.K. Choudhary and Hukam Singh had all led attempts on the peak. Finally, in 1973, Mahendra Singh's India-Tibet Border Police team reached the summit by the South-West Ridge.

Nineteen years later Panch Chuli II was climbed again, by two new routes from the east. Captain N.B. Gurung led a Gurkha regiment to success on the North-East Ridge from the Sona Glacier and Colonel Suraj Bhan Dalal's Kumaon-Naga regiment climbed the North Ridge from the Meola Glacier. Then in 1992 foreigners were allowed to explore the area for the first time in forty-one years. Chris Bonington and Harish Kapadia led an Indo/British expedition to attempt as many climbs as possible on the western side of the massif.

The 1992 expedition nearly ended in disaster when Stephen Venables fell 80m and broke both legs after an abseil anchor failed. The accident happened on the descent, with Dick Renshaw, Victor Saunders and Stephen Sustad, from the first ascent of Panch Chuli V (6434m), one of the peaks at the head of the previously untouched Panch Chuli Glacier. Coming on the last day of the expedition, when the team was

Stephen Sustad on day 3 of the Menaka-Rajramba traverse above the Uttari Balati Glacier, with Panch Chuli II floating serene above all the surrounding peaks. (*Stephen Venables*)

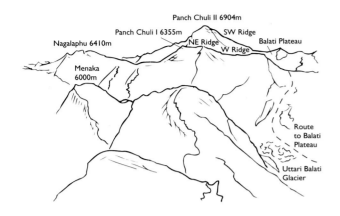

virtually out of food, isolated at the head of a previously unexplored valley, the accident was a reminder of how vulnerable alpine-style teams can be. Luckily, with Bonington providing extra support on the mountain, the Indian team members standing by in the village of Munsiari and the Indian air force able to provide highly skilled helicopter pilots, Venables was evacuated just four days after the accident.

Harish Kapadia, Monesh Devjani and Muslim

Contractor made the first ascent of Panchali Chuli (5220m) in the same cirque, but the earlier main thrust of the expedition was up the previously explored Uttari Balati Glacier. The Uttari Balati is an improbable gateway, with three chaotic icefalls to negotiate before one can reach the wide spaces of the upper glacier at about 4800m. In 1992 Chris Bonington and Graham Little climbed the steep spire of Sahadev East, while Renshaw, Saunders, Sustad and Venables made an extended ridge traverse of Rajramba (6537m), taking in unclimbed Menaka on the way. However, the main objective of the expedition, and our selected route here, was the South-West Ridge of Panch Chuli II.

From the upper basin of the Uttari Balati there are another 1000m to climb, up a slanting glacier ramp, to reach the Balati Plateau. (The obvious approach up the Dakshini Balati Glacier is hideous.) After negotiating the maze of crevasses on the plateau one sets foot at last on the elusive summit pyramid. In 1992 Bonington and Little climbed the blunt ice spur of the West Ridge, first attempted by Harrer in 1951. Meanwhile Muslim Contractor, Monesh Devjani and Pasang Bodh repeated the 1973 ITBP route up the South-West Ridge, without all the paraphernalia of fixed ropes and a large military team.

The South-West Ridge, like so many beautiful, elegant snow ridges, proves on close inspection to be annoyingly icy, with just a shallow snow crust, pitched at that awkward angle too steep for walking but too gentle for front-pointing; so the 800m climb from the col at the foot of the ridge feels surprisingly long. The attraction lies less in the actual climbing than in the line, a classic line on a beautifully proportioned peak, poised between Nepal to the east, Tibet to the north and the Nanda Devi range to the west.

(*Right*) Impromptu base camp in the Pyunshani valley, with the 1992 Indo-British team recovering after a long hungry day's jungle-bashing. Expedition leaders Chris Bonington and Harish Kapadia confer, while Victor Saunders and Stephen Sustad sort the remains of the rations for the attempt on Panch Chuli V. (*Stephen Venables*)

(*Below*) Looking across the Panch Chuli Glacier from Bainti Col to the South Face of Panch Chuli II. The long gully on the extreme left would make a very direct start to the South-West Ridge. On the right is Panch Chuli III, with Panch Chuli IV just showing extreme right. Both peaks were left unclimbed by the 1992 expedition. (*Monesh Devjani*)

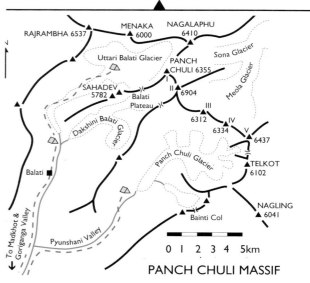

Future parties might consider an alternative approach from the Panch Chuli Glacier to the south-east. From the head of this glacier a single snow couloir rises about 1300m directly to the col at the start of the South-West Ridge. It is south-facing and partially threatened by séracs, so it would only work for a very fit party climbing at night. However, for those not attracted to the long, scenic meanderings of the Uttari Balati approach, this might be a better route. It also has the advantage of a base in the Panch Chuli Glacier cirque at the head of the Pyunshani valley, where fine climbs wait, not least the first ascents of Panch Chuli III and Panch Chuli IV. Perhaps the most exciting alpine-style challenge would be a continuous traverse of all five Chulis. There is still much to be done in this exquisitely verdant corner of the Himalaya.

(*Right*) The normal approach to Panch Chuli II up the enclosed icefalls of the Uttari Balati Glacier. The route pioneered by Heinrich Harrer in 1951 bypasses each of the three falls on the left. (*Stephen Venables*)

(*Far right*) Telkot (6102m) at dawn from Panch Chuli V. Behind Telkot are Nagling (left) and Bainti (right); all three peaks were left unclimbed by the 1992 expedition. (*Stephen Venables*)

PANCH CHULI MASSIF

SUMMARY STATISTICS AND INFORMATION

Mountain	Panch Chuli II
Height	6904m
Location	Eastern Kumaon Himalaya, Garhwal, India.
Route	South-West Ridge. An 800m high snow/ice ridge with a long and complex glacier approach.
First ascent of mountain	26 May 1973. 18 members of Mahendra Singh's ITBP expedition reached the summit.
First ascent of route	As above.
First alpine-style ascent of route	Muslim Contractor, Monesh Devjani & Pasang Bodh repeated the route in June 1992 in a single push from the Balati Plateau, after a steady build-up with porter support to that point.
Height of b/c	3200m at the snout of the Uttari Balati Glacier or, preferably, a km down the valley where there is no threat from perched boulders. This is a very low base camp and one really needs a well-stocked advance base on the upper glacier. For the South Face of Panch Chuli II and west flanks of Panch Chuli II, IV & V, there are delightful base camp sites below and above the Panch Chuli Glacier snout.
Roadhead	Madkhot, a hot, dusty village at the bottom of the Balati valley. Administrative centre and bazaar at Munsiari, high on the west bank of the Goriganga.
Length of walk-in	3 days with porters. Possible in one very long day.
Season	May offers the best spring conditions, but with frequent afternoon snow showers. In a good year autumn will have more stable weather, but snow conditions may be poor, with less freeze-thaw effect.
Permission	Indian Mountaineering Foundation, Delhi. This area may be reserved for joint Indian/foreign expeditions.
Success rate	The route was only climbed after seven attempts from the west. Modern expeditions, moving lighter and faster, with better knowledge of the route, should fare better.
Bibliography	The 1951 attempt from the east is described in W.H. Murray's evocative account of lightweight exploration in Garhwal, *The Scottish Himalayan Expedition* (Dent, 1951). The Harrer reconnaissance from the north is described briefly in *HJ* 18 and the 1973 first ascent in *Himalayan Club Newsletter* 29. The 1992 expedition is thoroughly documented in *HJ* 49 and, more idiosyncratically, in Victor Saunders' *No Place to Fall* (Hodder & Stoughton, 1994).

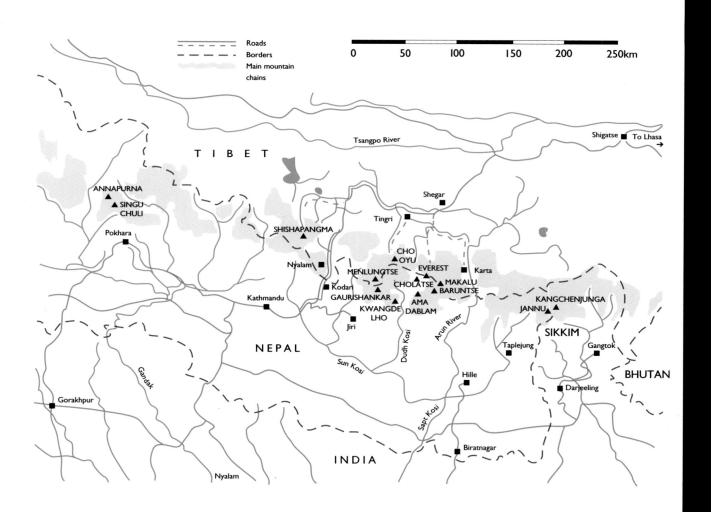

A young kharka-wallah tends
his sheep in the meadows of
Korchon, beneath the South
Face of Machapuchare.
(*John Cleare/Mountain Camera*)

NEPAL
AND
TIBET

SINGU CHULI 6501m

South Ridge / West Face

More trekkers visit the Annapurna Himal than any other mountain area of Nepal. The market town of Pokhara, with its famous lake, Phewa Tal, thrives on tourism, attracting as many travellers as the beaches of Mali or Goa. But the remarkable thing is that until 1949, when the government of Nepal began to open up the country's interior, no Westerners had visited this mountain paradise. Maurice Herzog's 1950 French expedition found a northern route up Annapurna I and claimed the first eight-thousander. Five years later a British Gurkha officer, Jimmy Roberts, arrived in Pokhara to explore the southern approach to the mountain.

Roberts had worked for years in northern India in sight of the Annapurna Himal. He had commanded Gurung and other Nepali tribesmen in his Gurkha regiment. Now at last he could see their county for himself and, at the same time, have the thrill of penetrating unknown territory.

Roberts was successful in 1956 in finding a route up the gorge of the Modhi Khola into the great enclosed cirque on the south side of Annapurna, the Sanctuary, and the following year returned with a British expedition led by Wilfrid Noyce, to attempt Machapuchare, the Fish's Tail. From a base camp inside the Sanctuary the team made a determined effort on the North Ridge, only to be stopped 50m from the summit by a combination of hard blue ice and poor weather. In Noyce's words, 'It looked as if the Goddess had drawn her firm line here, at least for these her two respectably married suitors.' He and David Cox retreated through the snowstorm and to this day the summit of Machapuchare remains, officially at least, untrodden, for it was declared off limits straight after the 1957 expedition.

Before leaving the Sanctuary, Cox and Noyce claimed a delightful consolation prize, a shapely summit which they called Fluted Peak and which is now known by its local name, Singu Chuli. Since the mid-seventies it has been classified as a trekking peak, meaning that it can be attempted by fairly informal parties, for a small fee, without all the rigmarole and expense of a major expedition. Trekking peak is a misleading term, for most of these peaks are serious

Singu Chuli or Fluted Peak, as it was called by David Cox and Wilfrid Noyce who made the first ascent as consolation for their near miss on Machapuchare in 1957. The South Ridge descends towards the camera, with the West Face in shadow on the left. (*Bill O'Connor*)

climbs, even by their easiest routes. Of the three in the Annapurna Sanctuary, Hiunchuli (6331m), which guards the entrance, is the most difficult. Tharpu Chuli, or Tent Peak (5500m), is the easiest and is climbed regularly by trekking parties. Singu Chuli (6501m) rises from the same spur separating the Annapurna South and West Annapurna Glaciers and is an altogether more serious proposition than Tharpu Chuli.

Cox and Noyce climbed Singu Chuli by the North-East Face and East Ridge, but most people visiting the Sanctuary will probably stay at Annapurna South base camp, from where the classic line of the South Ridge is the most obviously appealing route. It can be reached from the west, but most parties have approached the ridge from the east, traversing in underneath the fluted South Face, which is itself another option, to gain the fine, sharp-edged crest. For those who want something more modern, there is the West Face route, climbed by René Ghilini, Alex MacIntyre and John Porter in September 1982, as part of a very thorough acclimatisation programme to prepare for their audacious alpine-style attempt on the South Face of Annapurna. The route was excellent – alpine grade ED, following a mixed spur, then ice slopes directly to the summit, which is a strange detached pinnacle of ice sitting on a snow plateau.

Singu Chuli is a fine peak in its own right, but it is inevitably dwarfed by its giant neighbours which ring the Sanctuary. This is a situation which many relish, enjoying the ambience of big peaks like Annapurna I, Gangapurna and Tarke Kang, without having to experience the harsh reality of actually climbing them. For the more ambitious, both these routes on Singu Chuli – and some of the climbs on Tharpu Chuli and Glacier Dome – are a challenging and entertaining way of acclimatising for the gigantic South Face of Annapurna.

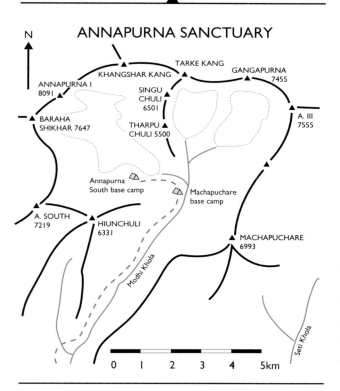

Local Gurung porters carrying loads up the Modhi Khola, heading for the Annapurna Sanctuary. (*Bill O'Connor*)

Mountain	Singu Chuli (Fluted Peak)
Height	6501m
Location	Annapurna Himal, Central Nepal.
Routes	South Ridge: classic snow/ice arête. West Face: mixed spur and steep ice climbing
First ascent of mountain	13 June 1952 by David Cox & Wilfrid Noyce (UK), via North-East Face.
First ascent of route	South Ridge – unknown. West Face – René Ghilini (Fra), with Alex MacIntyre (UK) & John Porter (USA).
Height of b/c	Annapurna South base camp is at 4250m beside the Annapurna South Glacier.
Roadhead	Phedi, 8 km west of Pokhara. It can be reached in a long day from Delhi.
Length of walk-in	Approximately 35km over 5 days.
Season	April/May or September/October.
Permission	Ministry of Tourism, Kathmandu, via a trekking agency.
Success rate	The peak still has very few ascents, so statistics are hard to come by.
Bibliography	*Climbing the Fish's Tail* by Wilfrid Noyce (Heineman, 1958). *Annapurna South Face* by Chris Bonington (Cassell, 1971). *The Trekking Peaks of Nepal* by Bill O'Connor (Crowood, 1989) and *Adventure Treks Nepal* by Bill O'Connor (Crowood, 1990).

ANNAPURNA 8091m

South Face

Of all nature's gigantic features, there can be few more impressive than the 3000m high South Face of Annapurna, the Harvest Goddess. For mountaineers, there can be few more attractive objectives.

In 1964, the last of the eight-thousanders, Shishapangma was climbed; of the others, only Everest and Nanga Parbat had been climbed by a second route. This marked the end of the Golden Age of Himalayan exploration and coincided with the closing of much of the Himalaya due to the political tensions within the host countries. In 1969 these restrictions were lifted and foreign climbers returned. There were still many virgin summits, but for mountaineers at the cutting edge the emphasis seemed now to be on trying hard new routes on the giant peaks which had already been climbed by their easiest lines. Everest's South-West Face was an obvious challenge which finally succumbed in 1975. Meanwhile, the first big successes came in 1970, when the Japanese climbed Makalu's long South-East Ridge, an Austro-German party forced the huge Rupal Face of Nanga Parbat and a British team succeeded on the South Face of Annapurna.

The Annapurna South Face expedition was led by Chris Bonington and the summit was reached by Don Whillans and a cult figure of British alpinism, Dougal Haston. Their moment of glory was the culmi-

nation of many weeks' effort by a team of eight climbers, supported by high-altitude Sherpas, supplying six camps along a continuous line of fixed rope. The route followed the left-hand of the three huge spurs on the face. The central ice ridge and the upper rockband gave some of the hardest climbing achieved so far at that altitude.

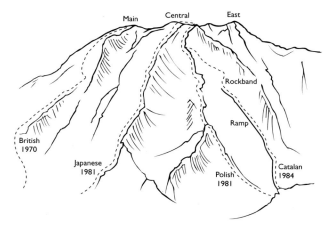

The stupendous South Face of Annapurna. It was the first of the giant Himalayan walls to be climbed, in May 1970, and it has remained a testing ground for the most ambitious Himalayan climbers. (*Enric Lucas*)

It was eleven years before this line was repeated, two Japanese climbers reaching the summit. And there was a further Japanese success in 1987 when four climbers summited on 20 December, making the first winter ascent of the face. Since then there have been several further ascents of the route, but none without fixed ropes. The other two prominent spurs were both

climbed in 1981 — the right-hand one in the spring by Ryzsard Szafirski's Polish expedition and the central spur by the Japanese again in the autumn. Both expeditions followed the British example, laying siege to the face with large teams of climbers.

Each of the three spurs is a magnificent line. So far no one has attempted any of them in alpine-style. On the British and Polish routes in particular, long sections of convoluted snow and ice ridge would make a fast ascent and unsecured retreat very difficult. Contenders in the modern idiom have turned instead to the huge open slopes and depressions to the sides of the spurs, where simpler terrain makes greater speed possible. The price, though, is greater danger from avalanche and stonefall. In 1992 Pierre Béghin and Christophe Lafaille were caught by a storm in the huge funnel between the British and Japanese routes and forced to retreat. Early in the descent an abseil anchor failed, plunging Béghin to his death and leaving Lafaille to make a desperate solo descent, bombarded by repeated rockfalls, as he struggled down with just ten metres of rope for protection. It was a falling rock on the same face which killed another prophet of alpine-style climbing, Alex MacIntyre, in 1982. His project was a great curving ramp line to the right of the Polish route. In his usual uncompromising style, he carried just the bare minimum of equipment; when he and René Ghilini reached a steep rockband at 7150m they were forced to accept defeat. During the descent a single stone sent MacIntyre plunging to his death.

Inspired by the style and line of MacIntyre's attempt, two Catalans, Nil Bohigas and Enric Lucas, arrived in the Annapurna Sanctuary in August 1984, determined to complete the route. They set up base camp at the regular site at 4250m, with accommodation for themselves, their liaison officer, cook and two friends from Barcelona, comprising just three tents and a cooking shelter! At the end of September, after first acclimatising on Fluted and Tent Peaks (as MacIntyre and Ghilini had done), they climbed the face in a single six-day push, reaching the summit on 3 October. The difficulties were extreme, up to V+/A2 and 80° ice. Bohigas and Lucas descended in a single day by abseil down the Polish spur, concluding one of the finest ascents of all time. We include their route in this book as an example of alpine-style bravura taken to its extreme.

The line is cunning, taking a leftward curving ramp which slices through the open slopes right of the Polish Spur, avoiding its intricate, time-consuming knife-edge ridges. Speed is paramount, for the start of the Catalan route is undeniably dangerous. Lucas commented on the stonefall danger on this section and cited this as a reason why he and Bohigas did not set foot on the wall until they were absolutely ready for a 'straightforward', i.e. fast, ascent. After bivouacking at the bergschrund at 5800m, they started the face at 10 pm. They climbed the initial section, which they

One of the last photos of Alex MacIntyre, who pruned equipment to the bare minimum in his quest for alpine-style commitment. Here, in 1982, faced with the difficulties of the critical rockband at 7150m, carrying just one ice screw and three rock pegs, he and René Ghilini had to admit defeat. It was whilst retreating down the exposed lower ramp that MacIntyre was killed by a falling stone. (*René Ghilini*)

compared to the North Face of the Droites, unroped for speed and soon after dawn they had reached 6800m, where the stonefall eased. Lucas described the risks to that point drily: 'Not huge, but numerous, the stones became an accepted rainfall of danger.'

took three falls before overcoming the difficulties and it took a whole day to surmount 50m in two pitches. They graded the rock V+ and A2; the ice was at least 80°.

Above the rockband, from 7200-7600m the route,

V+ have to be negotiated to reach easier terrain above.

The Catalans made their fifth bivouac on the wall above this barrier, then travelled lightweight to the summit ridge in five hours, emerging between the Central and East Summits. They reached the summit

(*Left*) Two years later, better ice cover on the rock and a bigger gear rack allow Enric Lucas to force the rockband. Both he and Nil Bohigas took leader falls and spent a whole day surmounting 50m in two pitches. (*Nil Bohigas*)

(*Above*) The following morning Lucas gets ready to leave the bivouac at 7300m and start a hard day's work on the huge central icefield. (*Nil Bohigas*)

As the ramp starts to curve left the route becomes safer but soon much harder as the rockband is reached. Ghilini and MacIntyre were thwarted by steep compact rock. The Catalans carried slightly more gear and found more ice overlaying the smooth rock. Nevertheless, when they started the step on the morning of the second day they found it extremely hard. Even climbing without their 25kg sacks they

on ice throughout, leads to a huge leftward traverse beneath another granite barrier 200m high (the Catalans made their fourth bivouac beneath a hanging sérac at 7460m which protected them from stonefall danger stemming from the granite above). The route now joins the Polish Spur, where the difficulties through the upper rockband appear fewest. Nevertheless, 160m of granite climbing up to grade

of Annapurna Central (8051m) at 12.30 pm where they spent ninety minutes before descending back to their top bivouac at 7800m.

The Catalans were well prepared for their descent, abseiling the Polish Spur and then the slopes immediately to its right in just sixteen hours to the base of the face! For this purpose they produced an 80m 7mm rope from their rucksacks to complement their 80m

On the fourth day the Catalans joined the upper part of the Polish Spur. Here Lucas follows a sensational pitch through the upper rockband at about 7700m, with clouds brewing in the Sanctuary 3000m below. (*Nil Bohigas*)

of 8mm rope, which they had doubled whilst climbing. For anchors, they used up all the climbing rack they had brought up to 7800m, making their last abseil on their last piton! Their descent had been rapid, audacious and relatively safe.

Few other viable options for descent exist if the climber wishes to return to the Sanctuary. The best descent to the north would probably be via the Dutch (1977) Spur to the left (facing) of the original route,

as Erhard Loretan and Norbert Joos (Swiss) did when they had reached the summit from the East and Central Summits on the first traverse of the peak, three weeks after the Catalan ascent.

Although the Catalans did not reach the true summit, their climb stands on its merit and its objective. As with Kurtyka's ascents of Gasherbrum IV West Face and Dhaulagiri East Face, it was the ascent of the face that counted, not the mountain top. The Catalan

Enric Lucas (left) and Nil Bohigas shortly after their brilliant raid on Annapurna. (*Ken Wilson Collection*)

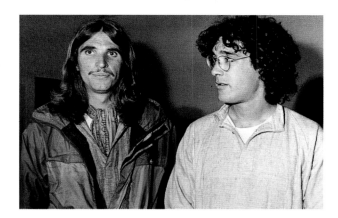

Lucas radios the girlfriends at base camp from the Central Summit of Annapurna. On the horizon behind on his left, 70km to the east, is Manaslu. On the far right, standing guard over the Sanctuary entrance, is the distinctive fishtail of Machapuchare. The 1957 team, operating with just three climbers and limited Sherpa support, almost completed the difficult North Ridge on the left. Since then the mountain has been out of bounds to expeditions. (*Nil Bohigas*)

SUMMARY STATISTICS AND INFORMATION

Mountain	Annapurna I
Height	8091m
Location	Annapurna Himal, Central Nepal.
Route	South Face (Catalan route). 2700m of ascent, mostly on steep snow and ice, but with passages of extreme difficulty (V+/A2 and 80° ice at 7200m and V+ at 7800m). Once committed on the route, descent is extremely difficult and dangerous until the line of the Polish Spur is reached.
First ascent of mountain	Maurice Herzog & Louis Lachenal (France) reached the summit on 3 June 1950.
First ascent of route	Nil Bohigas & Enric Lucas (Catalan), 27 September – 3 October 1984.
Height of b/c	4250m, on grassy meadows above the south bank of the Dakshini Annapurna Glacier, about 3km from the foot of the face.
Roadhead	Suikhet, an hour's drive north-west from Pokhara.
Length of walk-in	Approximately 50km, 5 days.
Season	The South Face has been climbed in spring, autumn and winter, though the Catalan route, so far, only in autumn.
Permission	Ministry of Tourism, Kathmandu, via a trekking agency.
Success rate	Only two partnerships have made serious attempts on this route, the first turning back at 7150m. Stonefall is a threat, particularly on the lower part of the face where Alex MacIntyre was killed on descent in 1982.
Bibliography	The first ascent is described vividly in Maurice Herzog's epic *Annapurna*, which has run to many million copies. Also a bestseller, Chris Bonington's *Annapurna South Face* (Cassell, 1970) gives a detailed account of the first ascent from the south. The Polish Spur is summarised in *AAJ* 1982 and the Japanese Spur in *Iwa To Yuki* 86 & 87. The Catalan route was widely reported, including a summary in *AAJ* 1985 and an article by Enric Lucas in *Mountain* 102.

route represents all the boldness and panache of alpine-style taken to extremes. Only a very fit, competent party will repeat it with any degree of safety and for even the fastest climbers the threat of stonefall will always exist, borne out by the Catalans' comments on the dangers in the first and second icefields and by MacIntyre's untimely death.

The South Face of the Annapurna overlooks some fantastic mountain scenery, notably the fishtail profile of Machapuchare and the serenity of the Annapurna Sanctuary. By any route the mountain is rich in historical resonance for it has seen three epoch-making climbs: the French ascent of the North-East Face in 1950, marking the first ascent of an eight-thousander; the British expedition of 1970 to the South Face, one of the first Himalayan giant wall climbs; and finally this exemplary climb in 1984, an expression of grand scale alpinism in the purest style.

GAURISHANKAR 7134m

West Face

Early explorers thought it was the highest mountain in the world and even today, when you land at Kathmandu airport and see its twin summits towering over the valley, it is easy to understand the mistake. Gaurishankar is a wonderful, holy mountain. The Buddhist Sherpas, who see just the South Summit from Sola Khumbu, revere the mountain as Jomo Tseringma. The Hindus of the lower valleys live in sight of both summits. They call the higher North Summit Shankar – a manifestation of Shiva, the god of creation and destruction, and the South Summit Gauri – the Golden Goddess, one of the many manifestations of Shiva's consort, which also include Parvati, Nanda and Durga.

Despite Gaurishankar's holy status, foreign climbers were permitted to attempt the mountain during the late 'fifties and early 'sixties. Raymond Lambert, who made an illegal foray to the Tibetan side in 1952, thus seeing both sides of the mountain, pronounced it unclimbable. With that irresistible provocation, a Japanese expedition tried the peak in 1959 and in 1964 Dennis Gray's British team forced a route from the Bhote Kosi, up the jungle-clad Rongshar Gorge to the North-West Ridge. The climbers traversed out on to the north, Tibetan, side of the ridge, where they were forced to retreat from about 7000m after avalanches swept away their fixed

ropes. Then came the clampdown on mountaineering in Nepal. When the doors reopened in 1970, Gaurishankar was out of bounds. It was only in 1979 that the mountain was again made available and, as one of the world's most desirable unclimbed peaks, it was now reserved exclusively for expeditions including Nepalese nationals.

Dennis Gray put in an application but later had to hand over leadership to his colleague Peter Boardman for an autumn attempt. Meanwhile the American Al Read, director of Mountain Travel Nepal, had got one step ahead with a permit for the spring season and it was his expedition, co-led by the famous Sherpa Pertemba, which had first pick at the mountain. Only the faintest traces remained of Gray's trail up the jungly Chumal Chu, leading tortuously from the Rongshar Gorge up to a col overlooking the Tseringma Glacier. Despite an earlier aerial reconnaissance, the team was awestruck by the view from the col. There in front of them, on the left, was their original objective, the North-West Ridge, now deemed to lie in Tibet and forbidden by the Nepalese government. On the right the 3km long knife blade of the wildly corniced South-West Ridge, swept up to the South Summit, separated from Shankar himself by a more wildly crenellated ridge. In between lay their only other option – the West Face. Gray had described

it as 'nine thousand feet (2800m) of precipice set at an incredible angle and swept by avalanches … a climbing proposition for generations to come'. Now, just fifteen years later, the young Pertemba looked at it and said, 'I think see Gaurishankar and die.'

Pertemba didn't die, nor did any of his Nepalese and American companions; together they achieved what may have been the hardest technical climb yet achieved in the Himalaya and, just one month after arriving at base camp, an American and a Sherpa emerged at the top of the West Face to stand on the highest summit of Gaurishankar. That left the alternative option, the South-West Ridge, for Peter Boardman's British/Nepalese/Swiss expedition in the autumn. Despite the spectacular difficulties, they too succeeded, using a moving 'capsule' of limited fixed rope to work their way along the surreal knife-edge, before cutting loose for an alpine-style dash to the top. Nine hard mixed pitches up the headwall led to a bitterly cold (8 November) bivouac on the snow plateau above. Early the following morning Peter Boardman, Tim Leach, Guy Neithardt and Pemba Lama climbed the final snow slope to the South Summit. In their extended state there was no chance of continuing along the connecting ridge to the North

The West Face of Gaurishankar's main summit by moonlight. *(Bill O'Connor)*

Summit, which they estimated at another three or four days' climbing.

The West Ridge has not been repeated in its entirety, but in 1985 a Slovenian team did re-climb the upper section after completing the first ascent of the South Face. The South-East Ridge, on the Tibetan frontier, has also been climbed, by Michio Yusua's Japanese team in 1983. The Chinese authorities have not yet permitted any attempt from the Tibetan side, which looks just as hard, if not harder, than the Nepalese flank. Of the routes in Nepal climbed so far, the most beautiful and direct — and probably most feasible alpine-style proposition — is the line of the first ascent, the West Face.

The key to the route was the long snow/ice rib running up the centre of the face. From Camp 1 at 5150m rock slabs and ice runnels led to the rib at 5500m. A second camp was dug into a crevasse halfway up the rib at about 6000m and things continued in similar vein to 6350m. Here, shortly before the rib abuts against the upper rock walls, John Roskelley and Pertemba traversed left, teetering on crampon

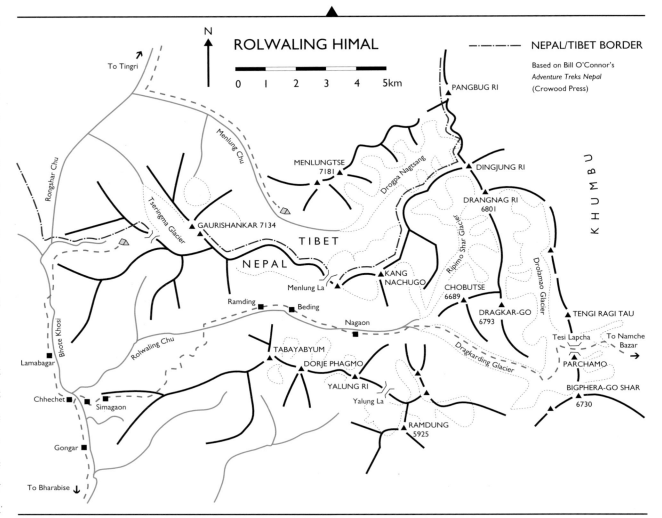

Gaurishankar's twin holy summits from the south-west, with, peeping out from the right, Menlungtse in Tibet. (Al Read)

points for 250m, occasionally using tension to overcome smooth slabs. The traverse landed them in a niche beneath a steep ice runnel, which was climbed for about 150m to a half-metre square platform on the left at 6500m – camp 3!

From the uncomfortable perch of Camp 3

Roskelley and Kim Schmitz fixed the next section. The key was a metre-wide ribbon of water ice, vertical at times, leading with some aid climbing through a rockband to a hanging icefield, which was fixed for 200m to the upper rockband. Dorje Sherpa accompanied Roskelley on the push through that final rockband

which culminated in an overhang surmounted on shifting pitons (A3), suspended directly above the 2500m void. It only remained to climb a snowfield, then follow the final few hundred metres of the North-West Ridge to the summit, completing a magnificent climb.

The 1979 ascent was sieged, with fixed ropes reaching close to the summit. Given the limited technical experience of some of the team, that was the best tactic at the time. Five years later another American, Wyman Culbreth, climbed a variation with Ang Kami Sherpa, in cleaner style. The pair moved supplies gradually up the rib, eventually establishing a Camp 3 at the point where the 1979 team moved left. Wyman and Ang Kami now continued straight up the headwall for about

(*Left*) Kim Schmitz at Camp 3 (6500m). He and John Roskelley spent four nights at this precarious perch whilst working on the upper wall. (*John Roskelley*)

(*Below*) The face in detail, photographed from the air, probably the hardest technical route ever followed to make the first ascent of a major Himalayan peak. (*Al Read*)

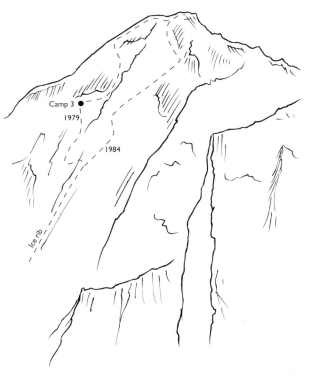

remarkable effort — before the pair continued down to base camp.

In January 1986 Ang Kami repeated his route, when he and the South Korean Choi Han-Jo made the first winter ascent of Gaurishankar. The original left-hand route remains unrepeated. Both routes are probably very similar, with sustained difficulties on very steep ice and granite. However, the right-hand version does traverse directly beneath the summit

(Above) A party enjoying a brilliant morning on Ramdung (5925m), a popular trekking peak above the Rolwaling valley. Gaurishankar towers above the horizon. The British 1979 route takes the South-West Ridge, profiled on the left, to the snowy South Summit, Gauri. On the right is the higher North Summit, Shankar, with the unclimbed shady East Face dropping into Tibet. (Glenn Rowley)
(Right) Chris Bonington with personal bearers in the Rongshar Gorge, en route for the 1987 attempt on Menlungtse, well into his third decade of Himalayan expeditioning. (Chris Bonington Collection)

250m then began a long rising traverse to the right which took them across the top of a large icefield to a vertical mixed gully in the large rockband above. Because there were no bivouac sites above Camp 3, the pair fixed ropes on this upper section to a point halfway up the rockband, before returning to sleep at Camp 3. Then, in a very long summit day, they reascended the ropes and continued up 200m of 80° hard water ice which eased to névé and, at last, the summit at 6.30 pm. After a long series of rappels in the dark they regained Camp 3 at 2.30 the next morning. That same day Ang Kami went back up to remove all the ropes used during the previous night's descent — a

hanging glacier. The lower ice cliff of this glacier rests on rock and threatens the whole right-hand side of the face. It is difficult to judge the extent of that threat, but it is significant that Roskelley, a man known for his fanatical interest in safety, chose the left-hand route. Perhaps the ideal line would continue from the top of the ice rib up the Culbreth/Kami route on to an upper rock rib, then diagonal left into the final rockband of the 1979 route. This would avoid both the long leftward traverse of the 1979 route and the risky rightward traverse of the 1984 route. It would involve some even harder climbing but, being direct, would be easier and safer to descend.

SUMMARY STATISTICS AND INFORMATION

Mountain	Gaurishankar
Height	7134m
Location	Rolwaling Himal, Eastern Nepal.
Route	West Face. 2800m of ascent from the Tseringma Glacier, up the central snow/ice rib to about 6300m, where the original route traverses left, while the 1984 variant continues straight up, then traverses right. Both versions involve sustained work on ice up to 90° and mixed pitches with aid up to A3. The rock is good granite. Descent by the same route.
First ascent of mountain	Dorje Sherpa (Nep) & John Roskelley (USA) reached summit 8 May 1979.
First ascent of route	As above.
First alpine-style ascent of route	The right-hand variation was climbed by Ang Kami Sherpa (Nep) & Wyman Culbreth (USA) in one continuous push, with limited help from a high-altitude porter and movable sections of fixed rope, reaching summit 16 May 1984.
Height of b/c	4950m at the tongue of a little glacier at the top of the Chumal Chu. From here it is necessary to cross a ridge and descend on to the Tseringma Glacier at 5200m to reach the West Face.
Roadhead	Charikot, on the Jiri road, about 6 hours from Kathmandu.
Length of walk-in	7 or 8 days, first up the Bhote Kosi, as for Rolwaling, then continuing north up the Rongshar Gorge, through the villages of Lamabagar and Bom, then east, climbing 3000m up the dense jungle of the Chumal Chu.
Season	The first two ascents of the face were made in spring when warmer conditions make the technical climbing more pleasant. However, by mid-May, the temperature rises further and the sun is longer on the face each day, increasing the risk of ice and rockfall. Autumn probably offers the safest conditions, but by late October strong, cold winds could make life very unpleasant on the upper face.
Permission	Ministry of Tourism, Kathmandu, via a trekking agency. All expeditions must be joint foreign/Nepalese.
Success rate	Three attempts on the original route and its variant have all been successful.
Bibliography	Dennis Gray's *Rope Boy* (Gollancz, 1970) and Don Whillans' *Portrait of a Mountaineer* (with Alick Ormerod, Penguin, 1973) describe the first concerted attempt in 1964. Peter Boardman's evocative *Sacred Summits* (Hodder & Stoughton, 1982) describes the first ascent of the South Summit by the spectacular West Ridge. The West Face is described in detail in Al Read's article in *AAJ* 1980 and Wyman Culbreth's in *AAJ* 1985.

MENLUNGTSE 7181m

West Face / South-East Face

Menlungtse is one of the most striking peaks anywhere in the Himalaya. It might better be described as a massif for there are two summits, one and a half kilometres apart, separated by a broad saddle dipping to about 6700m. It rises to the north of the main Himalayan chain, in Tibet, isolated like a massive island of granite at the headwaters of the Rongshar river. Protected by huge sérac barriers, knife-edge ridges and steep cliffs, it has always epitomised the elusive summit.

Menlungtse's natural defences are formidable and

until recently it was also protected by its political isolation. During the 1950s some climbers did sneak across the border from Nepal, most notably Raymond Lambert and Eric Shipton, who was enchanted by the peak and give it is unofficial name, Menlungtse (Jobu Garu is the correct Tibetan name). It was Chris Bonington who finally persuaded the Chinese Mountaineering Association to authorise a proper attempt on the mountain. In 1987, with Jim Fotheringham and Norwegians Bjørn Myrer Lund and

From the South Summit of Gaurishankar at 9 am, 9 November 1979 on the first ascent, with Menlungtse's icy flanks centre picture, and the Khumbu eight-thousanders beyond. (*Peter Boardman*)

Odd Eliassen, he attempted the obvious spur on the southern end of the West Face but was hampered by appalling weather and high technical difficulties, even below the vertical headwall at the top of the rib. A year later he brought a second expedition, intending to try the East Ridge, a beautiful direct line to the main summit. However, on closer inspection the team elected instead to try another route on the West Face. On this occasion they were successful and the West Summit was reached by Andy Fanshawe and Alan Hinkes after three days of alpine-style climbing.

Then in 1990, a strong American team of Greg Child, Jeff Duenwald John Roskelley and Jim Wickwire made a concerted effort on the East Ridge, which Roskelley had eyed up from Gaurishankar eleven years earlier. However, British doubts about the route were vindicated when Child and Roskelley were stopped at 6460m by bottomless snow on tottering cornices.

Both Americans and British dismissed the most simple, direct route to the main summit, the South-East Face. Guarded by a horrid looking icefall and threatened from above by batteries of séracs and some stonefall, this 2000m ice face appears extremely dangerous. However, that danger can be minimised by

a fast team and in 1992 one of the very best climbing partnerships in the world took the face by storm. The Slovenians Marko Prezelj and Andrej Stremfelj had only the previous year made their audacious alpine-style ascent of Kangchenjunga's South Ridge. On Menlungtse they were equally bold. On the early morning of 22 October they climbed in just five and a half hours from 5150m to 6150m, at which point they had to stop and shelter in a cave from falling rocks and ice. The following day they set off at 8.30 am and at 6.30 pm they reached the main summit of Menlungtse. Descending in the dark, they regained the bivouac by 2 am on the 24th and after a rest continued down, reaching the bottom by midday. They had spent a total of just fifty-three and a half hours on the face, with thirty-eight and a half hours' actual climbing.

(Above) Menlungtse from the south-east. The first attempt in 1987 was made up the left-hand ridge, leading to the West Summit (the West Face, climbed in 1988, is further round to the left). The 1990 American expedition attempted the beautiful but wildly corniced East Ridge on the right. The main summit was finally attained in 1991 by the Slovenians, Marko Prezelj and Andrej Stremfelj, who made a characteristically bold two-day dash up the South-East Face, emerging on the saddle just left of the summit. (Dave Bamford)

(Right) Andrej Stremfelj, master of alpine-style, travelling fast and light on the South-East Face at about 11 am on the first day. Shortly above the big séracs, he and Prezelj had to stop and shelter from ice and rockfall before resuming their climb the next day. (Marko Prezelj)

From Tingri on the Tibetan plain there is a tiny tractor road, open for just a few weeks of the year, which crosses the Fusi La (5200m), west of the Nangpa La and descends the Rongshar Gorge to the Sherpa village of Changbujiang, just 10km north of the Nepalese border. This road was built by the Chinese to place a garrison and an administrative centre in the village. Sadly, it has facilitated the removal of wood from the forests above the Rongshar Chu to the treeless Tibetan plain where the demand for building materials increases each year. From here a villagers' path leads up the Menlung Chu through rhododendron, bamboo and conifer forest to the base of the mountain.

The photograph on page 141, from the South Summit of Gaurishankar, shows the western and southern aspects of Menlungtse West. The Main

Future parties may well repeat the South-East Face, but it is worth remembering that the route's dangers were minimised by speed; not many people can match the panache of Prezelj and Stremfelj. The cold conditions of October may also have made the route safer than in the spring. The West Face route may be a more attractive option, but before describing it in detail let us look at the approach. Much of the charm of Menlungtse comes from its remote location and the journey to reach base camp on the meadows at 4400m between Menlungtse and Gaurishankar is one of the most enchanting in Tibet.

(*Above*) 6.30 pm, 23 October 1991. Andrej Stremfelj with Slovenian flag atop the elusive main summit of Menlungtse. Behind him are, left, the West Face of Cho Oyu, climbed the previous year by Kurtyka, Loretan and Troillet and, right, Everest, Lhotse and Makalu. (*Marko Prezelj*)
(*Right*) Andy Fanshawe at sunset on 23 May 1988, striding out along the final ridge to the West Summit. Travelling light without bivouac gear, Fanshawe and Hinkes decided wisely not to continue to Menlungtse's Main Summit. As it was, they had to make many abseils in the dark to regain their camp on the West Face late that night. (*Alan Hinkes*)

Summit of Menlungtse is just visible behind the less pronounced west top. The line of the West Face route is marked on the corresponding topo. A wide, easy-angled gully heading from scree up the left side of the North-West Ridge leads to a pronounced snowy apron. A 30m abseil leftwards reaches another slanting snowy line between séracs and the ridge crest which is followed in about ten rope-lengths to the Promontory at 5800m and a perfect basin for a bivouac. A broad terrace of snow traverses rightward across into the centre of the face. The route climbs straight up from there on snow turning a few easy séracs to a huge crevasse at about 6250m. Hard green ice is followed for six rope-lengths to another crevasse system, at 6500m the highest on the face (a good rack of disposable ice screws should be carried for descent). From the extreme south end of the crevasse system the route climbs straight up again for four steep (65°) pitches to the start of the headwall.

The key to the route is a deep gash at the very top of the headwall. The route reaches its base by following a broad rocky rib descending from its right for about five pitches (IV) on perfect granite. The chimney is loose and vertical (VI) and difficult to protect but leads to the summit ridge, 6950m at a point just beyond the last gendarme. The crest is followed on the north-east, snowy side to the West Summit at 7023m.

Andy Fanshawe and Alan Hinkes reached the West Summit at sunset. Having left bivouac gear down at the crevasse, they decided wisely not to continue down to the saddle and on to the main summit, rising as an icy steeple beyond the saddle. The return journey would probably have taken a full day. If future parties carried bivouac gear over the West Summit, this route could be the best way of reaching the Main Summit? It lacks the elegant directness of the Slovenian route but it is probably safer and has the added attraction of those superb mixed and rock pitches on the granite headwall. Whatever route climbers choose, Menlungtse will always be a difficult and challenging peak.

SUMMARY STATISTICS AND INFORMATION

Mountain	Menlungtse (Jobu Garu).
Height	Main Summit: 7181m; West Summit: 7023m
Location	Rolwaling Himal, Tibet.
Route	West Face of Menlungtse West. c.2000m of ascent, mostly on snow and ice but with steep rock climbing (up to VI) in the upper 300m headwall. Andy Fanshawe & Alan Hinkes reached West Summit on 23 May 1988 after three days climbing. The route had already been reconnoitred as far as the headwall.
First ascent of mountain	South-East Face of Main Summit climbed 22-23 October 1992, by Marko Prezelj & Andrej Stremfelj (Slovenia). 2000m ice climb, mainly 50° to 60°, but steepening to a 75° runnel through the black rockband at c.6400m.
Height of b/c	4585m, at Palbugthang on grassy meadows 3km from the snout of the Drogpa Nagtsang Glacier.
Roadhead	As far south as trucks can travel on the very rough track south from Tingri. In the summer and autumn it may be possible to drive all the way to Changbujiang; in spring one has to cross the Fusi La on foot.
Length of walk-in	8-9 days with the crossing of the Fusi La. 5-6 days from Changbujiang.
Season	Menlungtse seems to get more than its fair share of bad weather in the spring. Autumn probably gives a better chance of fine conditions.
Permission	China-Tibet Mountaineering Association, Lhasa or through an agent.
Success rate	Four expeditions up to 1995 have each taken a different route. Two of them were successful.
Bibliography	Apart form the usual journal reports, the two British expeditions are documented in Chris Bonington's *Mountaineer* (Diadem/Sierra Club, 1989) and the West Face route is described in Andy Fanshawe's *Coming Through* (Hodder & Stoughton, 1990). John Roskelley's *Last Days* (Stackpole Books/Hodder & Stoughton, 1992) takes a wry look at the yeti-hunting business and the horrendous conditions on the South-East Ridge.

(*Left*) Alan Hinkes following one of the crux pitches through the dramatic granite headwall. (*Andy Fanshawe*)
(*Far left*) The West Face of Menlungtse is on the extreme left. The 1988 route broke in from the left along the obvious glacier terrace, then climbed diagonally right up the steep icefield, breaking through the final rockband near its centre, before following the final ridge right to the obvious West Summit. (*Andy Fanshawe*)

SHISHAPANGMA 8046m

South-West Face

Shishapangma is the highest peak entirely in Chinese territory, yet, strangely, it is the nearest eight-thousander to Kathmandu, the capital of Nepal, and the only one visible from the town itself. It was the last of the fourteen to be climbed, a result of travel restrictions imposed in Tibet during the 'fifties. On the first ascent in 1964, ten Chinese climbers led by Hsu Ching reached the summit by the North-West Face and North Ridge. This may seem a large summit team, until you consider that there were 206 expedition members in all, including scientists and base camp staff!

Doors were not opened to non-Chinese parties until 1980 but in that year and 1981 another five ascents were completed, all of them following more or less the original route. It remains a popular expedition, with a high success rate, up what is probably the easiest eight-thousander.

The Tibetan name Shishapangma translates as 'the range (*shisha*) above the grassy plain', which is exactly how it looks when approached from the north. Part of this peak's attraction is its accessibility: it is possible to drive with jeeps and lorries to base camp at 5000m and from there yaks can be used to ferry loads right up to 5800m.

Cho Oyu, a few hours' drive south of Tingri, is similarly convenient and for this reason many expeditions to Tibet choose to climb both of these mountains in the same season. Once acclimatised on Cho Oyu, it is not unknown to spend less than a week on Shishapangma and still manage an ascent.

The South Face is steep and not quite so accessible, though by most peaks' standards the approach is short and kind. Travelling from Friendship Bridge on the Nepalese frontier, Nyalam is the first settlement on the Tibetan plateau that one reaches after a five-hour drive. It is from this dreary, dusty village, reminiscent of Spaghetti Westerns, that one starts the three-day walk up the Nyanang Phu Chu. The valley leads to a grassy base camp site at the far end of a boulder-strewn plateau above the north bank of the Nyanang Phu Glacier and directly opposite Pemthang Karpo Ri (6830m), one of the fine peaks on the Nepalese frontier. One advantage of climbing on this side of the mountain is that, instead of driving straight to 5000m, one starts walking in from around 3800m with a better chance to acclimatise.

This was the approach followed on the sixth ascent of Shishapangma in 1982. The party organised by Nick Prescott was the first to climb the mountain in pure alpine-style, tackling a face which had only before been glimpsed from across the frontier, in Langtang. Before setting foot on Shishapangma the three lead climbers, Doug Scott, Alex MacIntyre and Roger Baxter-Jones, made the first ascent over three days of Pungpa Ri, 7445m by its South-West Couloir and Ridge (45° ice and grade IV), cannily acclimatising and getting a close look at their projected descent route from Shishapangma. That was in mid-May. Then on the 28th, after three bivouacs on the South Face, they reached the summit of Shishapangma.

Roger Baxter-Jones and Alex MacIntyre nearing the top of the Peapod couloir on the first ascent of Shishapangma's South Face in 1982. In the background are the Langtang peaks on the Nepal/Tibet frontier. (*Doug Scott*)

(*Far left*) The old village of Nyalam, start of the walk-in to the East and South Faces of Shishapangma. (*Stephen Venables*)

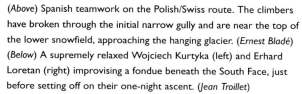

(*Above*) Spanish teamwork on the Polish/Swiss route. The climbers have broken through the initial narrow gully and are near the top of the lower snowfield, approaching the hanging glacier. (*Ernest Bladé*)
(*Below*) A supremely relaxed Wojciech Kurtyka (left) and Erhard Loretan (right) improvising a fondue beneath the South Face, just before setting off on their one-night ascent. (*Jean Troillet*)

Spanish climber, Areceli Segarra, approaching the South Face of Shishapangma in 1992, to repeat the Polish/Swiss route which ascends from behind her rucksack to the hanging glacier, then traverses left into the deep-cut couloir. The 1982 British route takes the extreme right couloir. The 1990 Slovenian route takes the harder buttress in the middle. (*Ferran Latorre*)

Their route takes a fairly direct line to reach a broad snowy couloir which emerges just east of the summit. For the most part on snow and ice, there is one section of quite hard mixed (Scottish 4) to reach the base of the final 'Peapod'. Although the overall angle of the face is not as steep as the team had expected, their route was quite sustained, with few obvious bivouac sites.

For twenty-eight-year-old MacIntyre, who died later that year descending the South Face of Annapurna, this route and his book co-authored with Doug Scott, *The Shishapangma Expedition*, will serve as a fitting memorial. He was a brilliant alpinist with a sharp mind, whose ideas and inventiveness led and inspired others — a cult-figure of modern alpinism.

MacIntyre achieved some of his greatest climbs,

such as the South Face of Changabang and the East Face of Dhauligiri, with the equally single-minded Pole, Wojciech Kurtyka, and it was Kurtyka who eight years later pioneered another route on the South Face of Shishapangma. The line he completed with the Swiss pair Jean Troillet and Erhard Loretan takes a similar gully to the Peapod on the 1982 route but on the left (west) side of the Main Summit. Entirely on snow and ice, never steeper than 55°, this route provides the shortest and quickest climb to the summit of any eight-thousander. The line heads for the col between the

▲

West and Central Summits, but it is best to break out right 200m beneath the col, taking a subsidiary couloir direct to the Central Summit. On the first ascent Loretan and Troillet, in characteristic fashion, climbed the face at night carrying no bivouac equipment and emerging on the summit ridge at dawn. Kurtyka also carried no equipment but was slower and decided to bivouac on the descent at 7800m. The night was 'pleasantly warm'.

'For a busy man or woman,' wrote Kurtyka, summing up the accessibility of this route, 'it is dream ground to flash an 8000m peak.' But, he added, does a busy man or woman have the necessary confidence and stamina for that kind of high-altitude exercise? The Polish/Swiss Shishapangma climb was completed just two weeks after the same trio had flashed their new route on Cho Oyu.

There is a third, harder, line on this face, pioneered in 1989 by one of the giants of Himalayan climbing, Andrej Stremfelj, and his fellow Slovenian Pavle Kozjek. This route, rated IV/V mixed and up to 65° on ice, weaves a beautiful varied line up the buttress between the two central gully lines and took three days on the first ascent.

The easiest descent from Shishapangma is the normal route to the north. However, most people will want to return to the southern base camp. Kurtyka, Loretan and Troillet reversed their route on the South Face. Other parties have chosen the original British descent, coming down the South-East Ridge to the 7300m col between Shishapangma and Pungpa Ri. This ridge has some knife-edged sections and needs care. From the col there remains a long, tiring descent of huge 45° snow/ice slopes, trending diagonally west to avoid big sérac barriers.

Shishapangma's South Face is a fine, sporting alter-

SUMMARY STATISTICS AND INFORMATION

Mountain	Shishapangma
Height	8046m
Location	Langtang Himal, Tibet.
Routes	South Face. Three parallel lines, each with 2200m of ascent on a 50° face. The 1990 route is on snow and ice throughout, whilst the 1982 and 1989 routes offer varying degrees of mixed ground.
First ascent of mountain	Summit reached 2 May 1964, by a Chinese party led by Hsu Ching.
First ascent of routes	25-28 May 1982 by Alex MacIntyre, Roger Baxter-Jones & Doug Scott (UK); 17-19 October 1989 by Pavle Kozjek & Andrej Stremfelj (Slov); 2 October 1990 by Wojciech Kurtyka (Pol), Jean Troillet & Erhard Loretan (Swiss).
Height of b/c	5400m, above the north bank of the Nyanang Phu Glacier opposite Pemthang Karpo Ri, 6830m.
Roadhead	Nyalam, 3800m.
Length of walk-in	Approximately 20km, 2-3 days.
Season	May or October, as in Nepal, appear to be the best months. In May the face will be drier and probably more prone to stonefall.
Permission	China-Tibet Mountaineering Association, Lhasa.
Success rate	Quite high.
Bibliography	*The Shishapangma Expedition* (Granada, 1984) is Scott's and MacIntyre's account of the first ascent of the face. Other (illustrated) references appear in *AAJ* 1990, pp 306-7; *AAJ* 1983, pp 35-9; *AAJ* 1991, pp 14-18; and *Mountain* 137. For accounts of attempts on the unclimbed East Face, see *AAJ* 1988 and *AJ* 1988/90.

native to the normal route from the north. The British route is an important landmark in Himalayan alpine-style history. The Swiss/Polish route is the easiest, whilst the Slovenian line offers perhaps the most technical and absorbing mountaineering adventure.

Luke Hughes warming up on a cold October morning at 7300m after making the second ascent of Pungpa Ri (7445m), off picture right. Behind is the South-East Ridge of Shishapangma, the usual descent route after climbing the South Face. From the col immediately behind the tent it is possible to drop back down the south side (left) to regain the foot of the face. (*Stephen Venables*)

John Longmuir and team at 7000m on the North-West Ridge of Cho Oyu, with Camp 2 in the ice barrier just beneath them. On the left horizon are the peaks of the Jugal and Langtang Himal, dominated by the unclimbed East Face of Shishapangma. (*Roger Mear*)

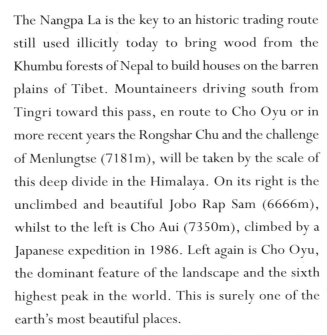

CHO OYU 8201m

North-West Ridge

The Nangpa La is the key to an historic trading route still used illicitly today to bring wood from the Khumbu forests of Nepal to build houses on the barren plains of Tibet. Mountaineers driving south from Tingri toward this pass, en route to Cho Oyu or in more recent years the Rongshar Chu and the challenge of Menlungtse (7181m), will be taken by the scale of this deep divide in the Himalaya. On its right is the unclimbed and beautiful Jobo Rap Sam (6666m), whilst to the left is Cho Aui (7350m), climbed by a Japanese expedition in 1986. Left again is Cho Oyu, the dominant feature of the landscape and the sixth highest peak in the world. This is surely one of the earth's most beautiful places.

More parties climb Cho Oyu from Tibet than Nepal. Access is much simpler, it being possible to drive to within a day of base camp, though this may of course present its own acclimatisation problems. Also 1982 border changes now mean that one's passage on to the lower slopes of the classic North-West Ridge, line of the first ascent, is unreasonably difficult from the south (assuming that one doesn't poach across the Nangpa La and then return south on the Gyabrag Glacier as Herbert Tichy and party did in 1954). Furthermore, many more routes have been opened on the Tibetan side of the peak, three of which are excellent technical climbs: the 2000m high North Face,

climbed by a Slovenian team in 1988; the Polish West Ridge (1986); and the West Face.

The West Face – first climbed in 1990 by that unstoppable team of Kurtyka, Troillet and Loretan, in just two days, including a descent of the North-West Ridge – is particularly attractive for the alpine climber. From the base of the face at about 6200m a broad, 45° couloir carries one high on to the face before a sustained section of mixed climbing (IV) on rock steps, punctuated by steep (60°) snowfields between 7000-7800m, leads one to a ramp line running rightward to the unclimbed South-West Ridge at 8100m. The summit plateau is met very near to its highest point which may be a blessing, though it must still be crossed in order to reach the start of the descent of the original route.

The Polish (West) Ridge that forms the left side of this face is easier, being mostly on steep snow and ice (up to 50°) though there is one 200m section of rock (III) to reach 7200m where it is possible to traverse on to the Tichy route. To stay on the ridge crest (the slopes of the original route hereabouts may be prone to avalanche in very snowy conditions) would mean joining this route higher up, nearer 7800m.

Being relatively safe, it will be interesting to witness the popularity of the West Ridge in coming years. To date it has been repeated only once, in the winter of 1989 by Carlos Buhler (US) and Martin Zabaleta (Spa) who comment favourably on the quality of the climbing.

At present, however, the original route is certainly the most popular. Herbert Tichy who led the first ascent was an exemplar of lightweight climbing and his story has a particular poignancy measured against modern trends of lightweight expeditioning. Philosopher and traveller first, mountaineer second, his aim was not solely to climb the peak, but to climb it specifically with a small team of friends. However, as the expedition progressed he became more and

more consumed by the summit, eventually risking the loss, at very least, of his already frostbitten fingers.

'As nearly all religions strive to take away the fear of death and make it seem acceptable, I may claim to have had a genuine religious experience,' he wrote. Others might simply call it anoxia and by most rational criteria his single-minded drive for the summit was foolhardy. However, as Diemberger once remarked, 'Everyone has the right once in his life to do something a little crazy.' Tichy got away with it, sustaining only minor permanent

injuries to his fingers. He attributed his remarkable healing not to religion but to the copious quantities of chang and rakshi that he drank on the way home.

Tichy preferred the company of his Sherpa friends, in particular Pasang Dawa Lama who had been almost to the summit of K2 with Wiessner in 1939, to other Austrians and accordingly there were just three Westerners on the expedition, one of whom had no designs on the summit. The Sherpas meanwhile were not employed in their traditional servant role but as

Erhard Loretan, a tiny speck, follows fresh tracks down the normal route below the ice barrier, having the previous day completed a lightning first ascent of the West Face with Kurtyka and Troillet. (*Wojciech Kurtyka*)

equal members of the climbing team and it was Pasang who really made the ascent possible. In the first push he led the route through the critical ice barrier at about 6800m; later, when news of a Swiss team also intent on Cho Oyu reached Pasang while he was travelling back from Namche Bazar with more supplies, he produced a super-human effort to ensure success. In three days he covered 50km and gained 4000m of altitude to rejoin Tichy and Sepp Jochler on the mountain and then drive them both on to the summit.

There will normally be fixed ropes in situ. From 7000m easy-angled snow trending leftwards leads to a steepening, in some years rocky, which is taken to gain access to final long snowslopes leading on to the rather featureless summit plateau. Only when the breathtaking view into the Khumbu is opened up and the Nangpa La trading route comes into sight, will climbers know they have reached the summit and be truly satisfied.

We cannot leave Cho Oyu without mention of one

SUMMARY STATISTICS AND INFORMATION

Mountain	Cho Oyu
Height	8201m
Location	Mahalungur Himal, Khumbu subsection, Tibet.
Route	North-West Ridge. 2200m of ascent on snow with a short section on steep ice and possible rock.
First ascent of mountain	Summit reached 19 October 1954 (the only eight-thousander to have its first ascent in the autumn) by Herbert Tichy & Sepp Jochler (Aus), Pasang Dawa Lama (Nepal).
First ascent of route	As above.
Height of b/c	5600m, above the north bank of the Gyabrag Glacier.
Roadhead	As far south from Tingri as trucks can travel, usually to about 4350m. In the post-monsoon period it should be possible to drive right up to 4800m, below the Fusi La.
Length of walk-in	Approximately 10km, 1 day.
Season	May/June or September/October.
Permission	China-Tibet Mountaineering Association, Lhasa.
Success rate	High. Over 50 per cent of expeditions visiting all routes on Cho Oyu succeed in reaching the top; on the North-West Ridge the success rate is higher. Over 400 people had reached the top by the end of 1993.
Bibliography	*Cho Oyu* by Herbert Tichy (Methuen, 1957) tells the story of the first ascent. There is an excellent condensed account of the 1954 expedition in Chris Bonington's *Quest for Adventure* (Hodder & Stoughton, 1981). For details of other routes see *AAJ* 1987 for the West Ridge, *AAJ* 1989 for the North Face, *AAJ* 1990 for the West Ridge in winter, *AAJ* 1991 for the West Face, *AAJ* 1986 and *Mountain* 116 (Zawada interview) for the South-East Face.

The massive bulk of Cho Oyu (left of centre) from near the Nangpa La. The North-West Ridge route follows the big snow scoop on the right. The shapely peak on the extreme right is Cho Aui (7350m). It was first climbed in 1986 by a Himalayan Association of Japan expedition, which followed the North-West Ridge on the right. (*Andy Fanshawe*)

On the whole route one small section of fixed rope was employed, through the icefall, and no supplementary oxygen carried. The expedition was remarkable and Pasang's achievement was comparable with Hermann Buhl's on Nanga Parbat the previous year.

The North-West Ridge is not technically hard but it is a long route, finishing well above 8000m. From the Gyabrag Glacier it ascends an easy moraine and rocky ridge to Pt 6446m (many climbers do this part of the route in lightweight training shoes). Next a long easy snow ridge is followed to the ice barrier. Conditions change but in recent years this has been negotiated by way of a hole left by a collapsed sérac.

more route, the colossal South-East Face in Nepal. The ascent of this face in the winter of 1985 was one of the great heroic feats of modern Polish mountaineering. This was no alpine-style dash, for the line up the huge central spur is long and intricate, with some very hard climbing on rock and ice. Faced with those difficulties and the extreme winter conditions on an 8000m peak, Andrzej Zawada led a concerted team effort with fixed ropes. Even with that kind of support, the second summit team of Zygmunt Heinrich and Jerzy Kukuczka ended up bivouacking in the open, high on the face, when they failed to find Camp 5 at the end of the short winter day.

Compared to the South-East Face in winter, the

shorter routes on the north side of Cho Oyu are all quite gentle propositions. The comparative ease of the North-West Ridge is well illustrated by statistics: by the end of 1993 over 400 people had reached the summit by this route. However, people do die here. Cho Oyu is a big mountain and anyone caught on its dome-like summit plateau in a storm could be hard pushed to find his way back down.

EVEREST 8848m

North Face Direct

It is over forty years since the first ascent of Everest, the world's highest mountain. Many, if pressed, would say that its summit is the one place they would most like to reach. Even those who scorn peak baggers cannot fail to understand its draw. So strong is it that some mountaineers are fully prepared to litter the mountain and its base camp sites with packaging, discarded tins of food, glass, ropes, oxygen cylinders and tents that will never decay – only rip in the wind or lie frosted, each year buried in snow and stripped again by winter winds.

Such desecration and disregard for Everest was sadly inevitable. In order to 'conquer' this peak, man has felt moved to disarm it, trussing it up in tens of kilometres of fixed rope. But many now consider such a siege style outdated and unacceptable. The emphasis among modern mountaineers, visiting peaks of any size, is not to reduce the mountain in this way but instead to raise themselves and climb it in a lightweight, environmentally sensitive manner.

Everest has witnessed every phase of the development of Himalayan mountaineering. That is not remarkable, but the scale of the achievements is. Its history is known well enough: seven determined efforts in the 'twenties and 'thirties reaching over 8500m on the North Ridge with a minimum of technological aids; the first proven ascent in 1953 from Nepal; the stupendous traverse by Tom Hornbein and

The Rongbuk Monastery, gateway for Everest expeditions dating back to 1921, is slowly recovering from the ravages of the Cultural Revolution. Here lamas help Sherpa Pasang Norbu make prayer flags to protect base camp. (*Ed Webster*)

(*Right*) Evening light floods the great sweep of Everest's North Face, photographed from the West Shoulder during an attempt on the West Ridge Direct in May 1985. In these spring conditions much of the rock is bare and the Japanese Couloir is only just discernible as a thin white line slanting through the lower rocks. Above the central snowfield, the Hornbein Couloir is more obvious – a deep cleft emerging just right of the summit. (*Ed Webster*)

Willi Unsoeld ten years later; the ascent of the South-West Face in 1975; the first ascent without oxygen assistance in 1978 by Peter Habeler and Reinhold Messner. Two years later Messner succeeded in making a solo ascent from the north in just three days, showing that a rapid time was possible if one could catch the correct conditions. Messner chose a calm spell at the end of the monsoon when the mountain had a heavy snow cover which had consolidated just enough to allow rapid progress. He took the pre-war route to 7800m and then made a long traverse across the North Face (below the level of the pre-war attempts) to gain the Great Couloir and thence the final summit pyramid. Earlier in the year a Japanese party had forced a route (using extensive fixed rope) directly up the right-hand side of the North Face to link up with the Hornbein Couloir. After the Messner ascent other climbs – notably the 1984 Australian ascent of 'White Limbo' – confirmed that by catching good snow conditions it was possible to reach the summit quickly and this point was powerfully confirmed by a rapid ascent of the face in 1986 by two of the world's greatest exponents of the art of extreme climbing in the Himalaya. This ascent more than any other in this book, and appropriately enough on the world's highest peak, expresses alpine-style in its most natural and powerful form.

The story, by its own design, is simple. Erhard Loretan and Jean Troillet (Swiss) with Pierre Béghin (French) crossed Tibet and approached the North Face of Everest in the monsoon season of 1986. They made advance base at 5850m on the Rongbuk Glacier and spent five weeks acclimatising, with only two forays to 6500m on neighbouring peaks. Then at 10 pm on 28 August they left advance base for the foot of the

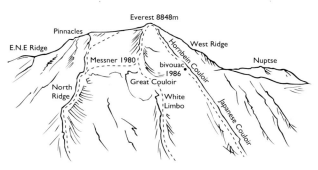

Japanese Couloir. They climbed through the night and by 11 am reached 7800m. Here they stopped, to spend the next ten hours of warm daylight relaxing and melting snow for drinks. At 9 pm they set off again, but at 8000m Béghin turned back. Unable to locate the snowcave where he had left his sleeping bag, he was forced to spend the night in the open, luckily with-

(*Above*) In 1986 Pierre Béghin felt too cold and tired to keep up with Loretan and Troillet. He returned to the North Face in 1987, when he took this shot of his Spanish companion, Luis Barcenas, starting up the Hornbein Couloir. The pair had to abandon the climb at 8700m. (*Pierre Béghin*)

(*Above right*) A bird's view of Everest's North Face, photographed from the summit of Changtse on the brilliant morning of 28 August 1986, the day before Loretan and Troillet started their remarkable ascent and speed descent of the North Face Direct. This picture contrasts radically with the spring photo on the previous page, showing how snow-plastered the face is in late summer. It was in similar conditions that Messner made his 1980 solo ascent and Tim Macartney-Snape's 1984 Australian expedition climbed White Limbo, the direct approach to the Great Couloir. (*Ed Webster*)

(*Far right*) Steve Bell fights his way up a tangle of old ropes on the last difficult step in the Hornbein Couloir before the angle eases off at 8550m. This picture was taken in spring, very different from the snow-smothered conditions of autumn when Loretan and Troillet made their historic ascent and record glissading descent. (*Andy Hughes*)

out ill effects. Loretan and Troillet continued up the Hornbein Couloir and at 8400m, after four hours climbing, they could go no further in the dark and were forced to wait for dawn. At 4 am they were again on the move and reached the summit at 1 pm. They lounged here for ninety minutes in the warmest part of the day. Finding the snow conditions perfect, they descended the entire face by sitting glissade in just five

hours – three hours to the snowhole where Béghin was resting and a further two hours to the foot of the face! Away from advance base for less than two days, they had been to the roof of the world and back.

They had climbed unroped, mainly at night. They took no tents, ropes or harnesses. They did not use bottled oxygen and they carried only lightweight sleeping bags and minimal food rations. Above 7800m they did not even carry a rucksack. It was, as Kurtyka quipped, 'night naked-ness'. They took nothing and left nothing.

Such pure expression of control on the world's premier peak requires more than a little fitness and confidence. It demands a full understanding of nature and of one's own physiology and psychology. It is interesting to note they only acclimatised to 6500m before

The summit of Everest on a magical October evening in 1984, showing the upper part of the Hornbein Couloir cutting through the Yellow Band. Two minuscule red figures can just be seen, immediately to the right and about 1 cm below the summit – Tim Macartney-Snape and Greg Mortimer completing their oxygenless ascent of White Limbo. (*Colin Monteath/Mountain Camera*)

starting their bold ascent and that they were then in the so-called 'death zone' for just sixteen hours.

This ascent of Everest, one of the very few in pure alpine-style, stands alongside Messner's solo ascent for its careful planning and confident execution. Both carried a bare minimum of weight in order to move fast and so limit the amount of time at high altitude. Messner, however, did carry full bivouac equipment, including a small tent. His climb was longer and, taking

Jean Troillet, back in Beijing after his historic ascent with Loretan, receives his official Everest certificate from the Chinese Mountaineering Association. (*Ed Webster*)

everything into account, probably more difficult.

The evening Troillet and Loretan descended Béghin made his attempt, but at 8300m, weakened by his night in the open, he decided that the task was too great and returned to the snowhole. At dawn he descended, taking two hours to reach the Rongbuk Glacier. An hour later a huge powder snow avalanche swept the entire couloir.

Béghin returned to the face in 1987 with a Spanish expedition. They pushed a new variation up the left

side of the Japanese Couloir and in a spirited effort Béghin and Luis Barcenas continued up the Hornbein Couloir and reached the West Ridge at 8700m before heavy snow stopped them.

All these ascents were made in August or early September, in short spells of settled weather at the end of the monsoon season. It is usually warmer at this time of year and there is more snow, too, which in good condition reduces the technical difficulty of the climbing and the risk of stonefall. The North Ridge is notoriously exposed to winds but, further right on the face in the lee of the West Ridge, the Loretan/Troillet route is usually more sheltered.

Our topo shows the line of Loretan and Troillet's route, the most direct on Everest. It is a hybrid of two other climbs. Up to 7800m the route follows the line of a wide curving gully cutting vaguely through two rockbands at c.6900m and c.7400m. This gully line was used by the Japanese in 1980, but they reached it by a rising traverse from the left side of the face to join the gully at the first rockband, whereas in 1986 Béghin, Loretan and Troillet climbed more or less directly up its right side. Above 7800 metres the route follows the Hornbein Couloir, as taken by the Americans in 1963. At its top, the route moves right to gain the West Ridge at around 8700 metres.

Between the bergschrund and the first band, the angle of the slope varies between 50° and 70°; above that the angle is kinder, averaging about 45° until it

Mountain	Everest: Sagarmatha (Nep)/Chomolungma (Tib).
Height	8848m
Location	Mahalangur Himal, Khumbu Subsection, East Nepal/Tibet.
Route	North Face (Loretan/Troillet variant)) 2600m of ascent from bergschrund, mostly on steep snow fields (in places up to 70°) but with some mixed ground (IV) possible in places.
First ascent of mountain	29 May 1953, by Edmund Hillary (NZ) and Sherpa Tenzing Norgay (India) as members of the British expedition led by John Hunt.
First ascent of route	Hornbein Couloir – Tom Hornbein & Willi Unsoeld (USA), May 1963. Japanese Couloir/Hornbein Couloir – Takashi Ozaki & Tsuneo Shigehiro (Jap), 10 May 1980.
First alpine-style ascent of route	By lower variant – Erhard Loretan & Jean Troillet (Swiss), 29-30 August 1986.
Height of b/c	5500 metres, near the junction of the East and Central Rongbuk Glaciers.
Roadhead	From Shegar on the Friendship Highway it is possible to take a truck to within a day's walk of base camp.
Season	Both the Japanese and Hornbein couloirs are technically easier after the monsoon snowfall. Comparatively warm weather in late August also aided the Loretan/Troillet ascent. However, they were lucky to find the right combination of consolidated snow and clear weather.
Permission	Chinese Mountaineering Association, Beijing.
Success Rate	This route has been climbed only once in alpine-style against a background of several serious attempts.
Bibliography	For a full Everest bibliography, see Walt Unsworth's definitive history – *Everest* (Oxford Illustrated Press, 1992). For details of this route, *AAJ* 1981 describes the 1980 Japanese ascent, *AAJ* 1987 the 1986 ascent and *AAJ* 1988 the 1987 Spanish/Béghin variation attempt. See also Wojciech Kurtyka's article 'The Art of Suffering' in *Mountain* 121.

steepens again in the Hornbein Couloir. In spring there are several awkward rock pitches in the couloir, but after the monsoon it is usually banked up with snow, leaving just two rock pitches at the top before the exit on to the West Ridge.

KWANGDE LHO 6187m

North Face

In the Gaurishankar chapter we touched briefly on the Rolwaling valley. In recent years this beautiful area has been re-opened to foreigners and has become quite a popular trek. Climbing south-east up the valley from Beding one passes the trekking peaks of Ramdung and Parchamo. The latter, harder, peak overlooks the Tesi Lapcha, the glacier pass linking Rolwaling to the famous Khumbu valley. For those prepared to risk the stonefall danger on the Rolwaling side, this is a dramatic climax to a delightful journey.

Descending into Khumbu, one passes right beneath the tremendous north faces of Tengkang Poche and the Kwangde peaks, which have, since the first foreign visitors came here in 1949, become the instantly recognisable backdrop to a million photographs of Thyangboche. Tengkang Poche has never been open to climbers but the three summits of Kwangde were declared trekking peaks, with minimal bureaucratic restrictions, in the mid 'seventies. First off the mark to take advantage of their new status were British climbers Roger Everett and Lindsay Griffin, who set up camp in the Nangpa Dzangpo valley in October 1978, intent on climbing the prominent North-East Spur of Kwangde Shar which, seen from Namche, appears as an inverted Y. Everett and Griffin followed the left arm of the Y, but this section could be avoided by a little glacier to the east, which would

Lindsay Griffin climbing perfect granite on the first ascent of Kwangde Shar's North-East Spur in 1978. The Everest group is immediately behind him, while Ama Dablam and the distant pyramid of Makalu dominate the right side of the main Khumbu valley. (*Roger Everett*)

also give access to the main stem of the Y, where the real meat of the climbing starts. In October 1978 there was a lot of unconsolidated powder snow overlaying the fine grey granite, giving testing mixed climbing. In a drier autumn or in spring, there would probably be more rock climbing. Either way, it is a fine route, culminating in a steep headwall which arrives abruptly

on the dramatic spiked summit. The best descent is down the original German route on the South Face into the rarely visited Lumding valley.

The North-East Spur of Kwangde Shar is a classic traditional line in a wonderful setting, facing out to Everest, Ama Dablam and Makalu. Immediately next door, with the same views but altogether more seri-

KWANGDE

Nupla 5886   Shar 6093   Lho 6187   Nup 6035   Tengkang Poche 6499   Panayo Tippa 6696

Nangpa Dzangpo valley

1. Griffin/Everett   1978
2. Lowe/Breashears   1982
3. Kearney   1989

ous climbing, is the dark, smooth North Face of Kwangde Lho. In summer it may be unclimbable without recourse to drastic bolting, but in the late autumn of 1982 a continuous line of ice runnels and smears enabled Americans David Breashears and Jeff Lowe to push a very hard route up the 1300m face. They

access to the rest of the face. There had been no riddle in the route-finding: ice was the quickest, easiest – and only – path. It was pure pleasure watching Jeff weave his way through the weaknesses of the pitch… His confidence and subtle technique obscured the fact that the ice was nearly vertical at 5600m. This was Jeff's

The magnificent new monastery at Thyangboche, rebuilt after it was destroyed by fire, with the famous backdrop of the Kwangde peaks to the south. (*Bill O'Connor*)

(*Right*) Jeff Lowe in his element, leading the crux pitch through the central rockband on Kwangde Lho's North Face in December 1982. The photo shows clearly the ephemeral nature of this route which depends on a continuous line of ice smears. (*David Breashears*)

started on 28 November, three days before the opening of the official winter season, following the second from the left of four thin ice ribbons which streak the lower wall. They spent five days on the face, with the crux halfway up, where a tenuous line of ice led rightward through the central rockband to snow and icefields above. Describing Lowe, the master ice craftsman, at work on this section, Breashears wrote in the *AAJ*: 'Jeff made a tremendous lead up a 160 foot pitch of water-ice over a rock band which barred

ideal – alpine-style over steep technical ground on a Himalayan north face in winter conditions.'

Since 1982 other hard climbs have been made on the Khumbu six-thousanders in late autumn and

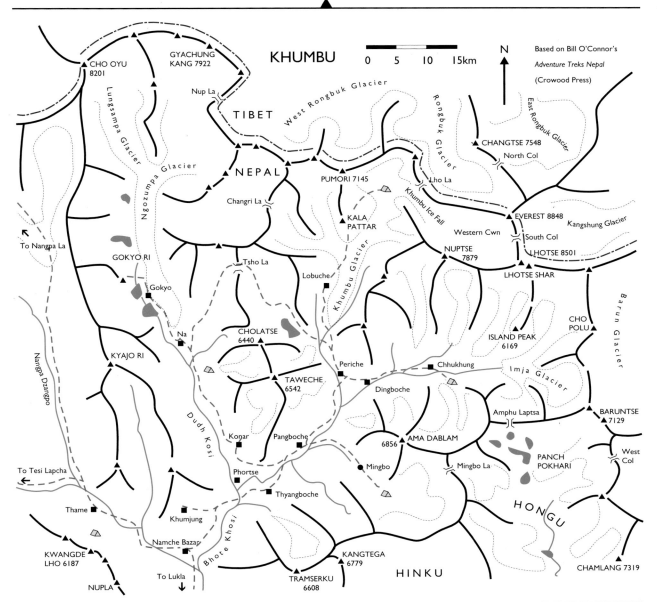

KHUMBU

Based on Bill O'Connor's
Adventure Treks Nepal
(Crowood Press)

0 5 10 15km

SUMMARY STATISTICS AND INFORMATION

Mountain	Kwangde Lho
Height	6187m
Location	Rolwaling Himal, Eastern Nepal.
Route	North Face. 1350m of sustained ice climbing. The average angle of the face is 65°, with many sections approaching vertical. Bivouac ledges virtually non-existent, so hammocks or portaledges are very useful.
First ascent of mountain	Summit reached from South Ridge 17 October 1975, by Lhakpa Tenzing, Sonam Gyalzen, Shambhu Tamang & Sonam Hisi (Nepal).
First ascent of route	18 November-1 December 1982 by David Breashears & Jeff Lowe (USA).
Height of b/c	c.3800m near the village of Hongu, in the Nangpa Dzangpo valley.
Roadhead	Jiri, 10 days trek to the south, but most people fly into Lukla, saving a week.
Length of walk-in	3 days from Lukla.
Season	Winter.
Permission	Ministry of Tourism, Kathmandu, via a trekking agency. All the Kwangde summits count as a single trekking peak, available on the same permit.
Success rate	The route has only been climbed once, but the face has been climbed by another line to the right. At least one party has arrived to find insufficient ice on the face.
Bibliography	The climb was described in an article by David Breashears in *AAJ* 1984. The best single source of information on the mountain is Bill O'Connor's *Trekking Peaks of Nepal* (Crowood, 1989).

winter, most notably perhaps, the Lowe/Roskelley route up the fearsome North-East Face of Taweche. November and December in particular give very cold, crystal clear weather, ideal for hard ice and mixed climbing. While the jet stream winds blast maliciously at anyone masochistic enough to attempt the highest peaks in winter, the lower summits usually remain calm. The Kwangde Lho North Face route is a good example of what can be done, although some strong parties have arrived to find insufficient ice. Conditions will inevitably vary on this ephemeral kind of route, but in a good year several similar lines may be possible; in 1985, for instance, Spanish climbers Angel Minoz and Juan Antonio Lorenzo climbed a new line to the right of the Breashears/Lowe route. In fact the whole Kwangde wall offers many possibilities, one of which, the North-East Buttress of Kwangde Nup, was soloed by Alan Kearney as a consolation prize, after he had to retreat from Cho Oyu in March 1989. Some consolation prize! And for those who prefer slightly gentler terrain, the routes on the south side – the South Ridge of Kwangde Lho in particular – are good climbs in their own right and they rise out of a remote and beautiful hanging valley which boasts one of the world's highest lakes. All of which proves that, even in the well-worked Everest region, adventure can be found just a stone's throw from the beaten track.

CHOLATSE 6440m

South-West Ridge / West Rib

In Sola Khumbu the mountaineer is spoilt for choice. Apart from the obvious challenge of Everest and its neighbouring giants, Lhotse and Nuptse, there is a wealth of smaller peaks, whose rock walls and elegant snow flutings and surreal ice sculptures offer every kind of technical interest at an altitude where the mountaineer is still in a fit state to enjoy his surroundings. Of all these peaks Cholatse was one of the last to be climbed, in the spring of 1982.

Peter Hackett led a very strong Anglo-American team, but had to drop out himself because of illness,

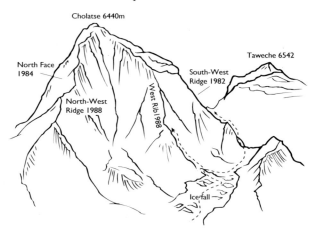

leaving Vernon Clevinger, Bill O'Connor, John Roskelley and Galen Rowell to push on up their chosen route, the South-West Ridge. They approached it from the west, siting their base camp on the meadows above the village of Na in the Gokyo valley. To gain the ridge from base camp they had to negotiate a vicious little

icefall, a miniature version of Everest's notorious Khumbu Icefall, which led tortuously up to an icy headwall and the col at the start of the ridge.

Once on the ridge they were safe from any avalanche threat but the climbing was, in Bill O'Connor's words, 'steep and technical on ice that

Cholatse and Taweche, two of Khumbu's most beautiful peaks, photographed from Gokyo Ri. (*Ed Webster*)
(*Left*) Ed Webster flying at a precarious bivouac site high on Cholatse's West Rib. Behind him are the Rolwaling peaks. The obvious skyline gap above his right hand is the Tesi Lapcha and the twin-summited peak above his left hand is Menlungtse. Down on the right are the rubble-strewn snout of the huge Ngozumpa Glacier and the much-visited turquoise Gokyo lakes. (*Glenn Dunmire*)

varied from hard blue green to brittle almost atmospheric soufflé'. On the first day they crossed a prominent rocky pinnacle and smaller pinnacles beyond it. Then on the second day, on the main knife-edge of the ridge, Roskelley, the undisputed ice master of the team, led pitch after pitch, frequently having to deviate on to the South-East Face to the right. The climax was a huge sérac barrier barring the way to the summit plateau, which gave two long pitches of very steep ice.

Beyond the plateau there were more awkward crevasses, delicate knife-edges of bottomless powder and a final spectacular pitch up the summit block of ice. It had been a long demanding day and the four had to bivouac in the open that night before making a series of abseils back down the ridge on the third day, completing a very rewarding expedition on 'the last virgin in the Khumbu'.

Like its neighbour Taweche, Cholatse presents

a formidable rocky northern aspect. On Taweche, the central plumb-line runnel of the North-East Face was climbed by Roskelley and Jeff Lowe in the winter of 1989.

Cholatse's North Face was climbed in April 1984 by Todd Bibler, Cathy Freer, Renny Jackson and Sandy Stewart, who spent seven days weaving a line up icy runnels through a maze of vertical granite walls. The face looks stunning, but the climbers' *AAJ* report on their first ascent was not encouraging: 'some hard rock, water ice, dangerous mushrooms and a lot of steep, rotten, unprotected snow-ice, where 'bollards were the only belay.' The route has not been repeated, but might perhaps be more amenable in winter.

Returning to the west side of Cholatse, in October 1988 Andy Selters and Thomas Walter climbed two new routes in the space of fourteen days. The West Face itself is a huge gully depression, threatened by

(*Above*) Whilst the high-altitude October winds bend the clouds over Everest and Lhotse, Cholatse's spectacular summit at 6440m is perfectly calm. (*Ed Webster*)
(*Far left*) Glenn Dunmire following the steep ice runnel during the first day on the West Rib. The icefall below is also the approach to the South-West Ridge. (*Ed Webster*)

batteries of séracs and scoured frequently by devastating avalanches. However, it is flanked on the left by the supremely elegant North-West Ridge. This was the second of the Selters/Walter routes; their first,

and easier line, climbed with Greg Collins, was the West Rib to the right of the suicidal gully. This route has now been repeated by three other parties, who confirm its quality as an interesting, safe and extremely scenic route up the mountain.

The approach is up the same icefall as for the South-West Ridge. From the top of the icefall, the route cuts left, underneath a prominent black outcrop, then back right and up icy runnels to the crest of the rib. Once on the rib, the steep crest leads to a long hard ice runnel, vertical in places, followed by some very exposed Alaska-style ridge climbing. The crux of the route is a 12m vertical icewall where the rib merges with the summit plateau, joining the South-West Ridge route.

Glenn Dunmire and Ed Webster, made the fourth ascent of the West Rib over three days in October 1993. While they were on the route, colleagues made the second ascent of the original South-West Ridge,

finding that in post-monsoon snowy conditions it was less extreme than the first ascensionists had suggested. Dunmire and Webster, taking advantage of their friends' tracks and anchors on the ridge, descended that route after completing the West Rib. The two parallel routes are quite similar in character. Apart from some danger on their common approach, they are both safe lines and combined they make an excellent traverse of this very appealing mountain.

SUMMARY STATISTICS AND INFORMATION

Mountain	Cholatse
Height	6440m
Location	Mahalangur Himal, Khumbu subsection, East Nepal.
Routes	South-West Ridge & West Rib. Steep snow and ice climbing with cruxes on vertical or overhanging sérac barriers. 900m of climbing (1500m from start of glacier).
First ascent of mountain	Summit reached 22 April from South-West Ridge, by Vernon Clevinger, John Roskelley, Galen Rowell (USA) & Bill O'Connor (UK).
First ascent of routes	South-West Ridge : as above. West Rib : Greg Collins, Andy Selters & Thomas Walter (USA) 7-10 October 1988.
Height of b/c	c.4700m above village of Na, immediately below Cholatse's West Face.
Roadhead	Jiri, 10 days trek to the south, but most people fly into Lukla, saving a week.
Length of walk-in	4 days from Lukla.
Season	Experience suggests that the colder, snowier post-monsoon conditions will suit both routes better than spring.
Permission	Ministry of Tourism, Kathmandu, via a trekking agency.
Success rate	Up to 1993, both attempts on the South-West Ridge had been successful. All four attempts on the West Rib, including one solo by Australian Adam Darragh, had been successful.
Bibliography	Articles on the first ascent appear in *AJ* 1983 (Bill O'Connor) and *AAJ* 1983 (Galen Rowell). The climb is also recorded in O'Connor's excellent guide *Adventure Treks Nepal* (Crowood, 1990).

AMA DABLAM 6856m

South-West Ridge / North-East Face

'A near perfect climb on a near perfect mountain', was how American Sue Giller described her ascent of the South-West Ridge of Ama Dablam in 1982; it is after all one of the true Himalayan classics. The South-West Ridge was the route of the mountain's first ascent in 1961 by an expedition led by Edmund Hillary, who had earlier declared it 'unclimbable', later modifying his view to 'fantastically difficult'. Today it is considered a much more reasonable proposition and is a justly popular route to Nepal's most shapely summit.

The main purpose of the 1961 expedition was in fact scientific, with the team spending ten months in Nepal at high altitude carrying out physiological tests to measure the relation between the negative effects of altitude and positive effects of acclimatisation. In May, after months living in the Silver Hut at 5700m on the Nare Glacier, Hillary's team made a serious attempt on Makalu, the world's fifth highest summit, without supplementary oxygen. American Tom Nevison, Sherpa Annullu and New Zealander Peter Mulgrew came within 120m of the top on the original 1955 French route before Mulgrew collapsed and was helped back down in an epic struggle, with Nevison also weakened by congestion on the lungs. Mulgrew developed appalling frostbite and later lost several fingers and both legs below the knees. In the desperate rout Hillary himself suffered a mild stroke

at 5800m and the British doctor Michael Ward collapsed into unconsciousness from oedema. No one actually died, but it was a close-run thing, illustrating graphically the deterioration brought on by extended stays above 5500m.

Makalu was a disaster but two months earlier, whilst still fit, the expedition had made a safe, controlled ascent of Ama Dablam. Michael Ward (UK), Wally Romanes and Michael Gill (NZ) and Barry Bishop (USA) took up the challenge. For three weeks they fixed around 500m on the ridge, hampered by very steep rock and ice climbing and the extreme cold. On 13 March they reached the summit – one of the few Himalayan summits to be climbed for the first time in winter – completing one of the most technical Himalayan climbs of its time, comparable to the difficulties met by Bonatti and Mauri in 1957 on Gasherbrum IV, though at lower altitude.

The name Ama Dablam means Mother's Charm Box. Ama refers to the arms of the mountain's long ridges protecting the Mingbo valley, like the enfolding arms of a mother. Dablam is the name of the double pendant containing pictures of the gods, worn by a Sherpa woman; it refers to two lumps of hanging glacier stuck on the upper part of the South-West Face. The upper hanging glacier is particularly prominent, giving this most photographed mountain much

of its distinctive character. However, it is also lethal, threatening the entire West Face. The 1961 team placed its final camp on a terrace formed by the lower piece of the Dablam, as have most of the increasing numbers of teams repeating the route since its second ascent in 1979. One consequence of all these ascents, many by commercial expeditions, is a yearly draping of fixed rope on the long horizontal section of the ridge, to facilitate what could otherwise be a very tricky retreat. This means that that elusive ideal, 'alpine-style', cannot strictly apply to this route, delightful as the climbing is. The good thing is that Sherpas usually come up from Pangboche in the autumn and remove the year's crop of rope for lucrative sales in the bazaar, leaving the ridge uncluttered for the first party up the next year.

For those who seek less popular routes, Ama Dablam has a wealth of other climbed and untried possibilities. In May 1979 Jeff Lowe made a remarkable solo ascent of the wildly fluted South Face,

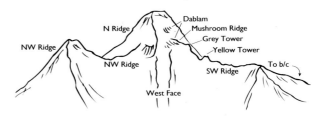

Ama Dablam's perfect symmetry seen from near Pangboche.
(*Brian Hall*)

emerging just beneath its vertical headwall on to the original route. That autumn a French expedition led by Louis Adoubert climbed the North Ridge, which

The surreal flutings of the South Face, soloed by Jeff Lowe in 1979. The Lagunak Ridge, first climbed by an Anglo-Spanish team in 1985, slants across from the right, while the original South-West Ridge is profiled on the left. (*Bill O'Connor*)

has since been repeated at least three times. It is a fine route, harder than the South-West Ridge, with rock at the start, and an extravagantly corniced snow ridge near the top. While the French were on the North Ridge, disaster struck a New Zealand team attempting the West Face, when a huge section of the upper hanging glacier crashed down, killing Ken Hyslop and

badly injuring Peter Hillary and his other two companions. This face would appear to be very dangerous but it has since been climbed, solo, by the well-known Czech climber Miri Smid in 1987.

Two routes were added in 1985. In November, Hooman Aprin and Randy Harrington (USA) with the Spaniard Martin Zabaleta climbed the South-East or

(*Left*) Dwarfed by the immense ice cliffs of the Dablam, a lone climber abseils back to the top camp from the summit icefield. The day this photo was taken a huge section of the Dablam peeled away, blasting the whole of the West Face. (*Alex McNab*)

(*Below*) A typical situation on the South-West Ridge, near the base of the Yellow Tower. Behind are the famous silhouettes of Kantega (left) and Tramserku. (*Bill O'Connor*)

Lagunak Ridge. Again, this ridge was slightly harder than the original route with the main difficulties on snow mushrooms and flutings. Where the ridge peters out against the South Face headwall, the team traversed left on to the top section of the South-West Ridge. The following month saw another accomplished alpine-style ascent, this time of the North-East Face. Tucked away at the back of the mountain, normally seen only by people climbing on Island Peak or Lhotse, or from high on Everest, this secret face was a formidable and potentially dangerous challenge.

The danger was minimised by tackling the face in winter, with daytime temperatures well below freezing; the technical difficulties were subdued by the very experienced team of Carlos Buhler and Michael Kennedy. They followed the prominent curving ice rib up the centre of the face. The difficulties were predominantly on ice over rocks, waterfall ice and unconsolidated snow. Describing the latter in the *AAJ*, Kennedy wrote: 'For a medium which most climbers

The East Face photographed by Michael Kennedy from Island Peak just before climbing the face with fellow American, Carlos Buhler, in December 1985. After crossing the dangerous gully from the right, their route followed the central curving snow-ice rib. Ten years later the route remains unrepeated, unlike the North Ridge on the right which has had several ascents. (*Michael Kennedy*)

regard as boring, snow displays an incredible variety of form, texture and consistency. And the techniques required, while perhaps not as elegant or as artistic as those on rock, are nevertheless complex and engaging in their own right. A good example is 5.10 snow. Usually found plastered over a hopefully-short band of steep rock, it generally has the consistency of wet sugar. Modern tools, for all their advantages on steep ice, are absolutely no use here. The preferred method is to punch the hands as far down into the snow as possible. The feet are then used to pack down a nebulous platform on which to stand.' This was definitely a route to sort out the sheep from the goats, but the deep snow meant that at least they could dig a comfortable ledge for each of the seven long, cold, winter bivouacs. Ten years on, the route has still not been repeated, but it will be in time, for the climbing is magnificent. For fast, competent ice climbers with the necessary mountaineering background, this could be the ideal direct route up Ama Dablam. However, it is probably only suitable as a winter climb and even then there will always be some risk crossing the huge right-hand couloir to get established on the ice rib.

The usual summer base camp on this side of the mountain is at about 5000m, near the foot of the North Ridge. Winter snow forced Buhler and Kennedy to camp lower down at the pasture of Shango. After their success on the North-East Face, they descended the normal route on the South-West Ridge, helped by some rope still in place

from the autumn. As this route becomes better known as a sure way off the mountain, it will probably be used increasingly by people descending from other lines.

The photo and topo on pages 168-9 show the main features of the South-West Ridge. Unlike most Himalayan routes it can be reached without setting foot on any glacier. Steepening slopes and scrambling on the south side lead to the main crest of the ridge at about 5800m. The ridge is then traversed horizontally for 500m with only 100m height gain. The climbing is mainly on rock, either on the crest or deviating just beneath, usually to the right, with difficulties from II to V. Above all, the climbing is enjoyable, with continuous interest on sound granite, culminating in a grade VI pitch up the Yellow Tower at the end of the horizontal section, where most parties place their second camp. Now, at last, one gains height. On the First Step of the Grey Tower there is more hard rock climbing with a grade VI overhanging crack. Steep snow and ice lead to the Second Step and above that is the critical Mushroom Ridge, forming a bridge from the lower ridge to the upper face. Camp 3 is normally sited on a broad terrace to the side of the Dablam.

The summit day is dramatic, with steep snow and ice climbing just right of the upper Dablam, leading on to the fluted snowfield above and so to one of the world's finest summits. Anyone who reaches this very special summit by the South-West Ridge can feel well pleased, for even this easiest route up the mountain is a difficult and committing enterprise. The other existing routes also have tremendous character and there are still major lines to be climbed, such as the fiercely steep North-West Face which has already been tried twice without success. Whatever route one attempts on Ama Dablam, the climbing, set right at the heart of Sola Khumbu, will always be inspiring.

Mountain	Ama Dablam
Height	6856m
Location	Mahalangar Himal, Khumbu subsection, East Nepal.
Routes	South-West Ridge: 1500m of climbing, at first on granite (up to UIAA VI) and later on snow with ice (c.50-60°) North-East Face: 1500m of climbing. A major ice climb, steep, with every consistency of snow and ice and some objective danger. Probably very dangerous outside the winter season.
First ascent of mountain	Summit reached 13 March 1961 by Michael Ward (UK), Barry Bishop (US), Wally Romanes & Michael Gill (NZ).
First ascent of routes	South-West Ridge: as above; North-East Face: 1-7 December 1985 by Carlos Buhler & Michael Kennedy (US).
Height of b/c	South-West Ridge: upper b/c when water is available at c. 5200m above Mingbo. North-East Face:5000m beside Ama Dablam Glacier, beyond Dingboche.
Roadhead	Jiri, 10 days trek to the south, but most people fly to Lukla, saving a week.
Length of walk-in	3 or 4 days from Lukla.
Season	South-West Ridge: better conditions appear to be in the dryer months - winter or pre-monsoon; the North-East Face is probably very dangerous outside the winter season.
Permission	Ministry of Tourism, Kathmandu.
Success rate	By 1992 there had been about 60 ascents of the South-West Ridge with about as many failures. The route is relatively safe. The North-East Face is unrepeated.
Bibliography	Numerous illustrated articles have appeared in the *AAJ* between 1980 and the present. The best were written by Tom Frost (1980) and Sue Giller (1983). Michael Kennedy wrote an article about the North-East Face in the *AAJ* 1987. Apart from journal entries, the 1961 expedition is recorded in Michael Ward's *In This Short Span* (Penguin, 1973) and Michael Gill's *Mountain Midsummer* (1969). There is also an interesting account of the expedition by Barry Bishop, in *National Geographic Magazine* (vol. 122, October 1962).

Carlos Buhler, with a lot of air beneath his feet, climbing through the elaborate sérac barrier near the top of the East Face. Across the basin of the Imja Glacier, Everest is partially screened by the huge South Face of Lhotse, one of the biggest mountain walls in the world and scene of numerous attempts during the 1980s, culminating in Tomo Cesen's controversial solo and the undisputed Russian ascent in 1990. (*Michael Kennedy*)

MAKALU 8463m

West Pillar

Dubbed the Walker Spur of the Himalaya, Makalu's West Pillar cuts a stupendous line to the summit of the fifth highest mountain in the world. Every mountaineer climbing high in the Khumbu is inspired by its bold architecture and this route is climbed more often than any other of comparable technical difficulty on an eight-thousander. One depressing result of this is the amount of fixed rope left in situ which following parties are inevitably tempted to use, if only as a guide to the route.

The mountain was first climbed in 1955 by Jean Franco's French expedition, following the route iden-tified from Everest two years earlier by Edmund Hillary – the Tibetan flank of the North-West Ridge, approached from the Makalu La. Sixteen years later, in the next great wave of 8000m exploration, it was another French expedition, led with equal verve and efficiency by Robert Paragot, that climbed the West Pillar, achieving what must have been the hardest tech-nical Himalayan climb of its era. The previous year, 1970, Makoto Hara's Japanese team had climbed the long South-East Ridge. The crux of the route was the formidable Black Gendarme at nearly 8000m, an obstacle which Doug Scott's 1980s attempts avoided by dropping down into the extraordinary hanging valley of the East Cwm. On the 1984 attempt with Jean Afanassieff and Stephen Sustad he came within about 150m of the summit, before making an exhaust-ing retreat when Afanassieff showed warnings of altitude sickness.

In contrast to the extended South-East Ridge, there are two really direct lines on Makalu. The South Face was first climbed in 1975 by a large Yugoslav expedition led by Ales Kunaver and repeated with a

(*Above*) Children watch another expedition caravan pass through. (*Andy Fanshawe*)
(*Left*) Chulilla, one of the villages in the Arun valley on the long and beautiful approach to Makalu. (*Ulric Jessop*)

direct start in 1989 by Pierre Béghin, who left his companions at 7000m to complete the face in a remarkable three-day solo. However, Makalu's true *direttissima*, and the subject of this chapter, is the West Pillar. The crux of the route is the great rock step between 7350-7750m, where Paragot's team of eleven climbers made their top camp in 1971, after two months hard rope-fixing. From here, on 23 May, Yannick Seigneur and Bernard Mellet, using oxygen,

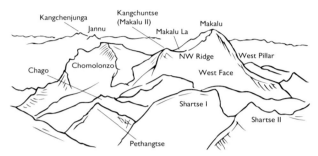

(Below) Makalu, the most architectural of all the eight-thousanders, photographed from near the summit of Everest, the view which convinced Edmund Hillary in 1953 that the easiest route on Makalu lay up the left flank of the North-West Ridge from the Makalu La. This was the route on which Jean Franco's French expeditions triumphed in 1955. Sixteen years later another French expedition took Himalayan climbing into a new realm with the ascent of the tremendous West Pillar on the right skyline. (*Kurt Diemberger*)

Chris Kopczynski, Kim Momb and Jim States traverse the Twins Arête on the initial section of Makalu's West Pillar. On the right is the South Face, scene of Pierre Béghin's extraordinary solo in 1989. The West Face on the left remains the quintessential 'Last Great Problem', with a headwall of smooth, bald granite starting at over 8000m. Some of the world's very best contenders have reached the upper icefield, but it remains to be seen whether anyone has the physiology for the sustained, icy cold difficulties on the headwall. (*John Roskelley*).

made their successful summit bid and were back at camp by 9.30 pm.

It has to be said that this route is supremely difficult to climb in genuine alpine-style and there have been precious few ascents in this fashion. In 1988 the Frenchman Marc Batard soloed the pillar in fourteen hours, an amazing feat, but he was basically jumaring back up the ropes fixed previously with his companions. More notably perhaps, in 1991, Erhard Loretan and Jean Troillet (Swiss) climbed the route on sight in a single push in just two days but they too were helped, this time by the ropes of a Spanish team on the Pillar.

Makalu dominates the head of the beautiful Barun valley which cuts south-east to the Arun, one of the Himalaya's great waterways. From the roadhead at Hille it is a twelve-day walk through glorious scenery, starting at very low altitude, but gradually gaining height to emerge on the far side of the Shipton La (4200m) on alpine meadows ringed by dozens of icy peaks. The best base for the West Pillar is a day further up the Upper Barun Glacier on the moraine of the Chago Glacier. From here the original route traces its way up the glacier, past the futuristic West Face, to the Makalu La, while directly opposite rises the West Pillar. Scree slopes around the base of the ridge lead to the French Camp 1 (5800m) where there are dozens of tent platforms and other relics of previous expeditions.

Many parties now start fixing ropes along the complex snow ridge (the Twins Arête) that leads over Pt 6420m to an exposed saddle at about 6400m, site of the French Camp 3. For the next 900m the route stays on the south (right) flank of the crest. The highlight, after about twelve pitches, is *la traverse terrible*, a wildly exposed ramp across the steepest portion of the South Face. Thereafter the route continues over mixed rock and ice slabs to reach the base of the rock step at 7350m.

Now the real fun starts – about eighteen pitches of extremely difficult climbing up to VI/A2. The line through a series of granite gullies, chimneys, grooves and off-widths will be marked in places by frayed relics of original French cable ladders and very near the top of the buttress a final loose-hanging ladder marks the crux off-width crack splitting a vertical wall. Another four pitches puts one beyond the last major difficulties.

A well-defined snowy ridge now leads to the junction with the South-East Ridge. Above that the ridge can be heavily corniced and a 25m rock barrier straddles the crest at 8500m. Further undulations over false summits lead to the pointed summit, which is probably, after K2, the most elusive of all the eight-thousanders.

Jim States on the lower section of the West Pillar. This was the first time that a small (four-man) team had tackled the pillar without oxygen but, like most subsequent parties, they decided to siege the route with fixed ropes. In the background, across the Barun Glacier, is Baruntse, with the South-East Ridge on the left. The elegant North-East Ridge, descends towards the camera from right of the summit, following the line between rock and snow. (*John Roskelley*)

Carles Valles tackling heavily iced granite at 7650m, near the top of the great rock step on the West Pillar. (*Manu Badiola*)

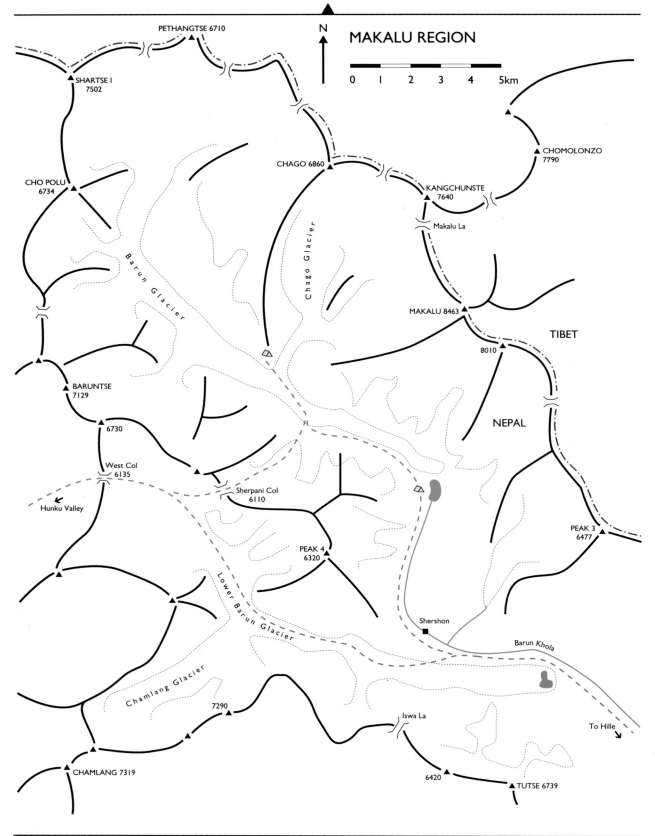

MAKALU REGION

N

0 1 2 3 4 5km

PETHANGTSE 6710

SHARTSE I
7502

CHO POLU
6734

CHAGO 6860

Chago Glacier

CHOMOLONZO
7790

KANGCHUNSTE
7640

Makalu La

Barun Glacier

MAKALU 8463

TIBET

8010

BARUNTSE
7129

NEPAL

6730

West Col
6135

Sherpani Col
6110

Hunku Valley

PEAK 3
6477

PEAK 4
6320

Lower Barun Glacier

Shershon

Barun Khola

Chamlang Glacier

7290

Iswa La

To Hille

CHAMLANG 7319

6420

TUTSE 6739

Mountain	Makalu
Height	8463m
Location	Mahalangur Himal, Makalu subsection, East Nepal.
Route	West Pillar. c.2800m of ascent on a perfectly defined pillar with rock climbing up to VI/A2 above 7500m.
First ascent of mountain	Summit reached 15 May 1955 by Jean Couzy & Lionel Terray (Fra) via the North-West Ridge.
First ascent of route	Summit reached 23 May 1971 by Yannick Seigneur and Bernard Mellet (Fra).
First alpine-style	Erhard Loretan and Jean Troillet (Swiss), October 1991, ascent of route aided by fixed ropes of Spanish team on route.
Height of b/c	5400m, beside the Chago Glacier.
Roadhead	Hille (there is an airstrip at Tumlingtar).
Length of walk-in	Approximately 120km and 12 days from Hille or 70km and 9 days from Tumlingtar.
Season	May or October.
Permission	Ministry of Tourism, Kathmandu.
Success rate	Quite high. Several small teams have succeeded on the route, but always with some degree of security from fixed ropes.
Bibliography	Excellent early potted history of the mountain by Gunther and Norman Dyhrenfurth in *Mountain* 64. The first ascent is recorded in Jean Franco's *Makalu* (Paris, 1955), and the first ascent of the West Pillar is covered in Paragot and Seigneur's *Makalu: Pilier Ouest*, with a summarised English translation by J. Russell (from the original account in *La Montagne*) in *AJ* 78. Other interesting ascents include John Roskelley's article in *AAJ* 1981, Doug Scott on the South-East Ridge in *Himalayan Climber* (Diadem/Sierra Club, 1992) and Kitty Calhoun Grisson's chapter in *Great Climbs* (Mitchell Beazley, 1994).

BARUNTSE 7129m

South-East Ridge

Mike Scott high on the South-East Ridge of Baruntse, one of several acclimatisation journeys Doug Scott and his companions made in 1984 before tackling the gigantic South-East Ridge of Makalu which forms the right-hand skyline plunging into the clouds. (*Doug Scott*)

In 1951 Eric Shipton's Everest reconnaissance expedition made a wonderful journey of exploration into the country east of Everest. Three years later one member of the team, Edmund Hillary, returned to that wild remote country with his Everest companion, George Lowe, and other New Zealanders to reconnoitre Makalu and indulge in an orgy of peak-bagging around the Barun Glacier. The expedition made no fewer than twenty first ascents and of these the most important was Baruntse.

Baruntse is a beautiful snow peak at the epicentre of three glacier valleys, the Imja, the Hunku and the Barun. The North Ridge of the lower North Summit was climbed from the more accessible Imja side by a Dutch team in 1983, but the first ascent of the Main Summit was made by the South-East Ridge, approached from the remote Barun. The most pleasant base camp for an ascent of this increasingly popular route is at 4900m on a small grassy terrace just below the snout of the Upper Barun Glacier and immediately below the 3500m South Face of Makalu. This site is quite remote from the base of Baruntse itself, but at a very welcome low altitude for resting from excursions on to the peaks hereabouts. Hillary's 1954 party chose to camp about 2km further up the glacier (on the true right bank) but at this site there is no grass and water is harder to come by.

Colin Todd and Geoff Harrow approached the South-East Ridge from the Upper Barun Glacier, at a point opposite the West Pillar of Makalu. From here they crossed the Sherpani Col to the large snowy plateau of the Lower Barun Glacier at a little over 6100m to the south of the peak. It is possible to reach this point more directly from the snout of the Lower Barun but route-finding through the icefall beneath Peak 4 can prove extremely difficult and at least one party has failed in this.

Once reached, the South-East Ridge has a height rise of just 1000m. The route is entirely on snow and ice and is not particularly technical, apart from a prominent ice cliff at c.7000m which gave a dramatic steep pitch to Doug Scott's party on the second ascent of the ridge in 1984. Cornices can also be a problem and the first ascensionists experienced a 60m section of ridge breaking away at the touch of an ice axe! So this is not a route to be taken lightly, particularly as it rises above a long, committing glacier approach.

Another excellent but harder route from the Barun side is the East Ridge, climbed by an American/Spanish expedition in 1980. It faces the great West

descent. However, perhaps the most ambitious traverse of the mountain would be an ascent of the North Ridge from the Imja Glacier, over the North and Main Summits and down the South-East Ridge. From the col at the bottom of the ridge one would have to drop down to the west, on to the Hunku Glacier, then climb over the Amphu Labtsa pass to regain the Imja Glacier, a committing undertaking.

The ascent of Baruntse from the Barun valley is a remote adventure, culminating in a relatively short climb to the summit of a beautiful seven-thousander.

SUMMARY STATISTICS AND INFORMATION

Mountain	Baruntse
Height	7129m; North Summit: 7057m.
Location	Mahalangur Himal, Makalu subsection, East Nepal.
Route	South-East Ridge (from east). c.1000m of ascent, mostly on snow with some ice and some corniced sections.
First ascent of mountain	Summit reached 30 May 1954 by Colin Todd & Geoff Harrow (NZ); North Summit: 1980 by Ubbink & Edwin van Nieuwkerk (Netherlands).
First ascent of route	As above.
Height of b/c	4900m, below the snout of the Upper Barun Glacier.
Roadhead	Hille (there is an airstrip at Tumlingtar).
Length of walk-in	Approx 120km and 12 days from Hille or 70km and 9 days from Tumlingtar.
Season	May or October.
Permission	Ministry of Tourism, Kathmandu.
Success rate	High. Several parties have climbed this ridge and with no reported serious accidents.
Bibliography	Edmund Hillary's *East of Everest* (Hodder & Stoughton, 1956) celebrates the joys of mountain wandering in the Barun region. See also Doug Scott's *Himalayan Climber* (Diadem/Sierra Club, 1992).

Early morning on the Lower Barun Glacier with Baruntse's South-East Ridge descending left towards the camera. The big ice cliff appears about a third of the way up the ridge. Fifteen kilometres distant, to the right of the foreground Pt 6730m, the day's first clouds gather above the fluted summit of Lhotse, the pinnacles of unclimbed Lhotse Middle and the white pyramid of Lhotse Shar. (*Doug Scott*)

Pillar of Makalu and is almost an easy miniature version of that route, sharply defined, with a short section of rock and mixed climbing to add interest. It emerges on the North Ridge between the North and Main Summits. The 1980 team fixed ropes, but an alpine-style ascent would be quite feasible, particularly if the South-East Ridge were in good condition for the

Although many parties have climbed the mountain within a fortnight of reaching base camp (including the Japanese party who made the first winter ascent of the peak in 1980), the length of the walk-in from the nearest roadhead (Hille) and the attractions of other peaks in the area means that most parties will be away from Kathmandu for at least two months.

South-East Ridge

You can see it in the famous view from Darjeeling — a slender, elegant summit piercing the horizon just to the west of Kangchenjunga's massive bulk. It was in Darjeeling, in 1955, that the bold idea of attempting Jannu was first formed. British climbers were celebrating their success on Kangchenjunga; their French drinking companions had just returned triumphant from the first ascent of Makalu. That night the French decided to take Himalayan climbing in a new direction with an attempt on the lower but much harder summit of Jannu.

Guido Magnone's 1957 reconnaissance confirmed suspicions that Jannu would prove a daunting challenge. The precipitous North and East Faces were deemed impossible and when Jean Franco led the first full attempt in 1959 it was from the south. From the Yamatari Glacier the expedition had to find a route on to the Throne — the high glacier basin beneath Jannu's granite headwall, enclosed between the giant encircling arms of the South-West and South-East Ridges. Any direct approach up the Throne Glacier was ruled out by avalanche danger, so the team chose a convoluted route up a parallel glacier on to the wild crest of the South Ridge, which led eventually to the elusive sanctuary of the Throne. From there difficult face climbing led back on to the crest of the South-East Ridge, where a sixth camp was placed at 7350m.

Brian Hall on the Tête du Butoir, the first big tower on the South-East Ridge, during the first alpine-style ascent of Jannu in October 1978. (*Roger Baxter-Jones*)

After weeks of exhausting work, tackling some of the most difficult and spectacular ice climbing yet attempted in the Himalaya, the team had to admit defeat on the difficult ridge just above Camp 6, but three years later Lionel Terray returned to lead another even stronger team to success. On 28 April 1962 René Desmaison, Paul Kellar and Robert Paragot climbed the final icy knife-edge to Jannu's precarious summit. The following day Lionel Terray reached the top with Jean Ravier and Sherpa Wangdi. For Terray the elusive summit of Jannu was perhaps the crowning moment of a remarkable mountaineering career.

The French route was repeated by Japanese climbers in 1974. They too organised a massive siege, with Sherpa porters, fixed ropes and camps, and oxygen equipment on the summit ridge, even though it lies below 8000m. However, in 1978 a team of young British climbers, each on his first visit to the Himalaya, climbed the route on sight in a single alpine-style push, carrying only minimal climbing gear and bivouac supplies. More remarkable was the fact that Brian Hall, Alan Rouse, Rab Carrington and Roger Baxter-Jones made their ascent from a base camp below the East Face (their original objective) which entailed three days extra walk over the Lapsang La to reach the base of the French route. With bivouacs at 4800, 5800, 6400, 6600 and 7000m (and two more on descent) they reached the top on 21 October. The ascent, completed in the bitter cold of late autumn, was a landmark in the development of alpine-style climbing, comparable to

Messner's and Habeler's ascent of Gasherbrum I (Hidden Peak) three years earlier.

By the 1980s the French route on Jannu, or Kumbhakarna as it was now officially known, had become a popular objective. Some teams opted for protracted sieges. Others travelled light and fast, most notably a Swiss team in 1984: after a preliminary recce, Daniel Anker, Bruno Rankwiler and Georg Rubin

elled alpine-style thereafter. The route, which takes the prominent spur on the left side of the face, is a superb climb, at first on rock (grade V) to a snow plateau and thereafter on an open mixed face to join the East Ridge at 7250m; it does however avoid the obvious challenge of the granite wall that falls directly from the summit. In 1989, the Slovenian Tomo Cesen claimed a more direct line, climbed solo, much of it

foray on to the face proper was made by Slovenian climbers Vanja Furlan and Bojan Pockar in 1991. They returned in 1992 to explore higher up this very steep mixed face. Over four days they climbed twenty-six pitches, with much vertical ice and rock difficulties to grade VII. However, they left untouched the formidable headwall and exited left on to the South-East Ridge at 7100m, from where they abseiled back down the

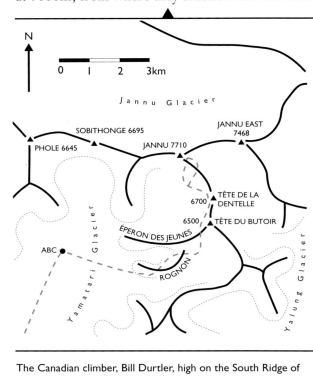

The Canadian climber, Bill Durtler, high on the South Ridge of Jannu in spring 1992. The blue ice of the Tête de la Dentelle is immediately behind him, with the upper basin of the Throne in shadow further back. The summit headwall is still over a kilometre distant. (*Rob Driscoll*)

climbed the entire route to the summit in just three days.

Meanwhile, during the 1970s other teams had been drawn inevitably to the awesome North Face of Jannu. New Zealanders tried the Wall of Shadows in 1975, followed in 1976 by a successful Japanese team, led by Masatsugu Konishi. The route was repeated twice in 1987 – by a six-man Dutch team and by French aces Pierre Béghin and Erik Decamp; both teams used fixed ropes on the lower buttress, but trav-

at night. Lack of photographic proof and other doubts over Cesen's career make it hard for some to accept the climb wholeheartedly. If his controversial ascent is to be believed, it was one of the most remarkable climbs of all time, but even his line had to avoid the gigantic overhangs of the central headwall.

Jannu's third face, the East Face, was to prove just as difficult. The 1978 British team reached the col between Jannu and unclimbed Jannu East, but the first

face. In 1993 another Slovenian attempt failed on this elusive face.

Jannu remains an inspiring challenge from every angle. Many will be drawn to the massive sombre architecture of the North Face; others will return to the tenuous ice runnels and flutings of the East Face; but here we look at the classic line of the first ascent – the South-East Ridge.

After their bold coup in 1978, the British alpine-

Jannu from the south-west, the view from near base camp on the Yamatari Glacier. Clearly visible in the centre of the picture is the great sérac barrier of the Throne Glacier, threatening any direct approach from this side. The immense South Ridge forms the right-hand skyline. The 1962 route approaches it from the far side, attaining the ridge crest at the Tête du Butoir. Once the Throne is gained there are two options: the original French route which regains the ridge crest below complex pinnacles, or the 1978 alternative which climbs more directly (and possibly more easily), through the headwall, to emerge on the final snow arête. (*Bill Durtler*)

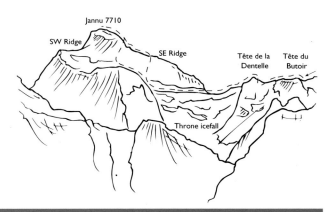

style team described the original route as 'not technically difficult', but we should remember that they were extremely experienced and dedicated alpinists, immersed in a tradition of misleading British understatement. Even they admitted that much of the route equated to Alpine TD, that it was very long and committing (at least 5km horizontal distance from the Yamatari Glacier) and that the summit ridge, climbed in late October, was very cold and exposed. Small

wonder that in 1962 the route had stretched France's best mountaineers to the limit. This easiest line up Jannu is no pushover.

The climb really starts from 4800m on the upper Yamatari Glacier, heading east up a subsidiary glacier via a rognon ridge, to an upper glacier plateau at about 6000m. This section can be heavily crevassed and in 1962 the French used a ladder to reach the plateau.

A steep mixed fluted face then leads on to the

Alan Rouse and Rab Carrington climbing the steep runnel from the shelf on to the Dentelle in October 1978 – much snowier conditions than those in the spring photo on p.182. (*Brian Hall*)

Éperon des Jeunes, the crest of the South Ridge. Spectacular cornices and ice towers adorn the ridge leading to the first big obstacle, christened the Tête du Butoir (the Buffer Tower) by the French in 1959. From here at last they could see into the elusive sanctuary of the Throne, but first they had to cross the

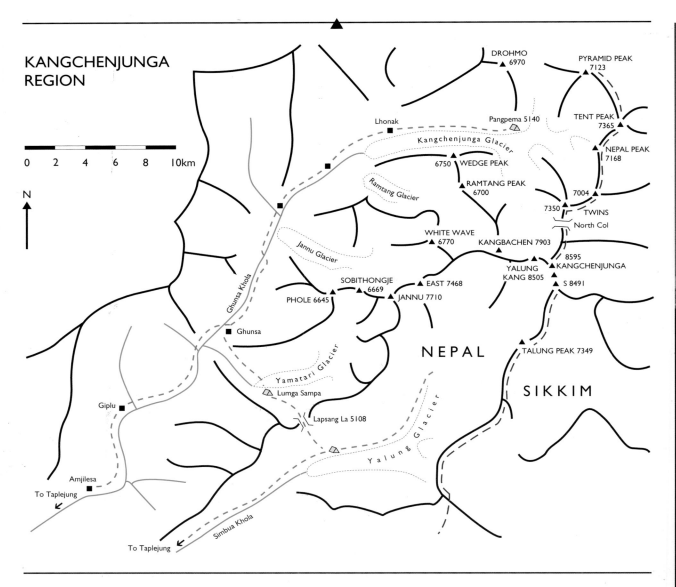

KANGCHENJUNGA REGION

0 2 4 6 8 10km

N

DROHMO
6970

PYRAMID PEAK
7123

Lhonak

Pangpema 5140

TENT PEAK
7365

Kangchenjunga Glacier

NEPAL PEAK
7168

6750 WEDGE PEAK

RAMTANG PEAK
6700

7004

Ramtang Glacier

7350

TWINS

North Col

Jannu Glacier

WHITE WAVE
6770

KANGBACHEN 7903

8595
KANGCHENJUNGA

YALUNG
KANG 8505

S 8491

SOBITHONGJE
6669

EAST 7468

PHOLE 6645

JANNU 7710

Ghunsa Khola

NEPAL

Ghunsa

TALUNG PEAK 7349

SIKKIM

Yamatari Glacier

Lumga Sampa

Giplu

Lapsang La 5108

Yalung Glacier

Amjilesa

To Taplejung

Simbua Khola

To Taplejung

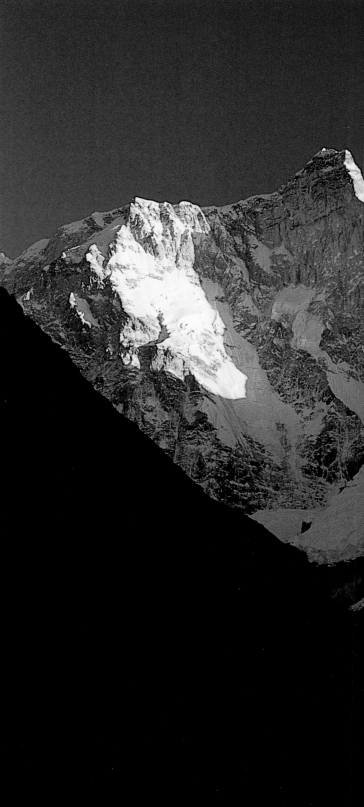

intricate tracery of the Tête de la Dentelle (the Lace Tower). The route they found traverses a hanging shelf on the left, then climbs a 65° runnel, sometimes ice, sometimes bottomless snow, which emerges close to the summit of the Dentelle. Beyond the Dentelle, the route leaves the ridge, descending left on to the Throne. In 1978 it took the British party a whole day to cross the Throne, breaking trail through deep snow. The terrain here is technically very easy, as Brian Hall remarked afterwards – 'just walking, but you're in a very, very serious position'.

From the Throne the French first ascent team climbed back right, to rejoin the ridge – now the South-East Ridge – at 7350m, where they placed Camp 6. It was the rocky pinnacles above here that gave them so much trouble in 1959. In 1978 the British team made their final bivouac right at the top of the Throne, at the higher bergschrund. From here they climbed in a single long day to the summit and back.

Jannu's awesome North Face (left), Sobithonge and Phole from the Jannu Glacier. The Japanese route on Jannu takes the sunlit spur on the left side of the North Face. (*Steve Razzetti*)

JANNU

Erik Decamp nearing the summit of Jannu after climbing the North Face in 1987. Behind are Jannu East (JE) and the Kangchenjunga massif: Kangbachen(1), Yalung Kang(2) Kangchenjunga Main(3), Central(4) and South(5). GS marks the Great Shelf, key to the first ascent in 1955. The great South Ridge of Kangchenjunga South, profiled on the right, was climbed alpine-style in 1991 by Andrej Stremfelj and Marko Prezelj. (Pierre Béghin/Foc Photo)

Their route crosses the bergschrund at the most convenient point and moves left around the base of an exposed granite spur which is followed on snow on its left side, leading to a faint hidden gully. Mixed climbing up this gully leads through the headwall to emerge on the final snowy section of the summit ridge at about 7550m, above the awkward pinnacles. A final snow arête, knife-edged in places, leads inexorably to the fairytale snow spike of the summit.

The 1962 route on Jannu, with minor variations, remains popular because it is a classic masterpiece of route-finding, weaving its way through fantastic ice scenery to a wonderful summit. It has been climbed several times in pure alpine-style. However, the route is very long and complex; retreat will never be easy and in 1992, when a Canadian climber fell ill at the Throne and had to be escorted down, his companion was very glad of fixed ropes on crucial sections of the route. The ideal, though, must be to keep any fixed ropes on this magnificent mountain to an absolute minimum and to remove them afterwards.

KANGCHENJUNGA 8595m

North-West Face / North Ridge

With the possible exception of Nanga Parbat, Kangchenjunga is the most massive and complex of the world's highest peaks and, like Nanga Parbat, it is steeped in mountaineering history, dating from the turn of the century. Despite stringent restrictions elsewhere in Nepal, Kangchenjunga, on the eastern border with Sikkim, was attempted from all sides long before other peaks were opened to foreigners in 1949. We can only touch on the highlights of pre-war exploration: Douglas Freshfield's epic journey round the mountain in 1902, Aleister Crowley's disastrous attempt on the South-West (Yalung) Face in 1905: Paul Bauer's spirited tunnelling up the surreal ice towers of the North-East Spur in 1929 and 1931; Gunther Dyhrenfurth's international expedition to the North-West Face in 1930.

When the mountain was finally climbed in 1955, it was by the Yalung Face from Nepal. After weaving a route through complex icefalls, Charles Evans' British team eventually attained the Great Shelf, seen so prominently from Darjeeling, 100km to the south. From there the route continued up the steep snow/ice Gangway before breaking right through a gully system to the prominent red pinnacles near the top of the West Ridge. It was here that Joe Brown, one of the world's very best rock climbers, led his famous crack, with his oxygen turned up to 6 litres a minute. He shared the summit honours with George Band; a day later Tony Streather and Norman Hardie also reached the top, avoiding the crack by what Streather jokingly called 'an easy walk round the back'.

The highest summit of the Five Treasuries of the Snows then remained untrodden for twenty-two years, until Narinder Kumar's 1977 Indian expedition retraced German steps up the wild North-East Spur from Sikkim. In 1931 a slope of lethal windslab had stopped the Germans crossing from the top of the spur to the upper North Ridge but in 1977 conditions were better, allowing Prem Chand and Naik Nima Dorje Sherpa to continue up the North Ridge to the summit, where, like the British twenty-two years earlier, they stopped two metres short of the final snow pinnacle out of respect for Sikkimese religious feelings.

Colonel Kumar had organised a large-scale siege to subdue the tortuous North-East Spur. The third ascent of Kangchenjunga used rather different tactics. Doug Scott and Peter Boardman had achieved international fame in 1975 with their summit successes on the Everest South-West Face campaign, but they wanted now to attempt one of the highest peaks without all the trappings of a full-scale siege. Joe Tasker, veteran of Changabang and Dunagiri, was equally committed to the lightweight approach, as was the fourth member, the Frenchman Georges Bettembourg.

the first of three gigantic tiers which give this huge face its distinctive character. The 1979 team decided to avoid the main face by climbing further left, up the West Wall of the North Col – 900m of mixed climbing which they compared to one of the best routes at Chamonix, the

ful escape, retreating 3000m in a single day, demonstrated their prowess at altitude and, perhaps, strengthened their resolve and confidence on the final summit bid, after a few days recuperation at the idyllic Pangpema base camp. This time Bettembourg

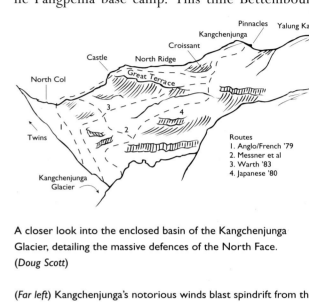

A closer look into the enclosed basin of the Kangchenjunga Glacier, detailing the massive defences of the North Face. (*Doug Scott*)

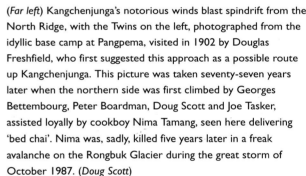

(*Far left*) Kangchenjunga's notorious winds blast spindrift from the North Ridge, with the Twins on the left, photographed from the idyllic base camp at Pangpema, visited in 1902 by Douglas Freshfield, who first suggested this approach as a possible route up Kangchenjunga. This picture was taken seventy-seven years later when the northern side was first climbed by Georges Bettembourg, Peter Boardman, Doug Scott and Joe Tasker, assisted loyally by cookboy Nima Tamang, seen here delivering 'bed chai'. Nima was, sadly, killed five years later in a freak avalanche on the Rongbuk Glacier during the great storm of October 1987. (*Doug Scott*)

Scott's survival of an oxygenless bivouac at 8700m on Everest in 1975 and the Habeler/Messner oxygenless ascent three year later had proved what was possible at extreme altitude. Now, in 1979, the new art of the possible came to Kangchenjunga, via the North-West Face.

This was the route which Dyhrenfurth's international team, including such luminaries as Erwin Schneider and Frank Smythe, had attempted in 1930, ending in disaster when a giant section of ice cliff avalanched, killing Sherpa Chettan. That ice cliff was

North-East Spur of the Droites. So, by the equivalent of a major alpine wall transposed to much higher altitude, they reached the start of the North Ridge. Given the length and complexity of the project, they chose understandably to fix ropes up this initial wall. Above the North Col they only fixed the occasional short section, like the steep rocks of the Castle.

The first summit bid nearly ended in disaster when Bettembourg, Boardman and Scott had their tent destroyed by Kangchenjunga's notorious winds, at about 8000m in the middle of the night. Their success-

dropped out and Tasker climbed with Boardman and Scott, skirting below the ridge, across the huge scree terrace at the top of the North-West Face, to join the original 1955 route at the Pinnacles on the West Ridge. They reached the summit late, at 5 pm, but managed to regain their top snowcave by 9 pm and two days later were safely down at base camp.

Peter Boardman later described the Kangchenjunga climb in an article entitled, provocatively, 'No More Himalayan Heroes'. The inference that four ingenues had casually sneaked up the mighty Kangch is of course

▲

misleading. The team was exceptionally strong and highly motivated. Despite good planning and judicious use of fixed rope, they had some close shaves. The following year, climbing directly through the three giant terraces of the North-West Face, Masatsugu Konishi led a traditionally massive Japanese expedition to success without serious incident but in 1982, when Ang Dorje, Reinhold Messner and Friedl Mutschlechner climbed hybrid between the Japanese and Anglo-French routes,

The cold reality of life at 8000m plus. Peter Habeler (left), Martin Zabaleta and Carlos Buhler back at their Camp 4 on the Great Terrace, after reaching the summit of Kangchenjunga in deteriorating weather on 3 May, 1988. By now, 4 May, a metre of new snow had fallen. Later that day the climbers found their Camp 3 destroyed by avalanches. On the final day of their harrowing retreat they discovered that Camp 2 had also vanished without trace. (*Carlos Buhler Collection*)
(*Right*) A perfect summit day for Peter Boardman and Joe Tasker on 16 May 1979, as they round the base of the Croissant into the couloir which gains the upper slopes. Below them can be seen the Great Terrace, leading round to the concealed North Col with the Twins rising immediately behind. Further back the frontier peaks, all over 7000m, are highlighted against the distant brown hills of Tibet. (*Doug Scott*)

they only just got down alive through fierce storms. In 1988 when Carlos Buhler, Peter Habeler and Martin Zabaleta climbed a similar line, they also had a fierce struggle back from the summit, with two of their camps destroyed by avalanches.

There have now been many attempts and quite a few successes on this side of the mountain. The Japanese direct route is the hardest and possibly the most danger-

ous. The Messner route starts up the same Ice Building which caused the accident in 1930, before breaking back left, to reach the North Ridge near the Castle. Several parties have reported that the 1979 line to the North Col is actually quite badly affected by rockfall. Two

upper face. The final section past the Pinnacles, round on the South-West Face, involves some awkward mixed climbing which, at nearly 8500m without oxygen, must demand the utmost care.

Kangchenjunga has never been climbed from the

After traversing round the Pinnacles on to the Yalung Face of the mountain, Joe Tasker follows up the last few metres to Kangchenjunga's highest summit. Behind him on the left is the connecting ridge to Kangchenjunga Middle and South (the furthest point), first traversed in 1989 by a highly successful Soviet expedition led by Eduard Myslovsky. Two teams of five climbers traversed the four 8000m summits of Kangchenjunga on consecutive days, in opposite directions, after first establishing a comprehensive chain of communication on the Great Terrace. The traverse awaits an alpine-style, oxygenless, ascent. (*Doug Scott*).

American expeditions have followed a line further right and Hermann Warth's 1983 German expedition pioneered another line up the corner between the West and North-West Faces. All these routes eventually converge on the Great Terrace. Most parties follow the Anglo-French option, skirting beneath the obvious Croissant rock buttress, but Messner's team went left on to the East Face before traversing back on to the

north in genuine alpine-style, in a single push with no fixed ropes. The original route up the South-West Face was soloed by Pierre Béghin in 1983 and in 1991 Andrej Stremfelj and Marko Prezelj climbed on sight up the stupendous South Ridge. Their ascent must be one of the boldest efforts of all time and the route is probably the finest line on Kangchenjunga. However it leads to the South, not the Main Summit. For those

SUMMARY STATISTICS AND INFORMATION

Mountain	Kangchenjunga
Height	8595m
Location	Kangchenjunga Himal, East Nepal.
Routes	North-West Face and North Ridge. 2600m of ascent from the upper Pangpema Glacier. Several lines of varying directness. On the main face there can be hard ice climbing through sérac barriers. The difficulties on the Anglo-French and Warth routes are concentrated on more mixed terrain.
First ascent of mountain	Summit reached 25 May 1955 by George Band & Joe Bown (UK).
First ascent of routes	North Ridge via West Face of North Col – Peter Boardman, Doug Scott & Joe Tasker (UK), May 1979. North-West Face left-hand route – German expedition led by Hermann Warth, May 1983 (not completed to summit). North Face Direct – Japanese expedition led by Masatsugu Konishi, May 1980.
Height of b/c	5140m at Pangpema meadows.
Roadhead	Basanthapur (there is an airstrip at Suketar, 2500m above Taplejung).
Length of walk-in	Approximately 100km and 10 days from Taplejung. Another 3 days from Basanthapur.
Season	April-May seems to offer a better chance of success than the autumn season.
Permission	Ministry of Tourism, Kathmandu, via a trekking agency.
Success rate	About 30 per cent of expeditions have succeeded on this side of the mountain since 1979.
Bibliography	There is a huge literature on Kangchenjunga, starting with Douglas Freshfield's classic *Round Kangchenjunga* (Arnold, 1903). The best concise history of the mountain is the feature by Gunther and Norman Dyhrenfurth in *Mountain* 68. The 1979 ascent is comprehensively documented in Peter Boardman's *Sacred Summits* (Hodder & Stoughton, 1982), Joe Tasker's *Savage Arena* (Methuen, 1982) and Doug Scott's *Himalayan Climber* (Diadem/Sierra Club, 1992). For the Messner variant see *All 14 Eight Thousanders* (Crowood, 1988). Other routes on the North-West Face are well documented in the *AAJ* and *HJ*.

who aspire to the highest of the Five Treasuries by an interesting, varied and highly adventurous route, the various lines up the North-West Face and the North Ridge offer a fantastic challenge.

MOUNTAINEERING REGULATIONS & PEAK FEES

Pakistan

Access to all peaks under 6000m is free, unless they lie in a restricted area (eg the Upper Baltoro Glacier), when a trekking permit and liaison officer are required.

All peaks above 6000m require a permit, for which application should be made by 31 December of the preceding year (two years in advance for K2) to:

The Government of Pakistan, D.O. No.1 (21)/79-ME (PtII), Tourism Division, Islamabad (Fax 51 817 323).

Royalties are as follows (1994 prices):

		supplement for each member beyond 5
K2	$9000	$1000
8001-8500m	$7500	$700
7501-8000m	$3000	$300
7001-7500m	$2000	$200
6000-7000m	$1200	$150

The liaison officer must be equipped with the same equipment as expedition members. In addition to the royalty, the expedition must pay a $200 environmental levy. A recoverable bond of $4000 must be banked in Islamabad, against the possibility of rescue. Porters and liaison officer should be insured with a Government-approved insurer in Pakistan.

India

There is no official lower height limit for peaks requiring royalty payments, although a handful of 'trekking peaks', such as Stok Kangri in Ladakh, can be climbed with minimal restrictions. Climbing in the Eastern Karakoram and some other sensitive areas is restricted to joint Indian-foreign expeditions. Permits for all peaks should be sought at least six months in advance from:

Indian Mountaineering Foundation, Benito Juarez Road, Anand Niketan, New Delhi 110 021 (Fax 91 11 688 3412).

Royalties are as follows (1994 prices):

Eastern Karakoram and other restricted areas	$3000
Nun & Kun	$2250
Other peaks 7001m and above	$1800
6501-7000m	$1350
6001-6500m	$900
Below 6000m	$500

If more than one peak is attempted, the royalty for the second peak is at 50%. The expedition liaison officer must be supplied with the same standard equipment as the expedition members.

Nepal

Climbing is permitted only on designated peaks, but the current list of about a hundred available peaks is growing. Climbing on the so-called 'trekking peaks' involves only minimal complications and a permit fee of $300. Application should be made to:

Nepal Mountaineering Association, PO Box 1435, Kathmandu.

Applications for other peaks should be made to:

HMG Ministry of Tourism & Civil Aviation, Mountaineering Division, Kathmandu.

Royalties are as follows:

Everest	$50,000
(for 5 members, with $10,000 per extra member, with a maximum total of 7)	
Other peaks over 8000m	$8000 (maximum 9 people)
7501-8000m	$3000 (maximum 9 people)
7001-7500m	$2000 (maximum 9 people)
6501-7000m	$1500 (maximum 9 people)
Below 6500m	$1000 (maximum 9 people)

The liaison officer must be equipped to the same standard as expedition members. There is also a requirement to employ, pay and insure a sirdar (headman) and kitchen staff. Most expeditions arrange staff and applications through a local trekking agency.

China

After many misunderstandings by officialdom in the 'eighties, mountaineering in Chinese-controlled Tibet and Sinkiang has recently become much less frustrating. Prices are now closer to real market value; nevertheless all services such as fees, hotels, transport, porterage etc. are still controlled by the Chinese Mountaineering Association, which is responsible for the expedition from the moment of entry until it leaves China. Prices must be agreed in advance when the 'protocol' is signed and before any extra service is supplied (even a round of beer!) the price has first to be agreed with the liaison officer. In addition to the LO, an interpreter is attached to the expedition.

Permits can be sought from Beijing at:

Chinese Mountaineering Association, 9 Tiyuguan Road, Beijing, or direct from the Sinkiang Mountaineering Association in Urumchi or from the Tibet Mountaineering Association, No. 8 East Linkhor Road, Lhasa, Tibet (Fax 86 891 36366).

Only a limited number of peaks is officially open and royalties are as follows:

Everest	$5500
Other 8000m peaks	$3000
7000-7999m	$2160
6000-6999m	$1350
Below 6000m	$30 per climber

These costs are for a maximum of 20 members. Unclimbed peaks and new routes carry higher royalties, some very expensive.

THE HIMALAYAN CODE OF CONDUCT

Prepared by the British Mountaineering Council in consultation with the Himalayan Environmental Trust.

Campsite Remember that another party will be using the same campsite after you have vacated it. Therefore leave the campsite cleaner than you found it and replace turfs and stones.

Limit deforestation Make no open fires and discourage others from doing so on your behalf. Where water is heated by scarce firewood, use as little as possible. When possible, choose accommodation that uses kerosene or fuel-efficient wooden stoves. Above the treeline and in thinly forested areas be self-sufficient in fuel supplies.

Rubbish Burn dry paper and packets in a safe place. Bury other paper and biodegradable material, including food. Carry out all non-biodegradable litter. If you come across other people's rubbish, remove it as well. Give away to local people what can be usefully and safely recycled.

Water Keep local water clean and avoid using pollutants such as detergents in streams or springs. Dig latrines at least 30m from water sources and bury all waste.

Plants It is illegal to take cuttings, seeds and roots in many parts of the Himalaya. Avoid damaging vegetation. Avoid all unnecessary disturbances to birds and animals.

Conservation Minimise erosion by keeping to paths, where they exist. Do not allow the cooks and porters to throw rubbish in the nearby stream or river.

Local culture As a guest, respect local traditions. When taking photographs, respect privacy; ask permission and exercise restraint. Respect holy places, preserving what you have come to see. Never touch or remove religious objects. Remove shoes when visiting temples. Refrain from giving money to children, since it will encourage begging. A donation to a project, health centre or school is a more constructive way to help. Respect for local etiquette earns you respect. Loose, lightweight clothes are preferable to revealing shorts, skimpy tops and tight-fitting action wear. Hand-holding or kissing in public are disapproved of by local people.

A SELECT BIBLIOGRAPHY

The literature of Himalayan climbing and exploration is huge and only a few pointers can be given here. Specific books and journal references are mentioned in each chapter. For general reference, the following are particularly useful:

Abode of Snow Kenneth Mason (Diadem, 1987) The definitive history of climbing and exploration up to 1954.

Sivalaya Louis Baume (Gaston-West Col, 1978) A chronicle of the attempts and ascents of the 8000m peaks, with full bibliography, up to 1977.

High Asia Jill Neate (Unwin Hyman, 1989) Invaluable, scholarly guide to all the 7000m peaks.

The Trekking Peaks of Nepal Bill O'Connor (Crowood, 1989) Expert guide to the 17 so-called 'trekking peaks'.

Adventure Treks Nepal Bill O'Connor (Crowood, 1990) Much useful tangential advice and sketch maps on mountaineering in Nepal.

Hidden Himalaya Soli Mehta and Harish Kapadia (Hodder & Stoughton, 1990) A historical guide to the Indian Himalaya and Karakoram by two acknowledged experts.

Pakistan Trekking Guide Isobel and Ben Shaw (Odyssey, 1993) A labour of love, accurate and very readable, describing all the known trekking routes in the northern areas of Pakistan.

The world's most comprehensive single source of information on the Himalayan peaks is probably the Alpine Club Himalayan Index, a computer database, updated annually. Enquiries to:

The Alpine Club, 55 Charlotte Road, London EC2A 3QT
(Telephone 44 171 613 0755).

Maps

Many of the best Himalayan maps are produced by the host countries' military authorities and are not available to civilians. However, there is a growing number of maps produced specifically for climbers and trekkers. Amongst the most useful are:

Pakistan
Karakoram Orographical Sketch Map, 1:250,000, 2 sheets. Published by the Swiss Foundation for Alpine Research
The Baltoro Glacier, 1:100,000. Published by Yama-Kei Publishers Co. Ltd., Japan
Nanga Parbat, 1:50,000, Alpenvereinskarte. Published by the Austrian and German Alpine Clubs

India
Ladakh-Zanskar, 1:50,000. Published by Pegasus, Switzerland
Garhwal Himalaya, sketch maps and diagrams. Published by Jan Babicz, Klub Wysokogorski, Gdansk, Poland

Nepal
East Nepal, 1:50,000 series. Published by Nelles Verlag, Munich, Germany
Everest, 1:50,000. Published by National Geographic. The definitive map, masterminded in the 'eighties by Bradford Washburn.